Lio

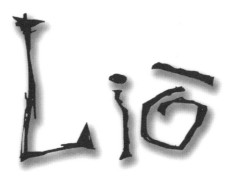

Lio

Happiness Is a Squishy Cephalopod

A MARK TATULLI COMIC

**Andrews McMeel
Publishing, LLC**

Kansas City

LIŌ is distributed internationally by Universal Press Syndicate.

 For information, write Andrews McMeel Publishing, LLC, an Andrews McMeel Universal company, 4520 Main Street, Kansas City, Missouri 64111.

07 08 09 10 11 WKT 10 9 8 7 6 5 4 3 2 1

ISBN-13: 978-0-7407-6849-1
ISBN-10: 0-7407-6849-2

Library of Congress Control Number: 2007925338

www.andrewsmcmeel.com

To Mom and Dad who (despite what some newspaper readers may think) raised me right.

Love – M̄T.

Foreword

Being what they call "edgy" on the comics page means taking a lot of crap.

Readers accustomed to years of G-rated, milquetoast family fare wince at any joke that's not about eating big sandwiches or running over the mailman.

For young cartoonists trying to appeal to the same generation that watches *The Daily Show*, *Family Guy*, and *South Park*, this creates an almost impossible task. Be funny and generate angry letters to the editors, or suck. (By the way, you can't say "suck" on the comics page either, at least not without losing a paper or two.)

About the best you can hope for is that other young cartoonists try to push the envelope as much as you. The reason for this is that when you're the only inmate climbing over the jailhouse wall, you're an easy mark for the guard in the tower (or in our case, the retired octogenarian with the pen).

What you want is a full-on jailbreak. After all, they can't shoot all of us.

Get Fuzzy is one of those fellow inmates for me. As is *Doonesbury*. As was *The Boondocks* while it ran. *The Boondocks* was great. Aaron didn't only try to escape; he gave the finger to the guard. I could always count on him to do something more outrageous than me, meaning that he drew three complaints to the editor that week, as opposed to my mere one or two.

But then he up and left, leaving my flank exposed.

And into this gap marched LIŌ.

No big sandwiches here.

No, this one was dark. Cute things died. Oh, I know what Tatulli says, which is that he doesn't actually show them dying. Your imagination has to supply that part. But that's crap. He's killing these things.

And the strange part about Tatulli is that for years, he had been a model inmate. He had been drawing a family strip, for God's sake. It was like seeing the kindly old prisoner who for years had been whittling driftwood suddenly stab the warden.

What did this all mean?

It meant cover.

On days I was showing my crocs biting off someone's arm, LIŌ was gathering corpses from a graveyard. On days where I had my characters discussing nuclear war, Tatulli showed the nuclear war. And on days where I was killing talking flies, Mark was killing puppies.

And suddenly, the guards weren't just shooting at me. There was this big, fat new target lumbering over the prison wall, and his pants were caught on the barbed wire.

And that is a wonderful thing.

Stephan Pastis
Creator of *Pearls Before Swine*

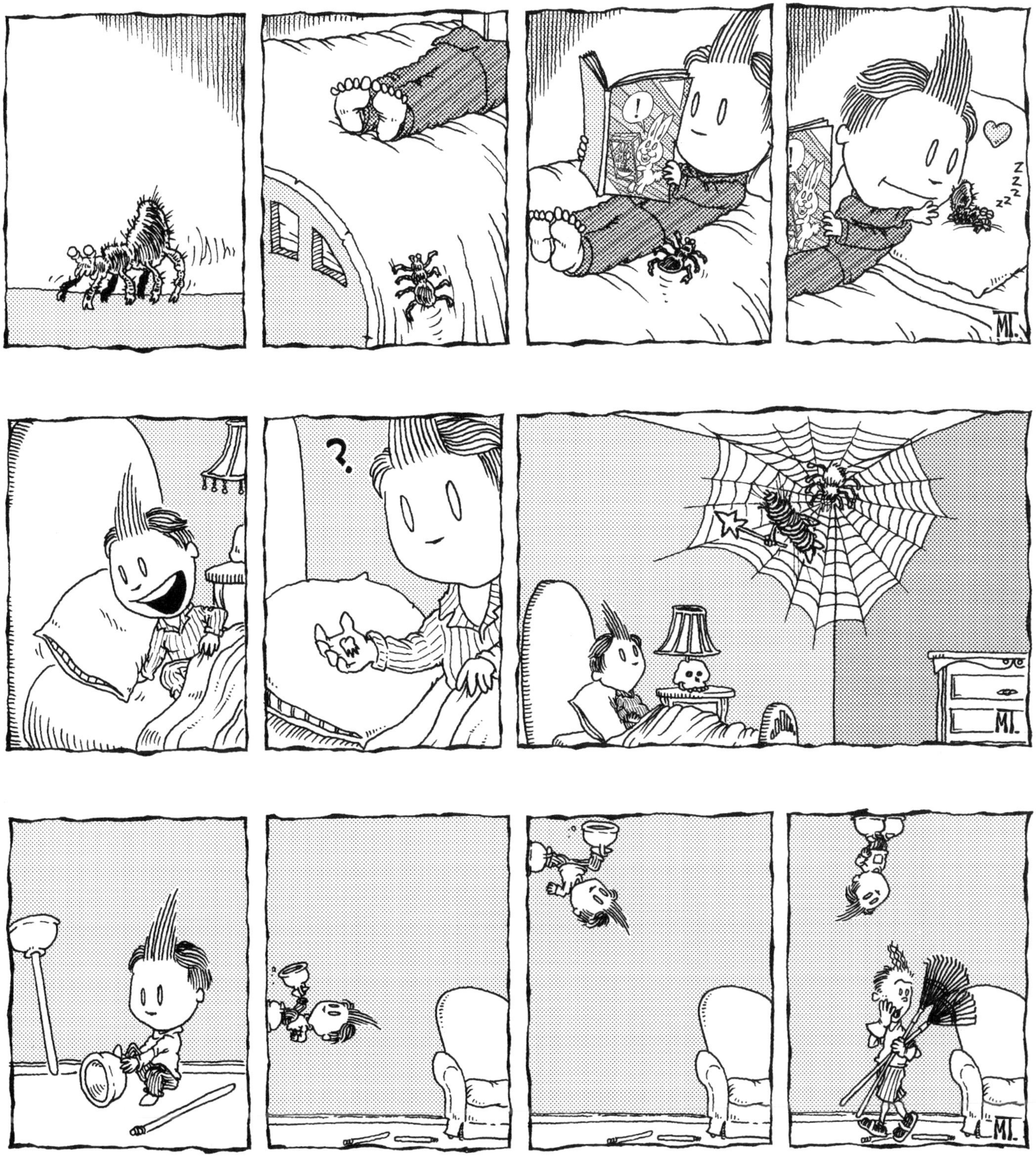
!
ZZZZZ
?

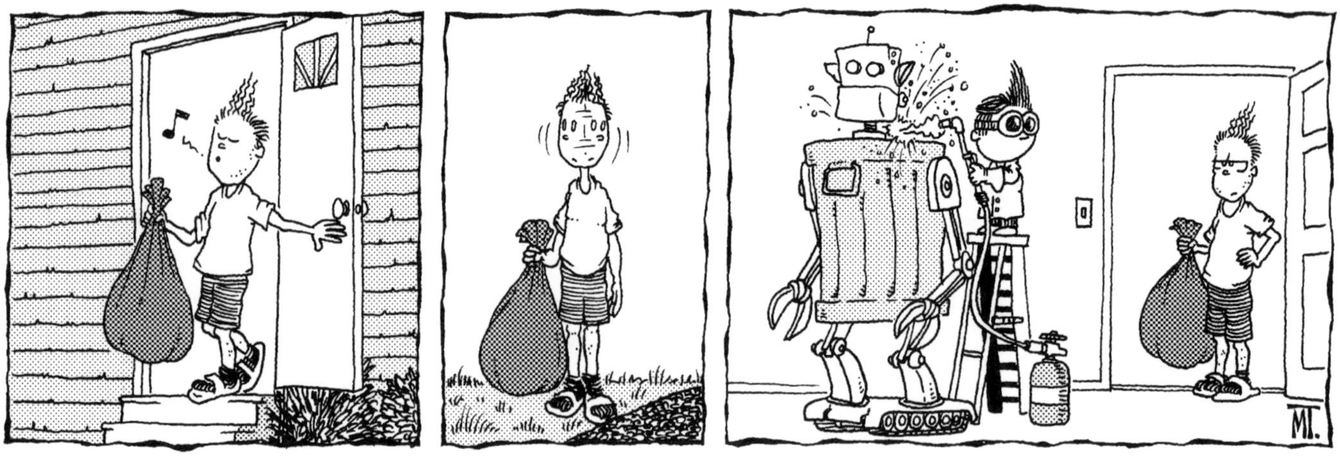

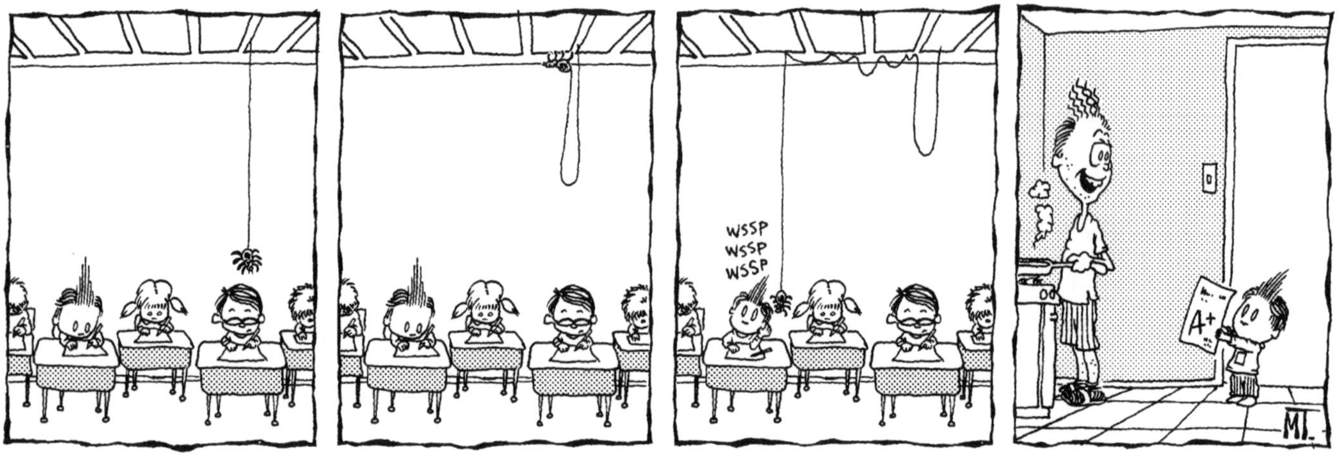
WSSP
WSSP
WSSP
A+

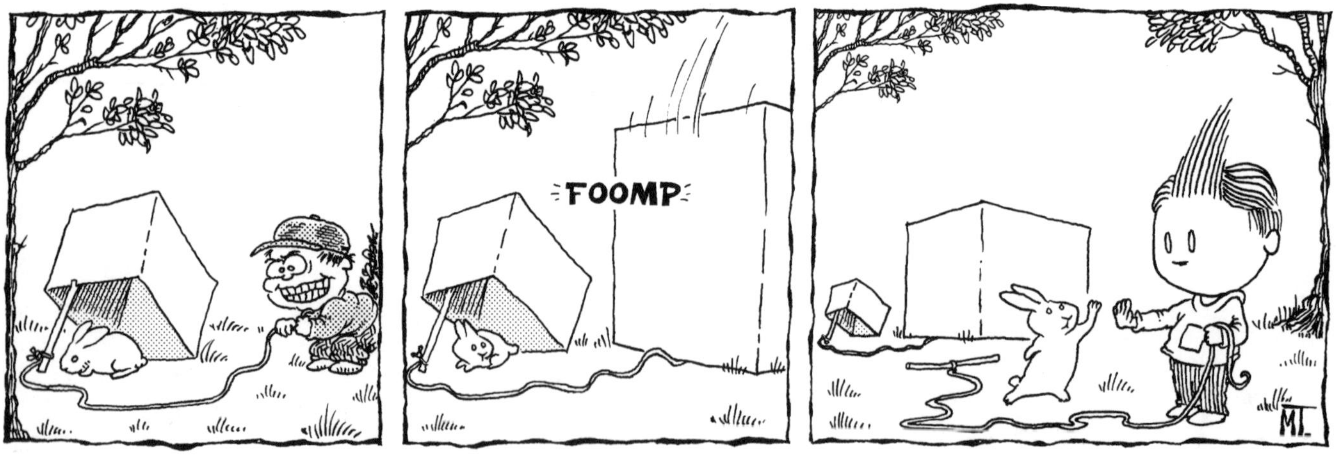
FOOMP

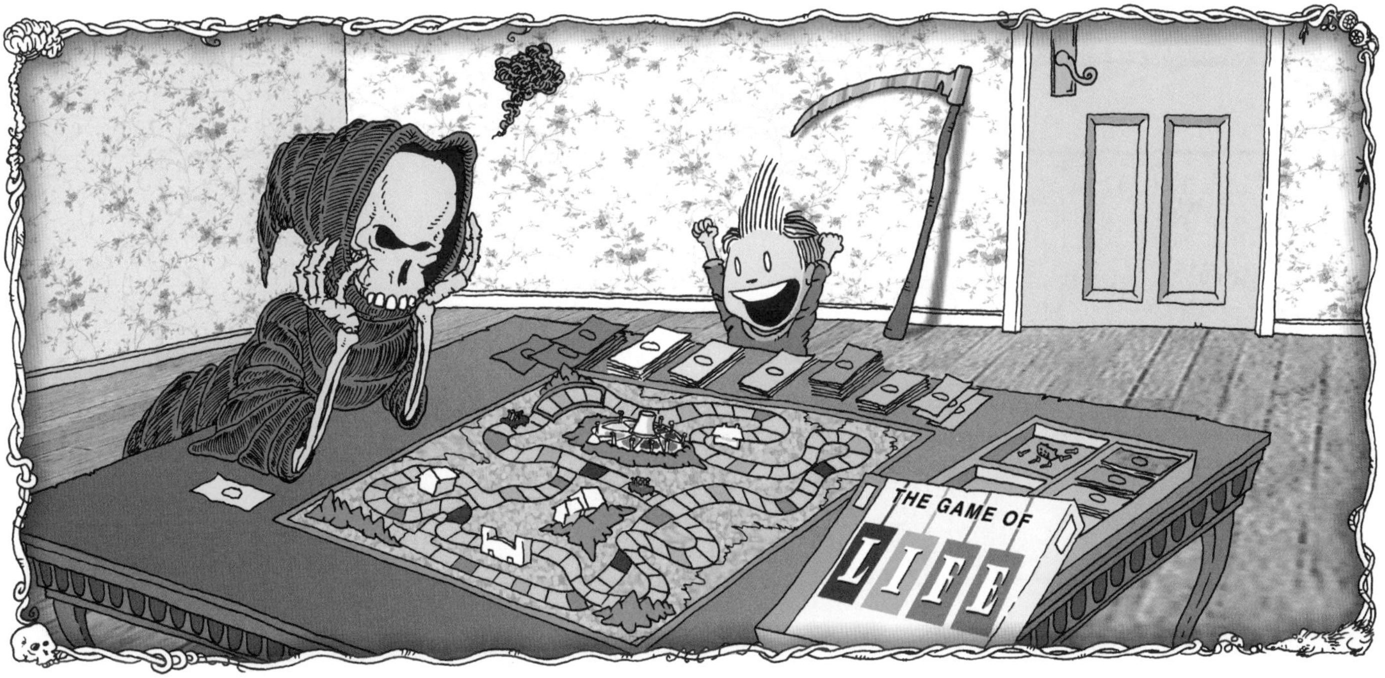
THE GAME OF
LIFE

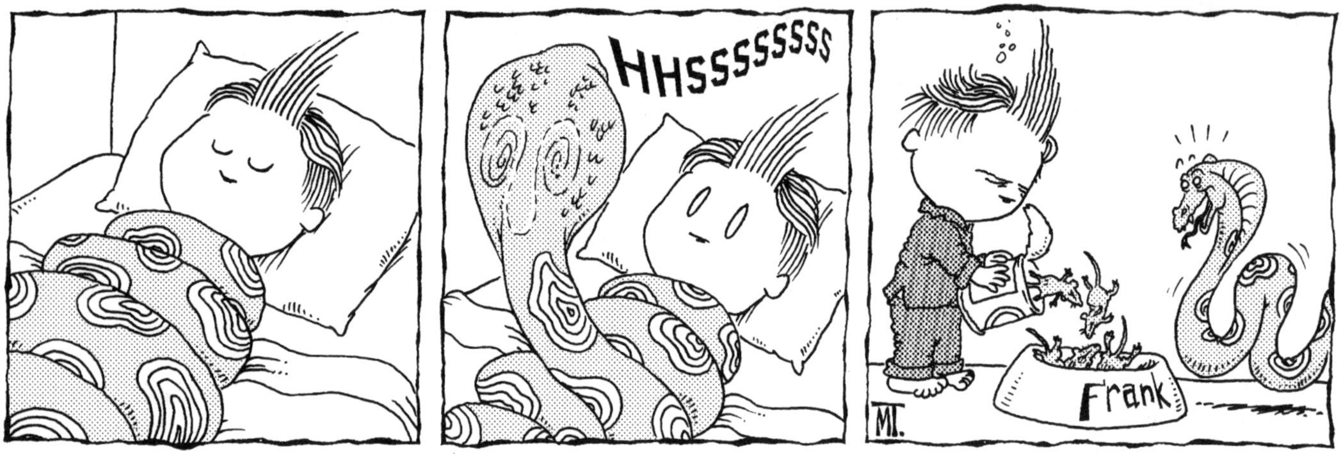
HHSSSSSSSS
Frank

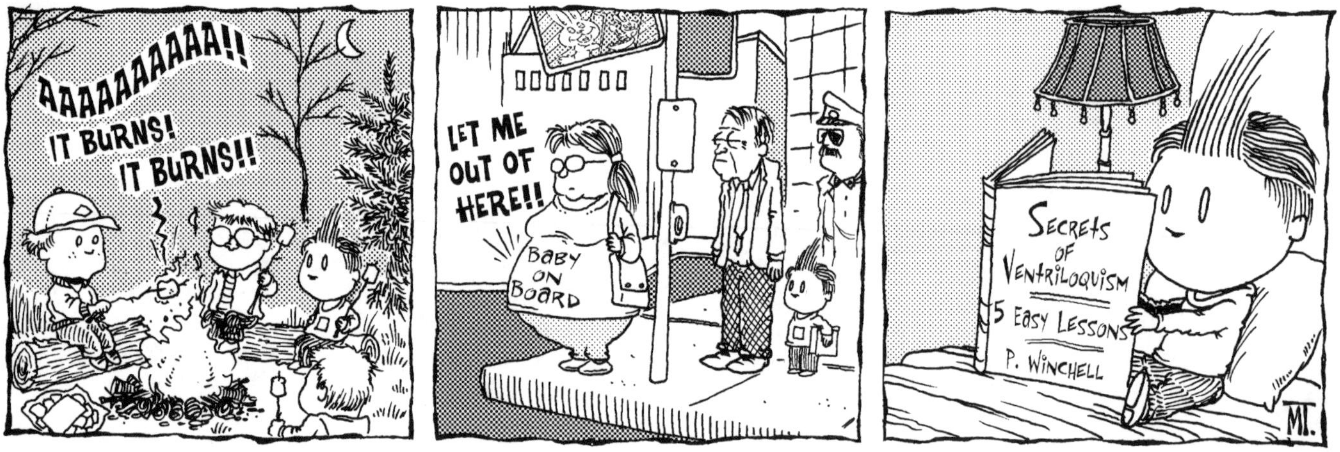
AAAAAAAAAA!!
IT BURNS!
IT BURNS!!
LET ME OUT OF HERE!!
BABY ON BOARD
SECRETS OF VENTRILOQUISM
5 EASY LESSONS
P. WINCHELL

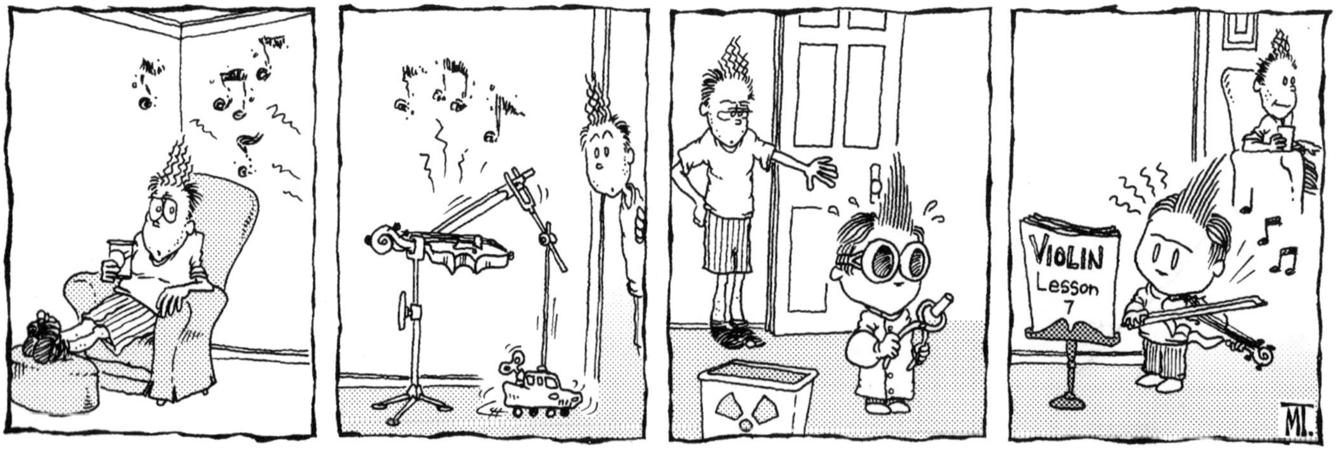
VIOLIN Lesson 7

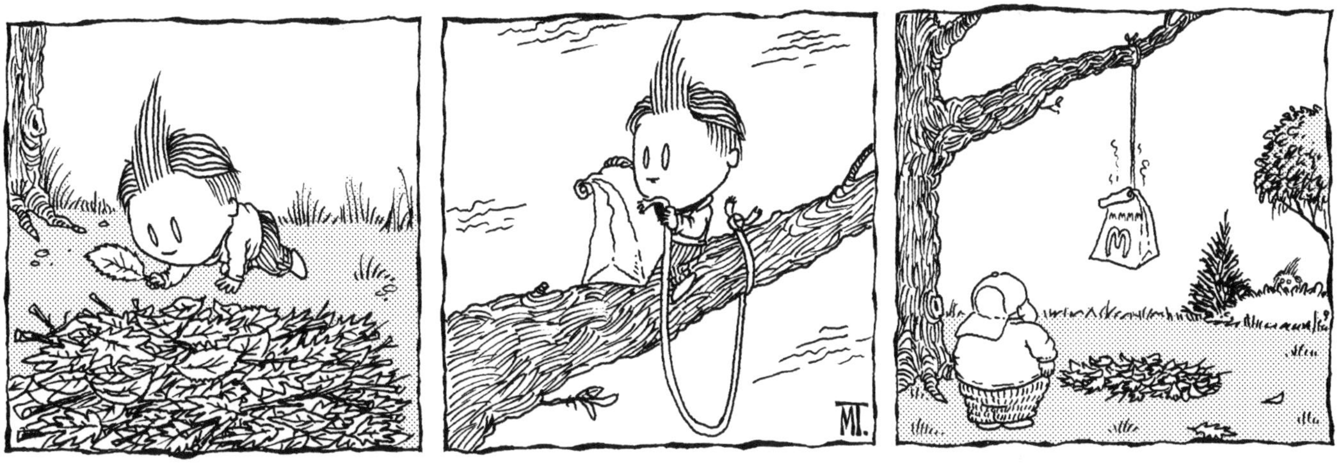
MT.

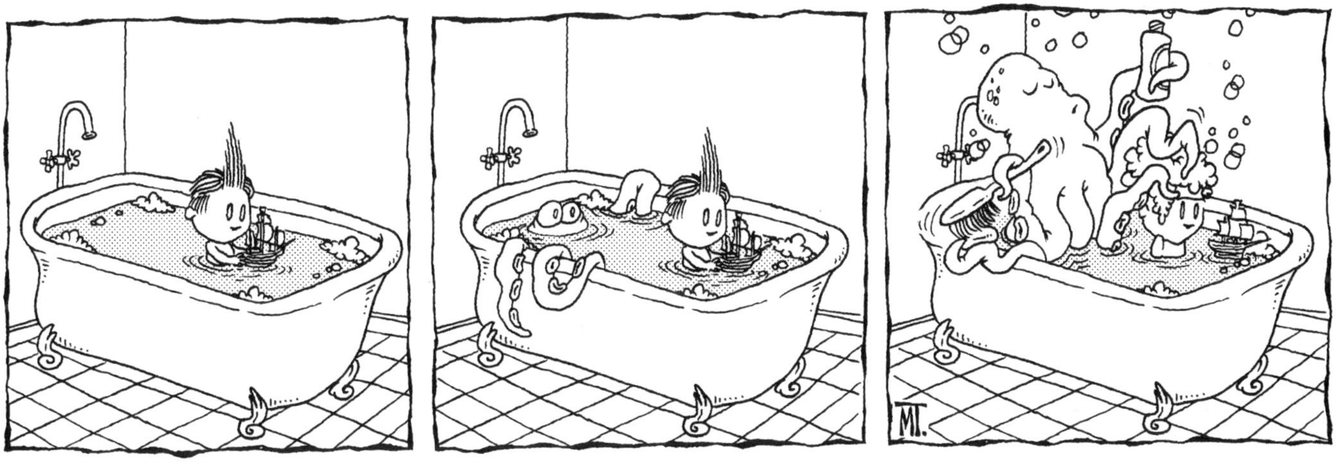
MT.

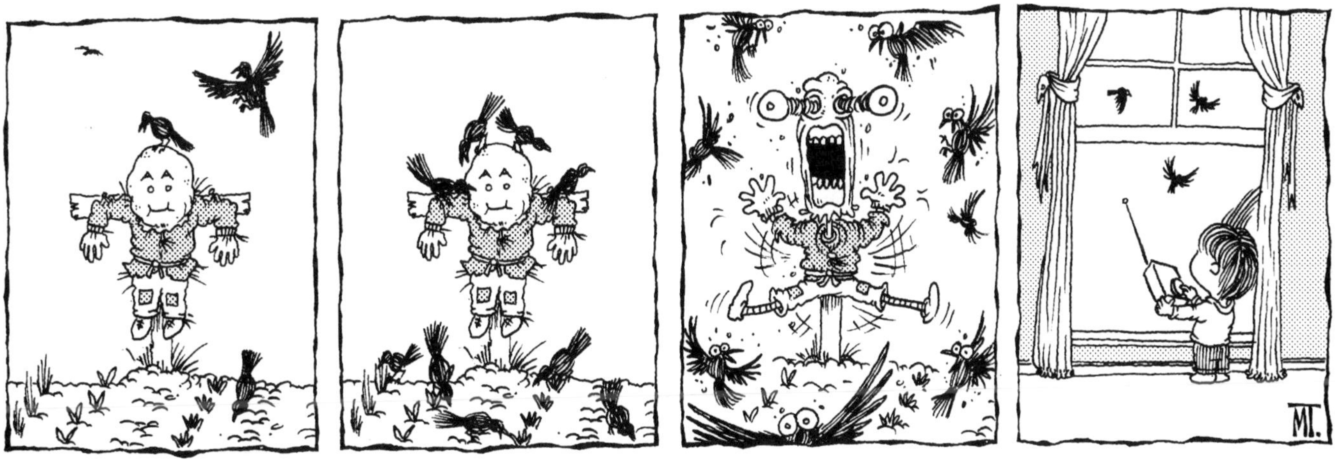
MT.

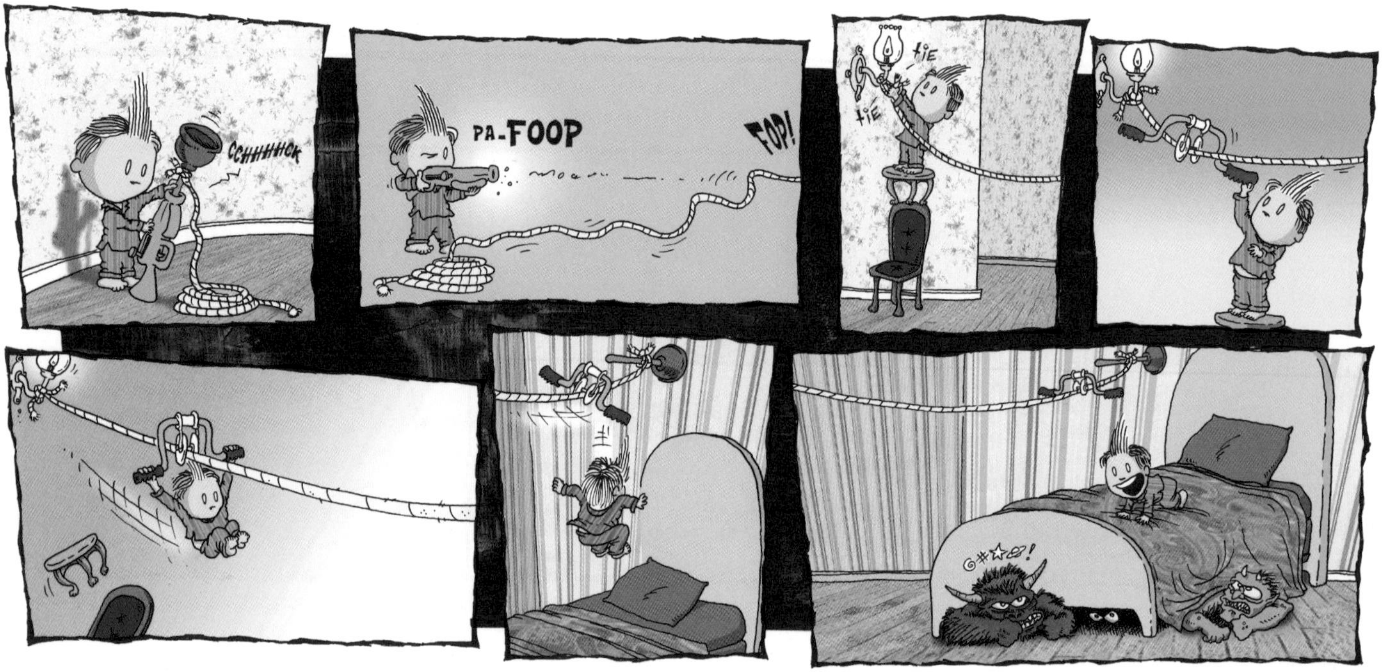
CCHHHHCK
PA-FOOP
FOP!
tie
tie

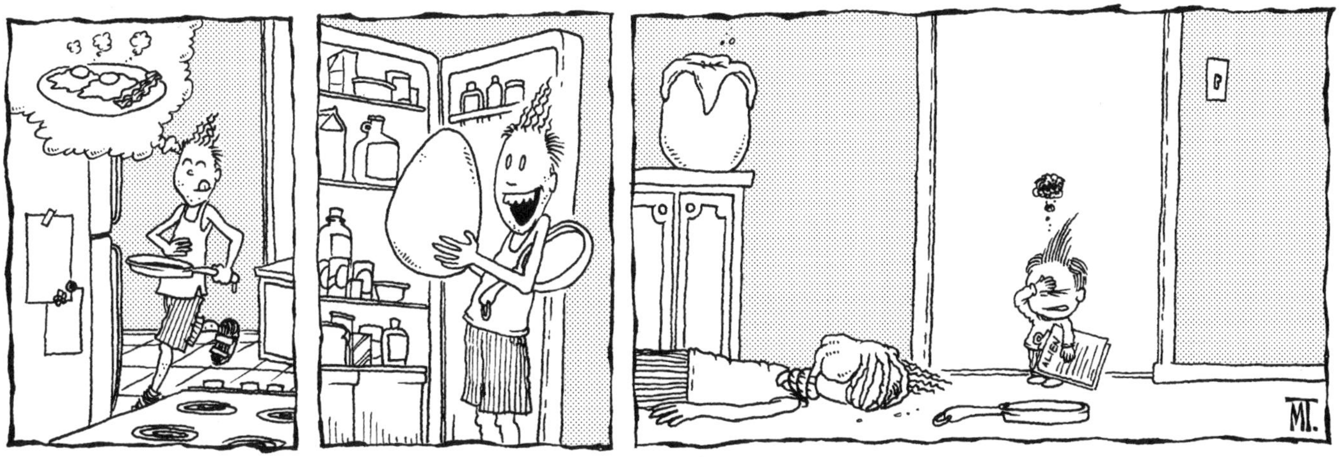
MI.

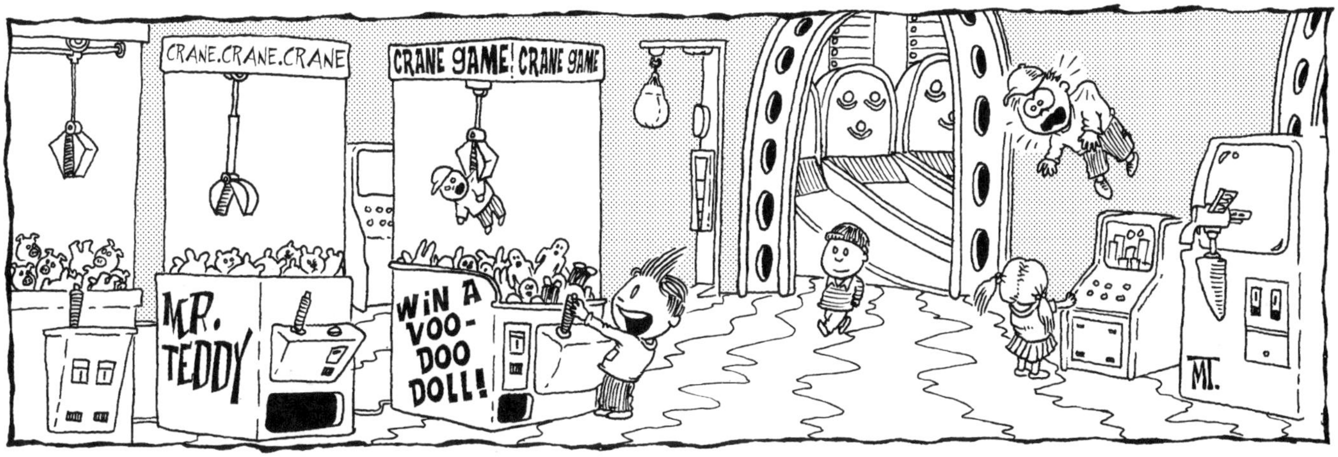
CRANE.CRANE.CRANE
CRANE GAME! CRANE GAME
MR. TEDDY
WIN A VOO-DOO DOLL!
MI.

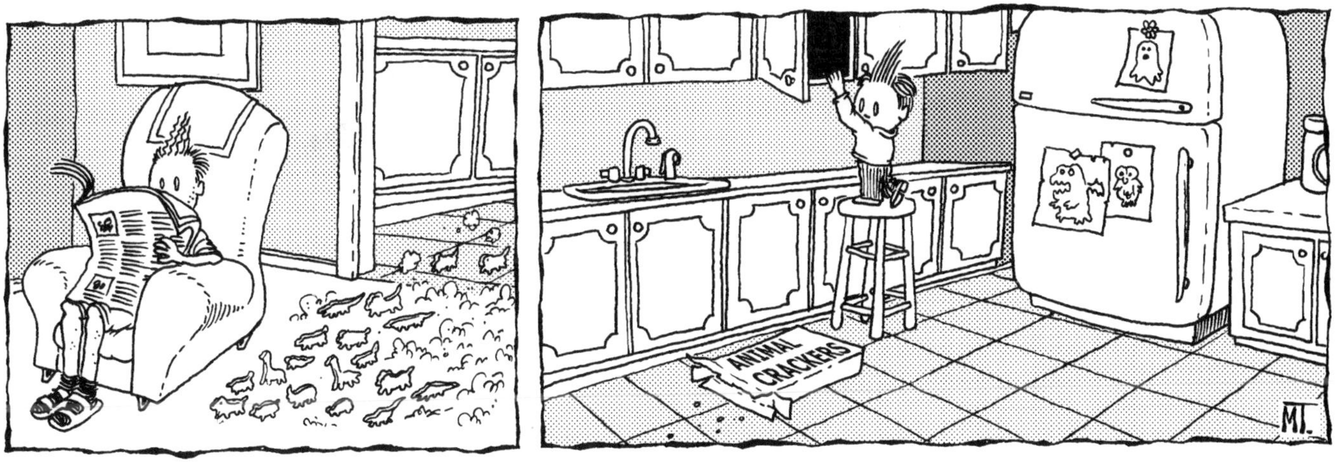
ANIMAL CRACKERS
MI.

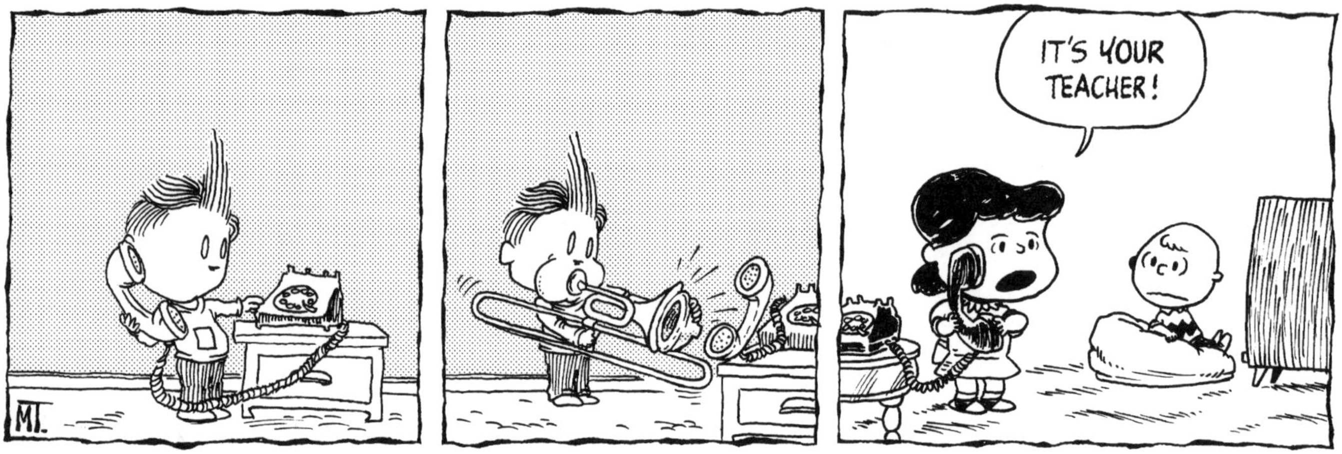
IT'S YOUR TEACHER!

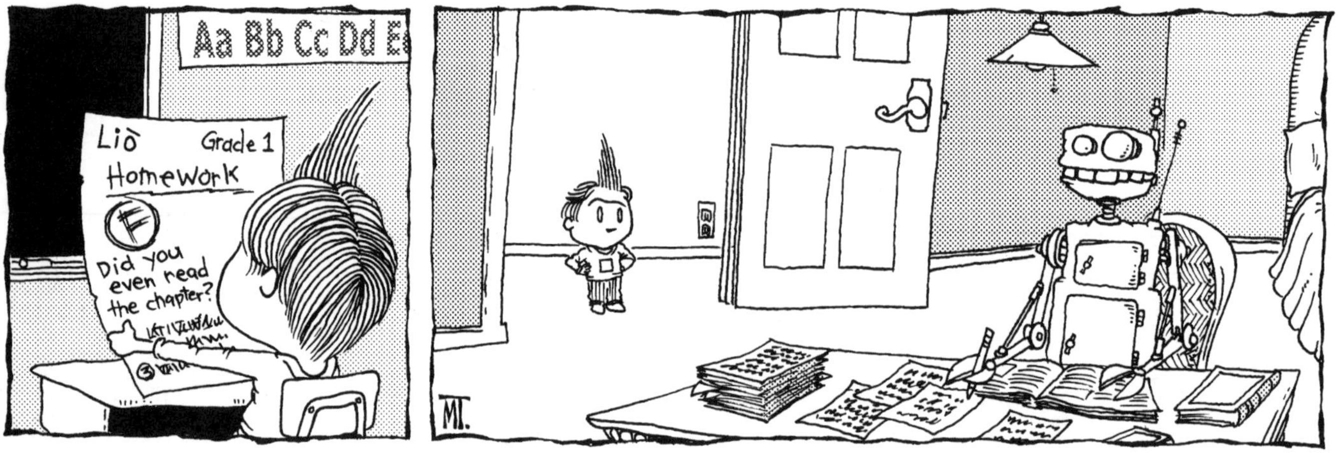
Aa Bb Cc Dd E
Liò Grade 1
Homework
F
Did you even read the chapter?

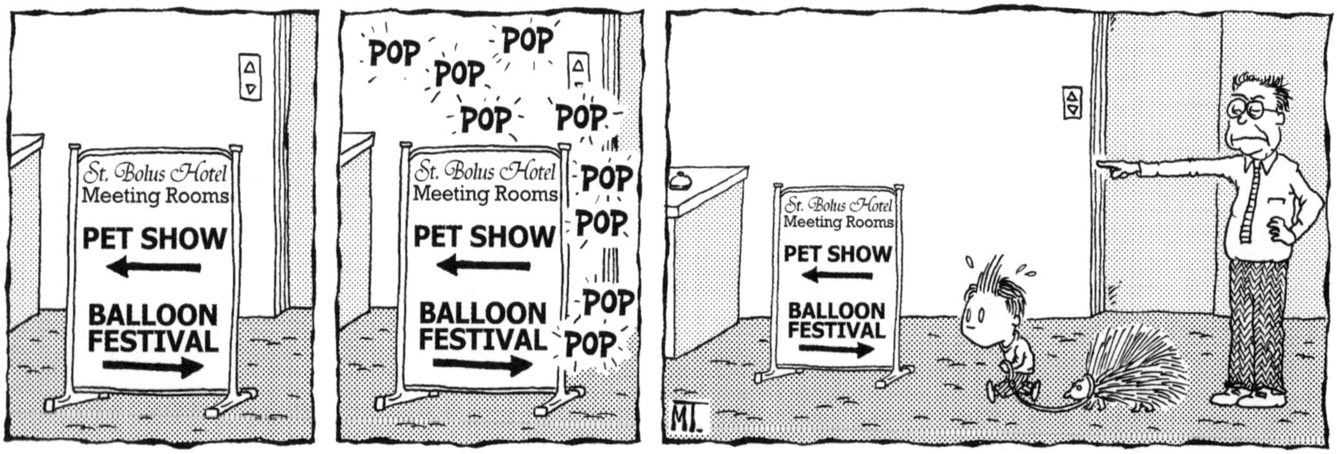
St. Bolus Hotel
Meeting Rooms
PET SHOW
BALLOON FESTIVAL
POP POP POP POP POP POP POP POP POP
St. Bolus Hotel
Meeting Rooms
PET SHOW
BALLOON FESTIVAL

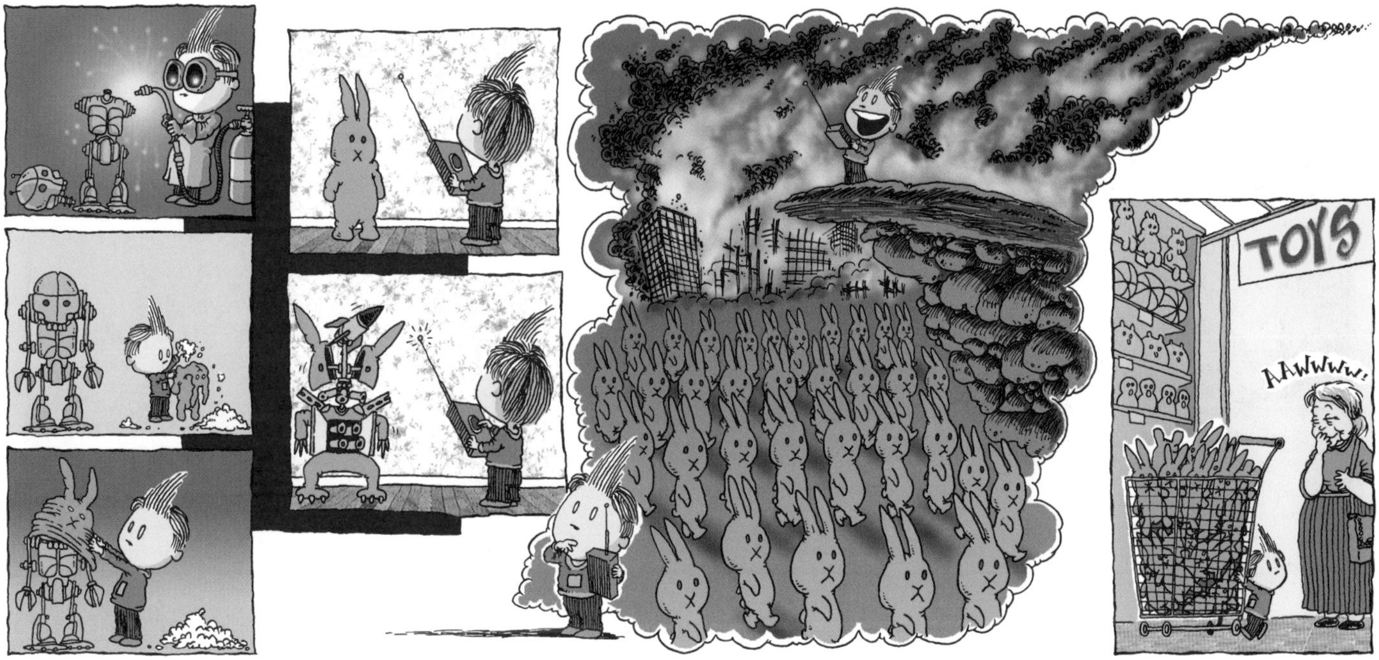
TOYS
AAWWWW!

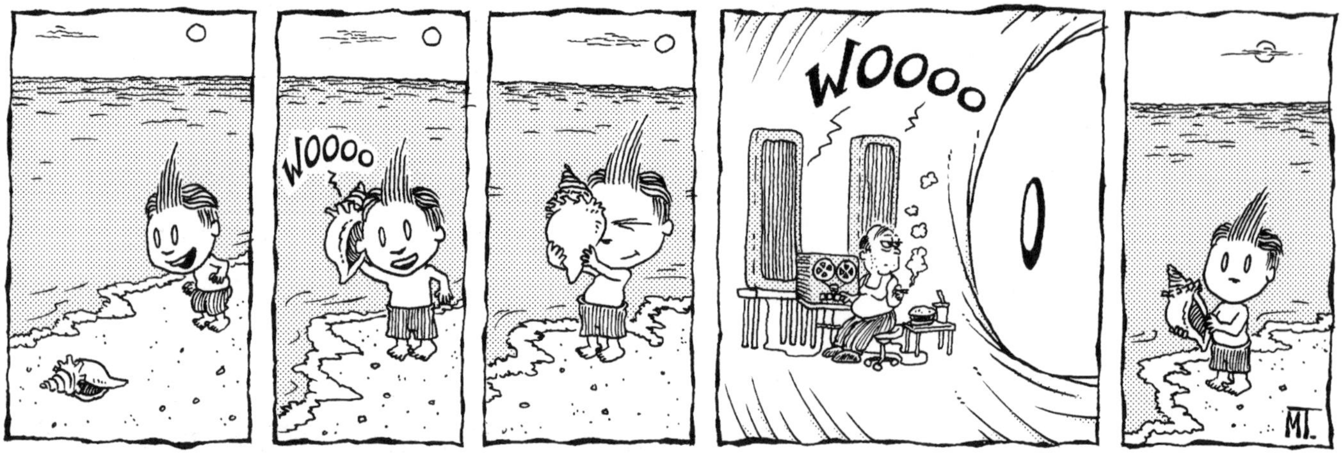
WOOOo
WOOOO

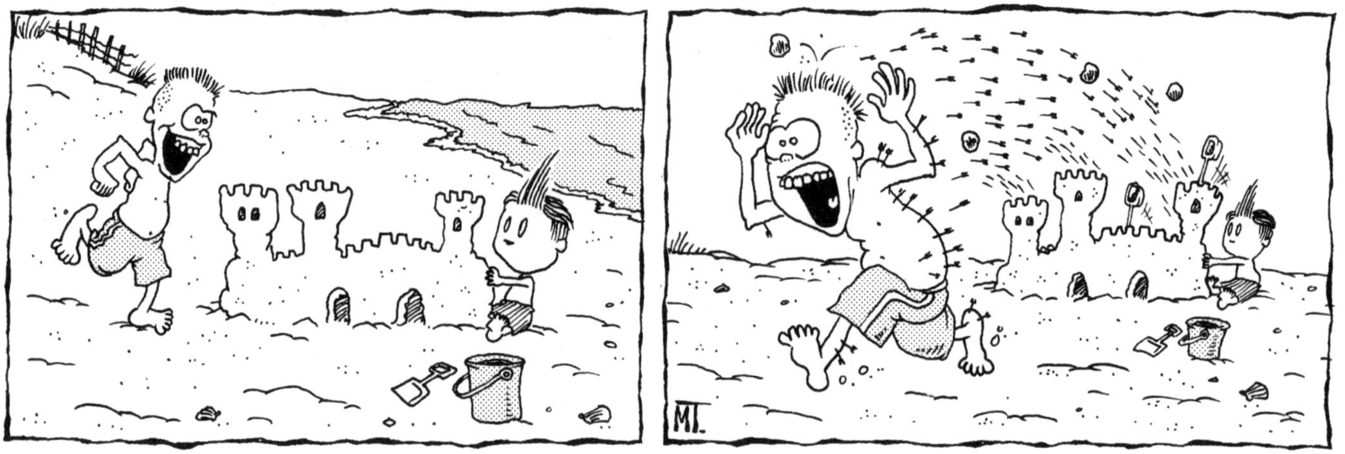

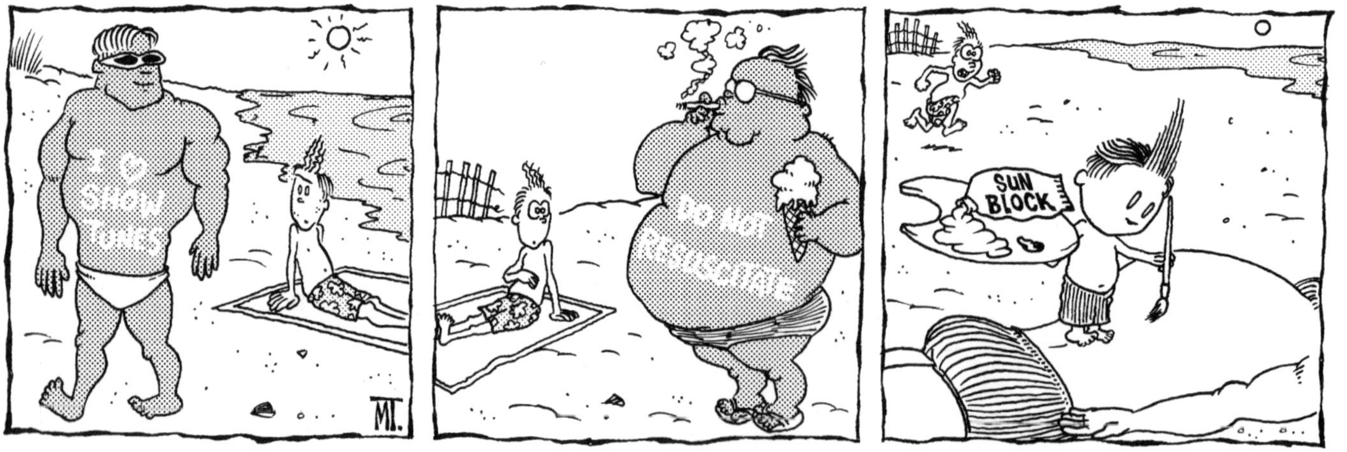
I ♥ SHOW TUNES
DO NOT RESUSCITATE
SUN BLOCK

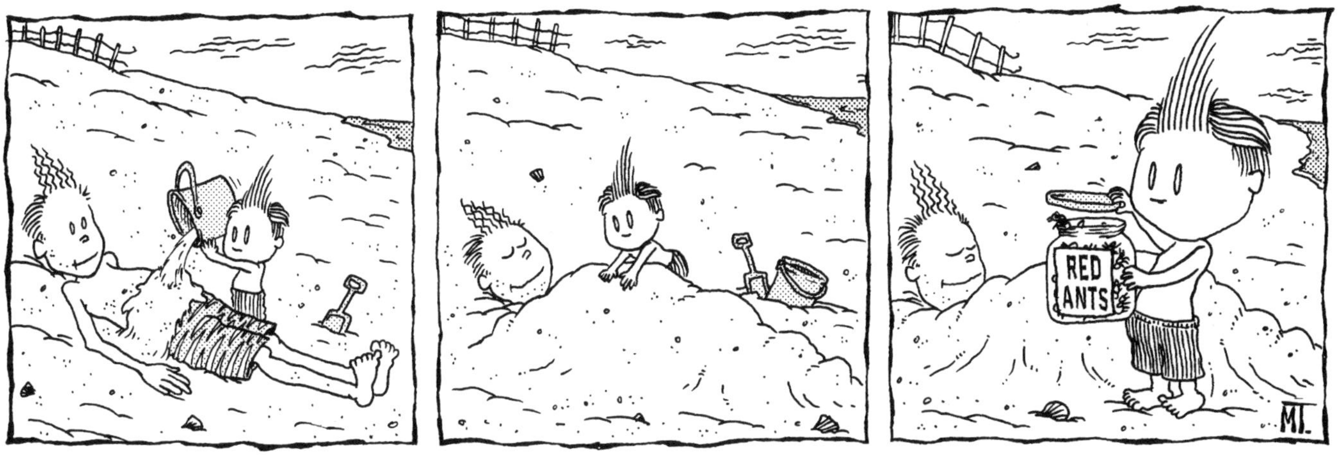
RED
ANTS
MT.

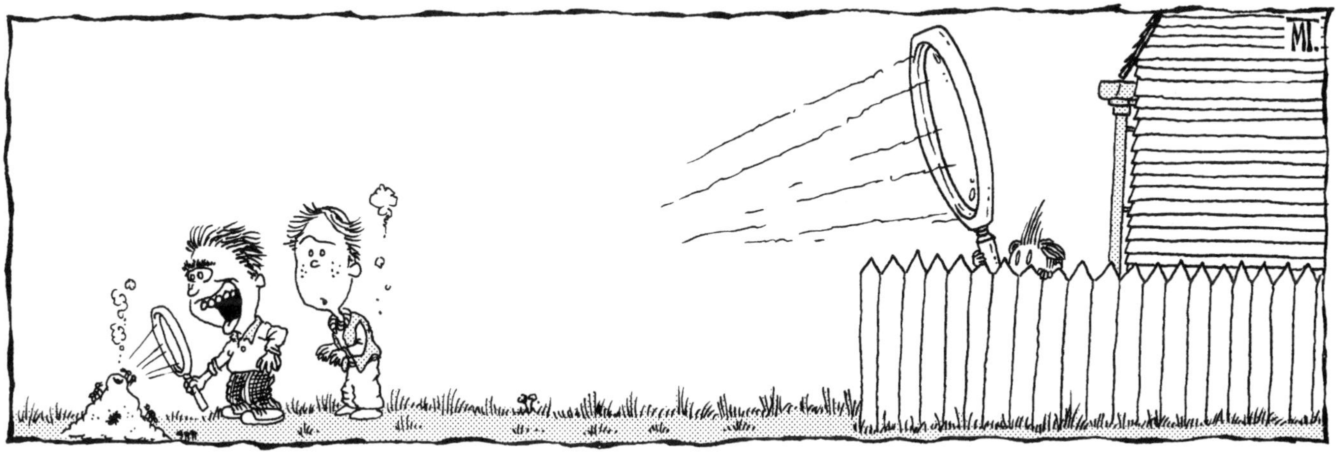
MT.

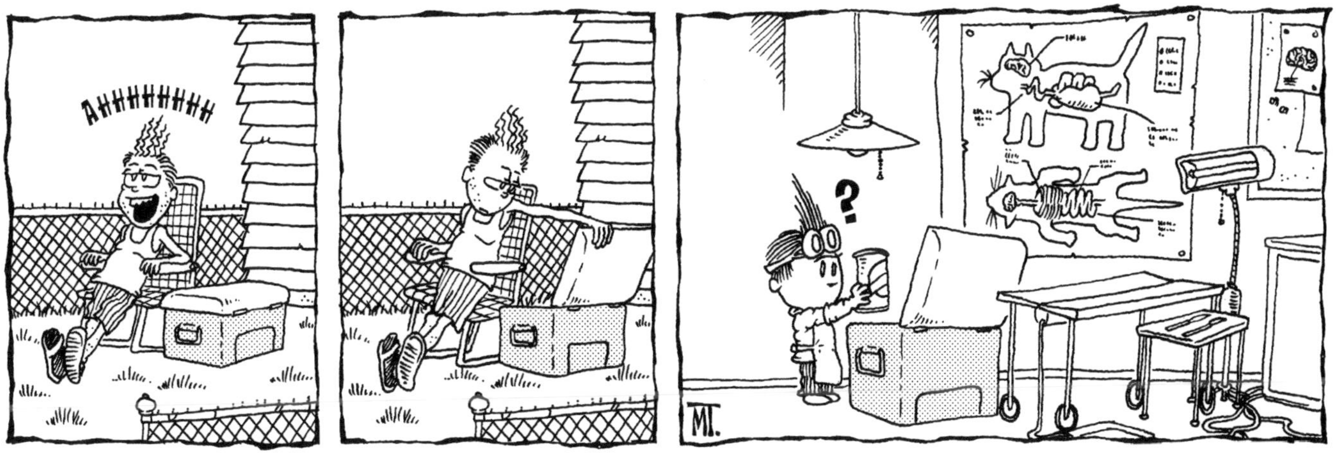
AHHHHHHHH
?
MT.

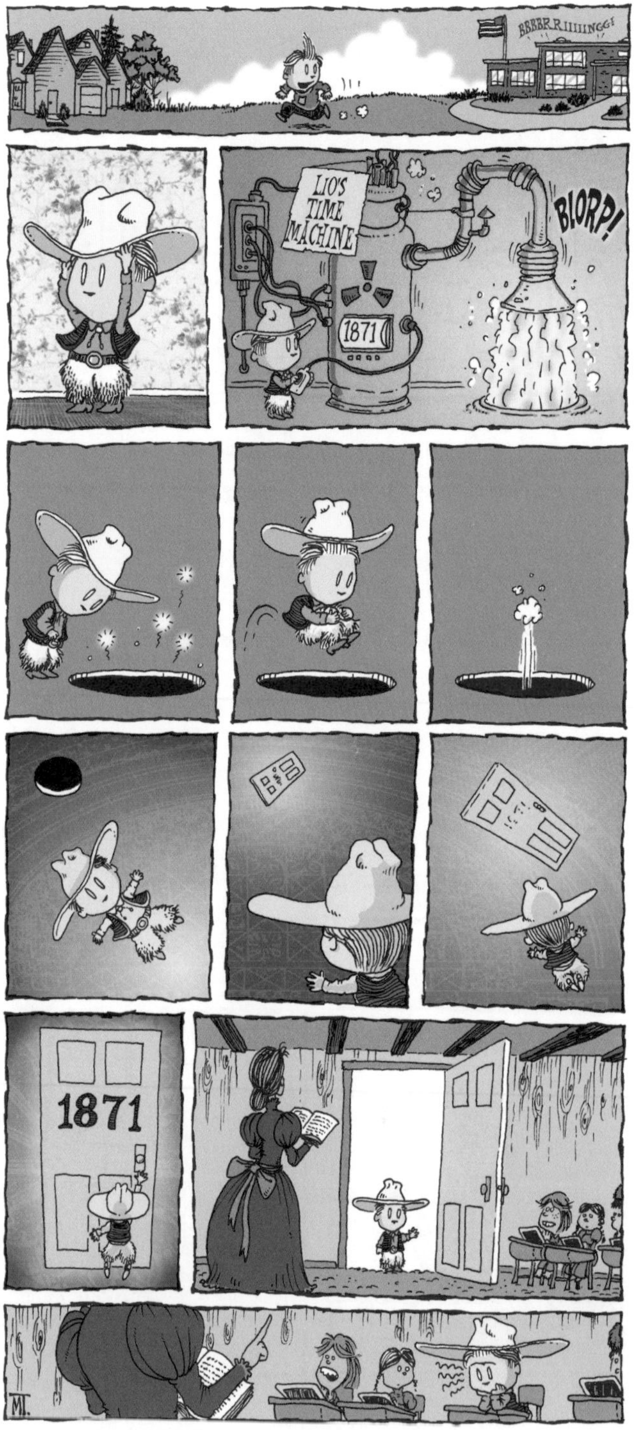
BBBBRRIIIIINGG!
LIO'S TIME MACHINE
1871
BLORP!
1871
MT.

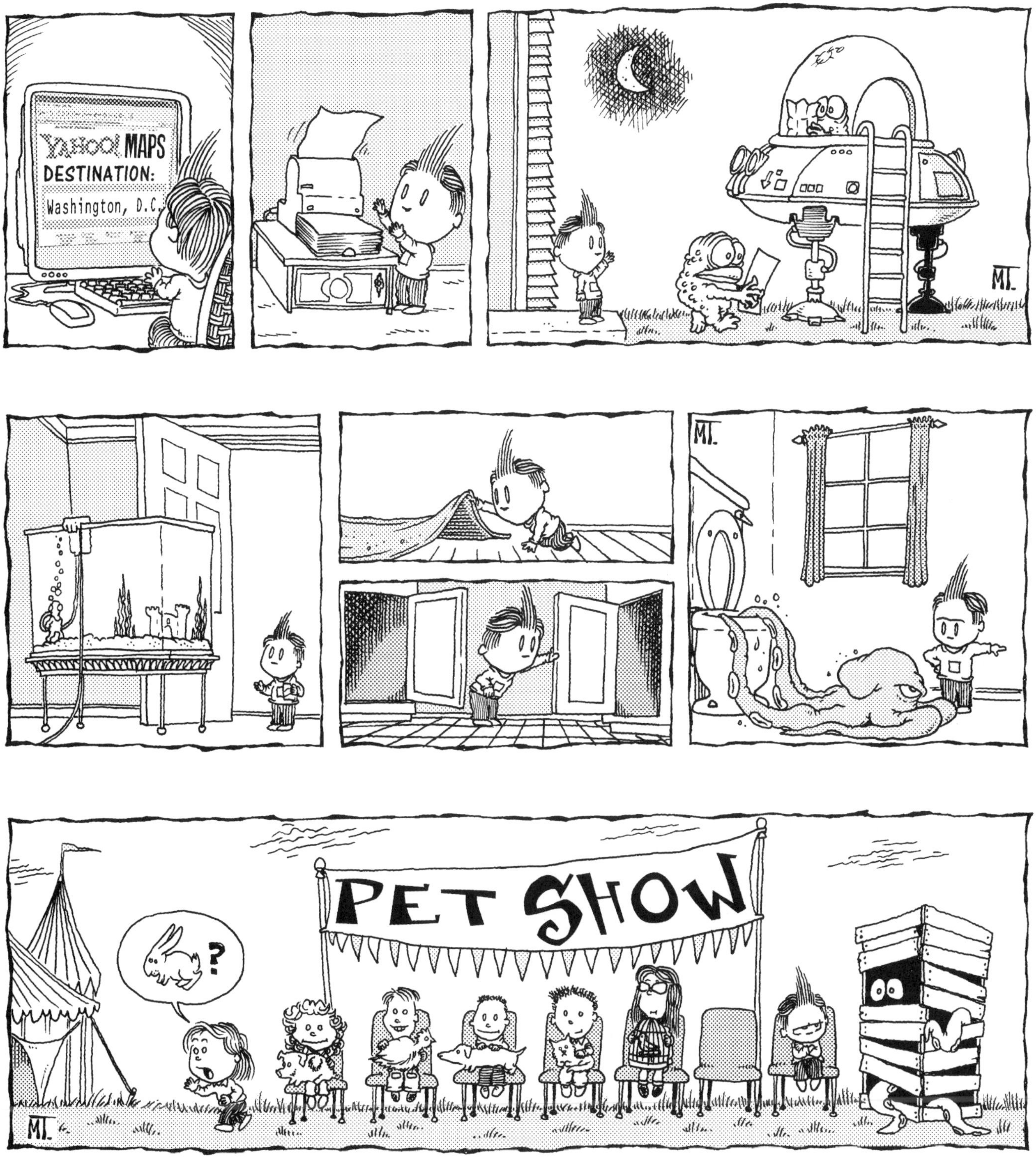
YAHOO! MAPS
DESTINATION:
Washington, D.C.
MT
MT
PET SHOW
?
MT

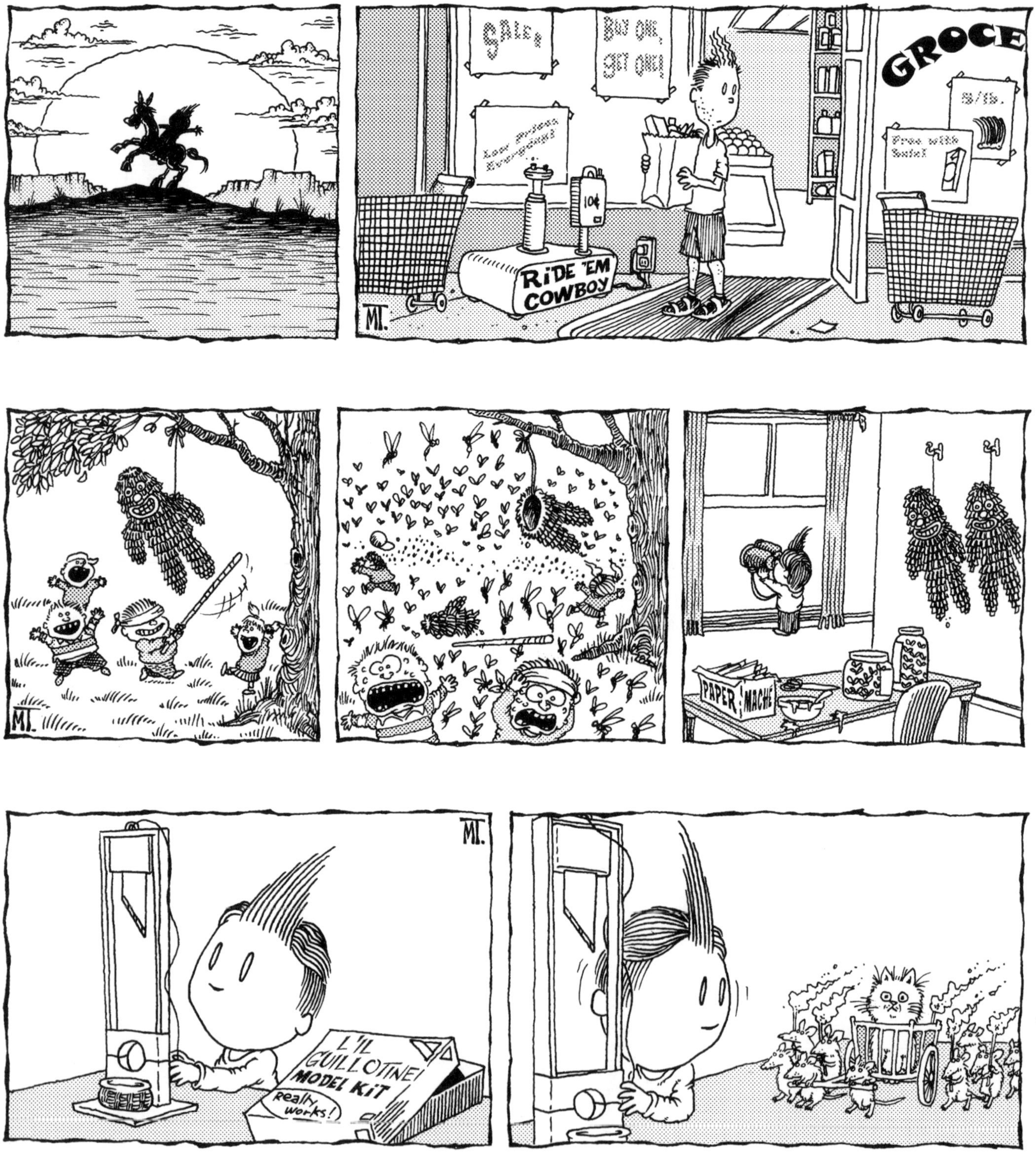
SALE!
BUY ONE, GET ONE!
10¢
RIDE 'EM COWBOY
GROCE
MT.
MT.
PAPER MACHE
MT.
L'IL GUILLOTINE MODEL KIT
really works!

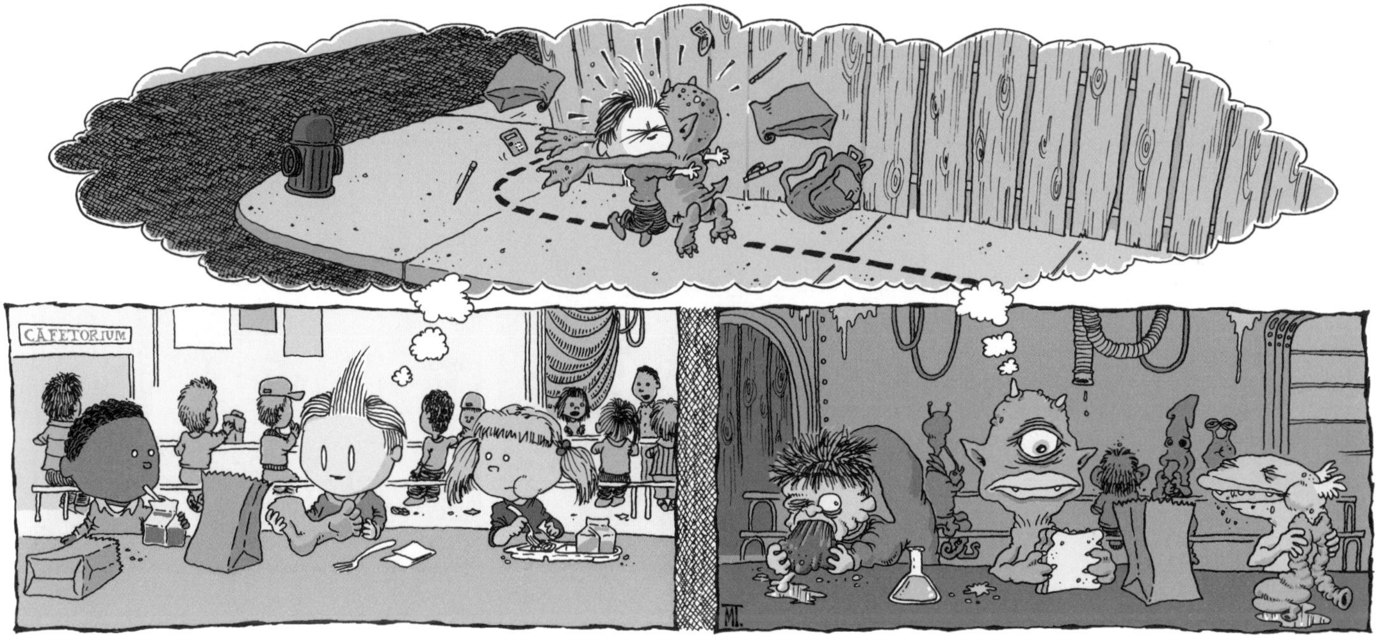
CAFETORIUM

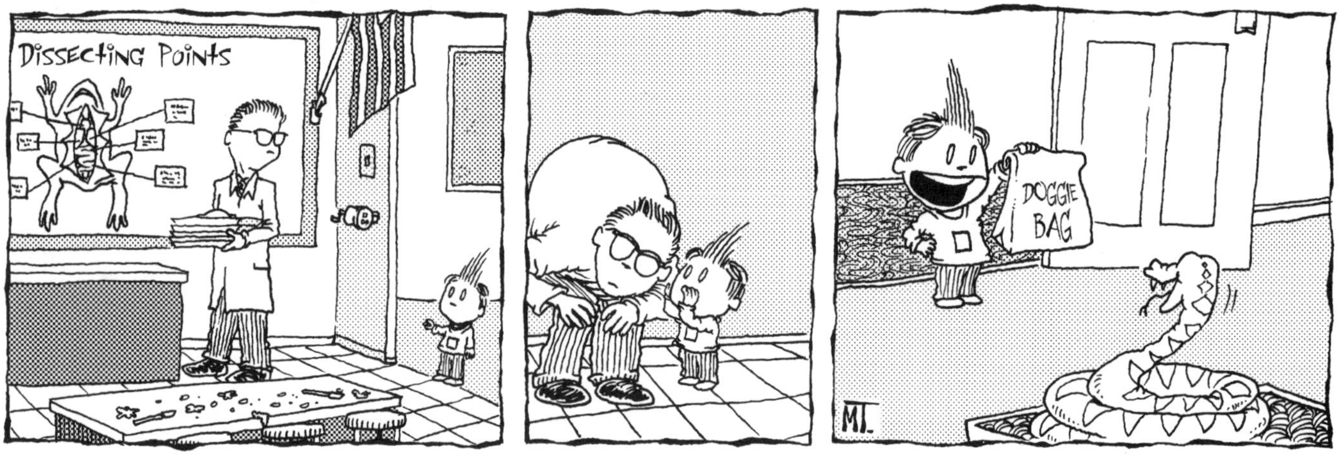
Dissecting Points
DOGGIE BAG

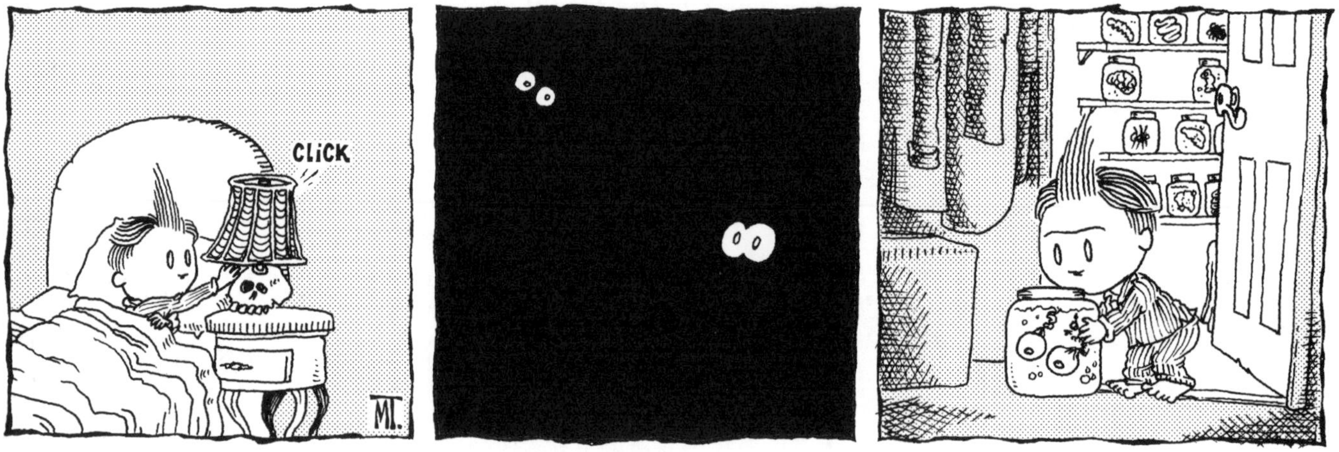
CLICK

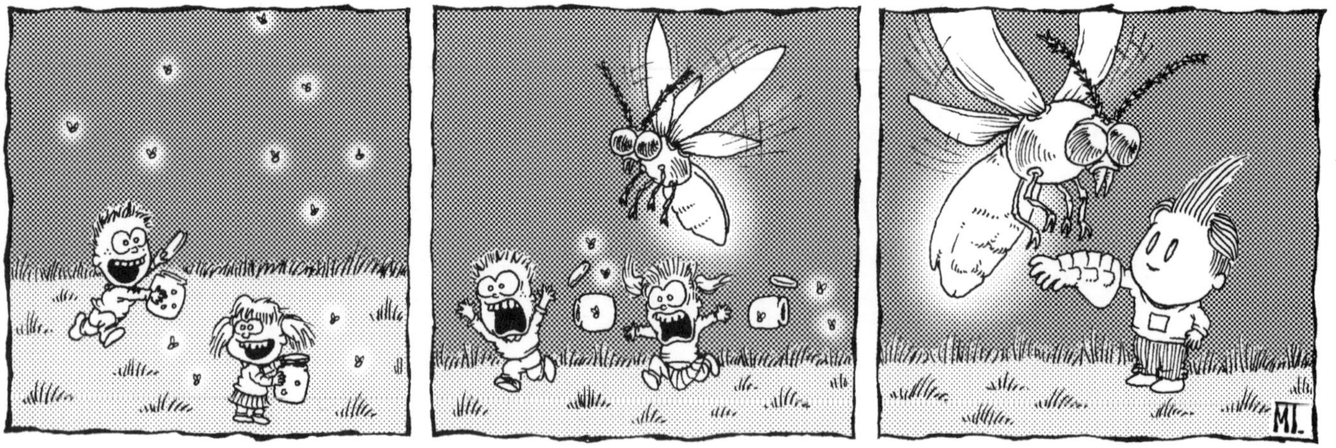

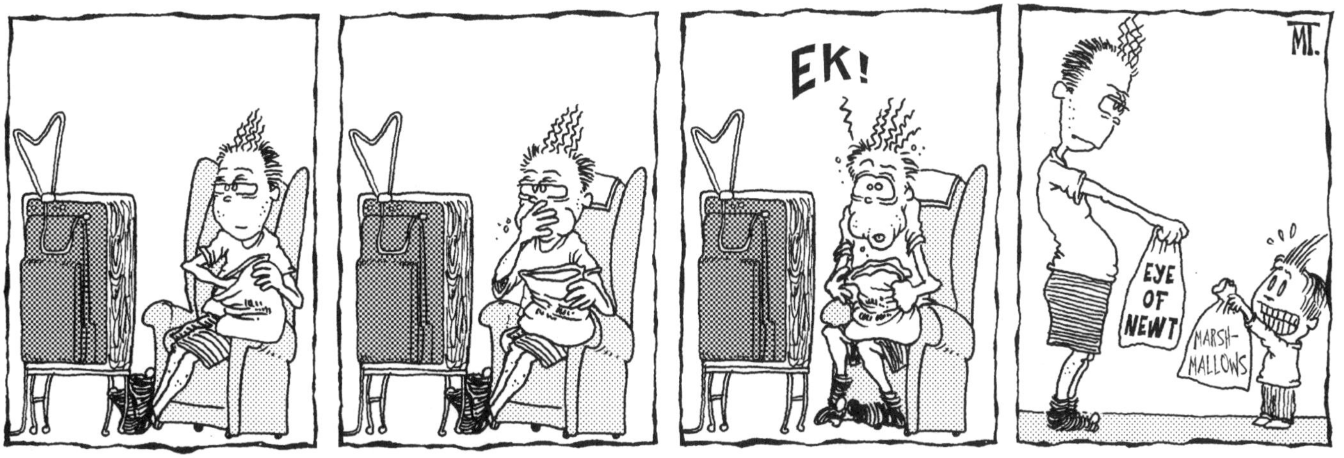
EK!
EYE OF NEWT
MARSH-MALLOWS
MT.

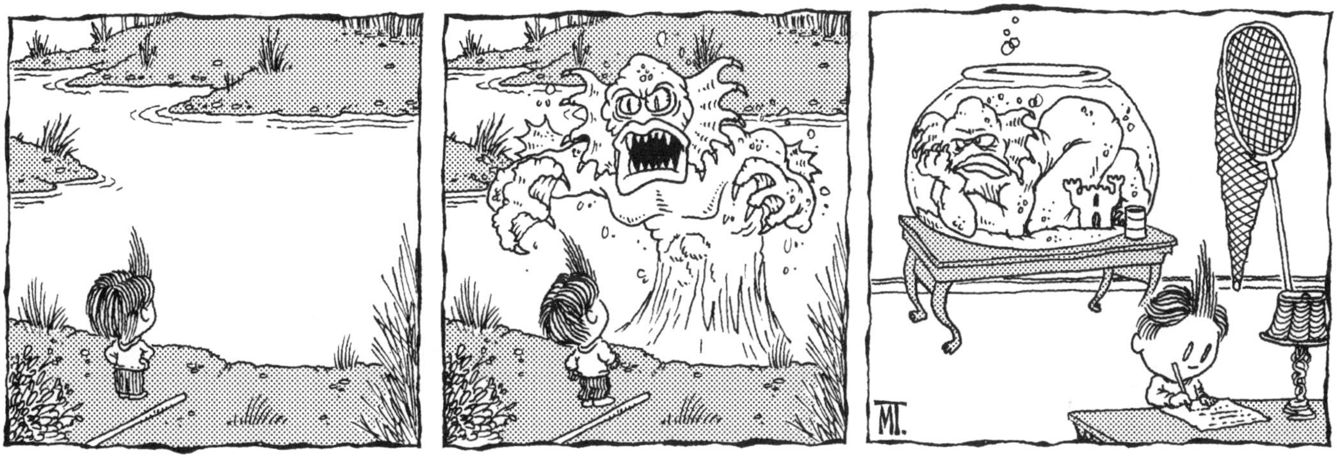
MT.

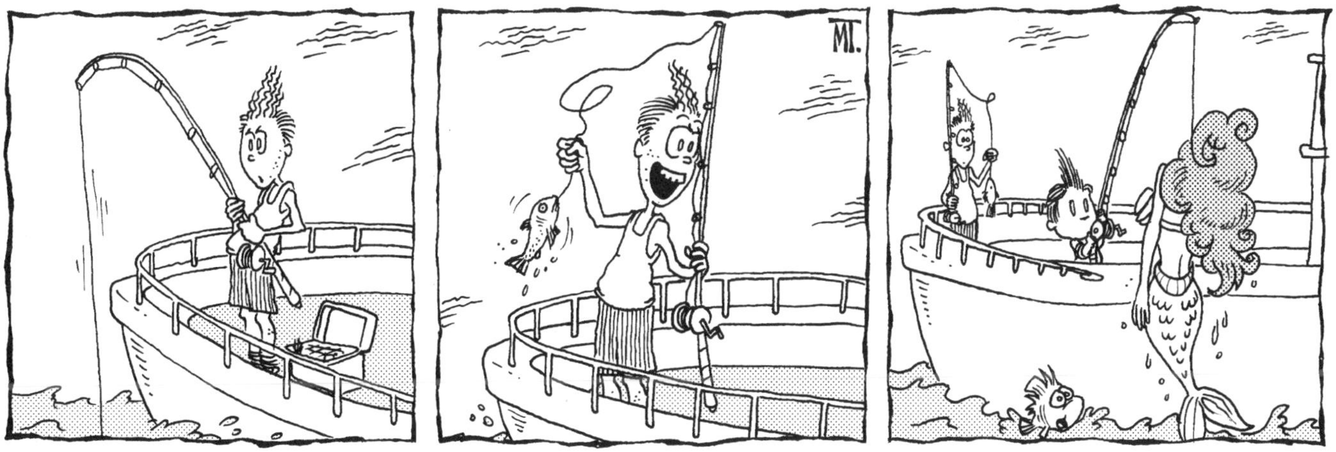
MT.

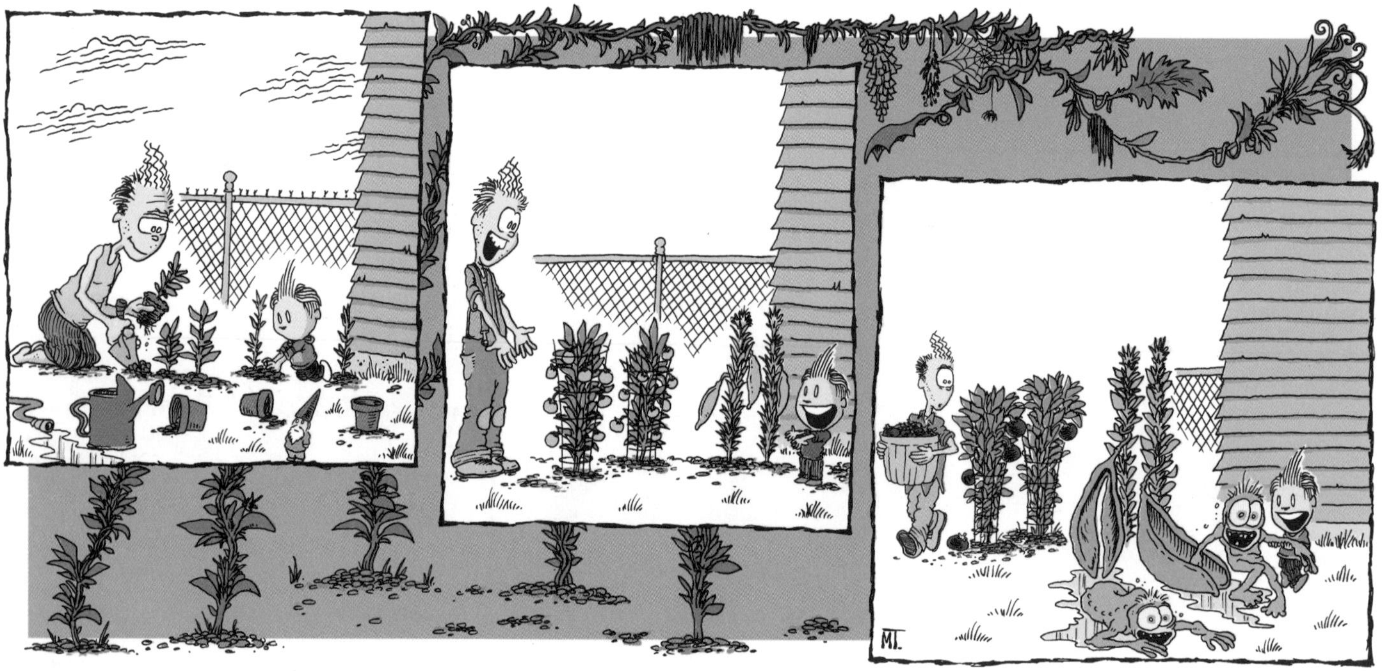
MI.

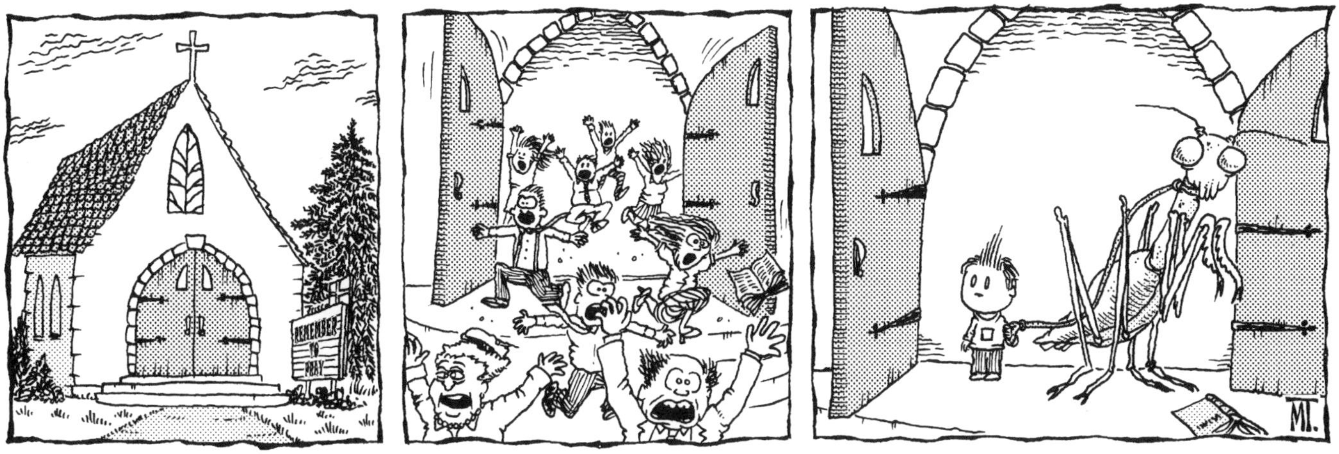
REMEMBER
TO
PRAY
MT.

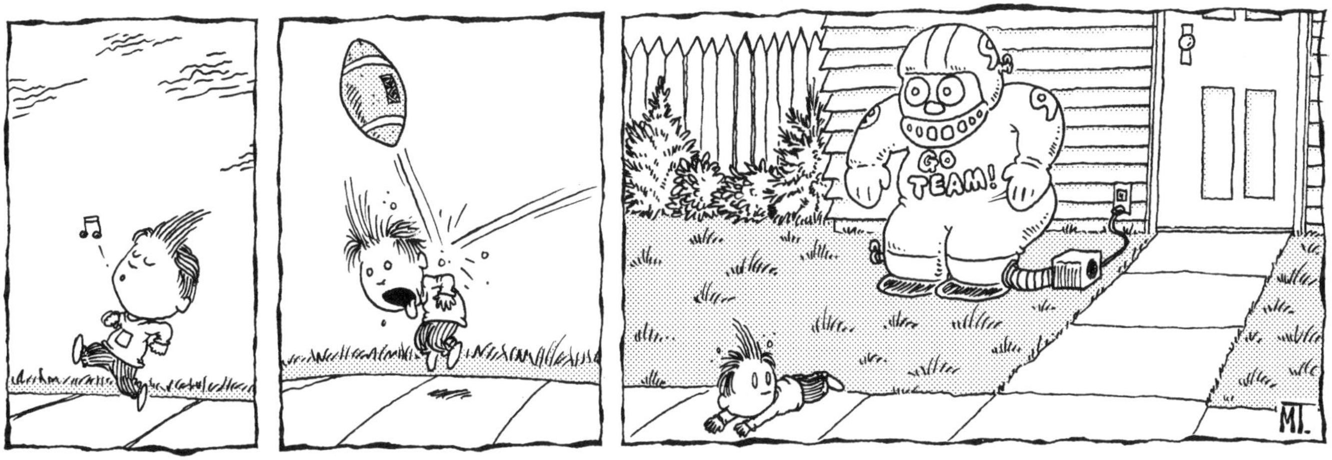
GO TEAM!
MT.

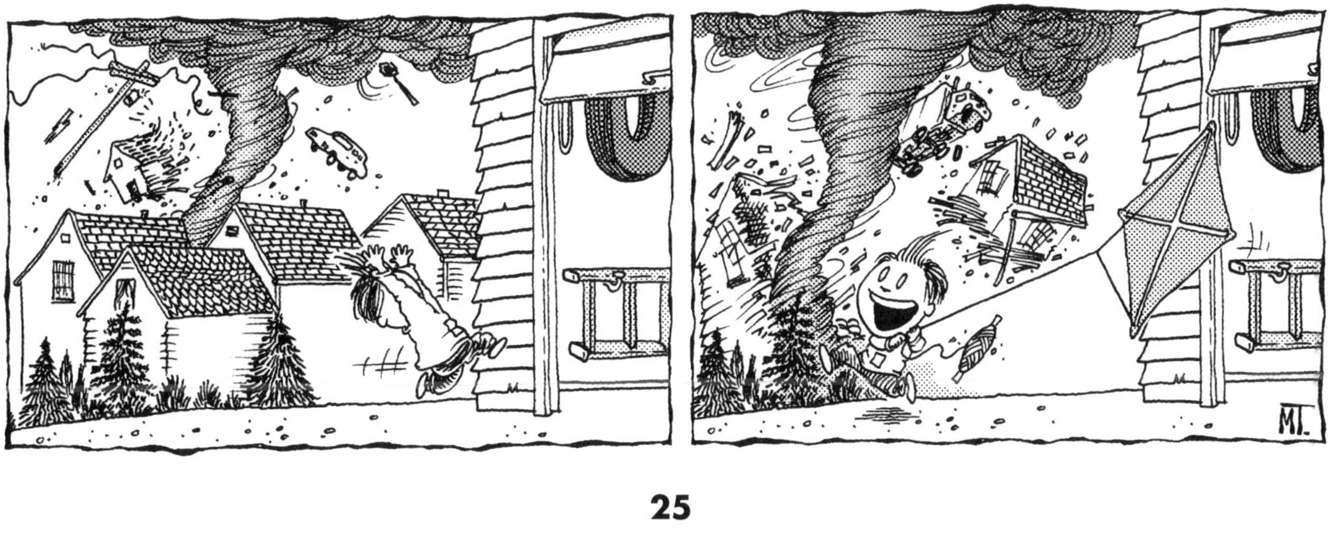
MT.

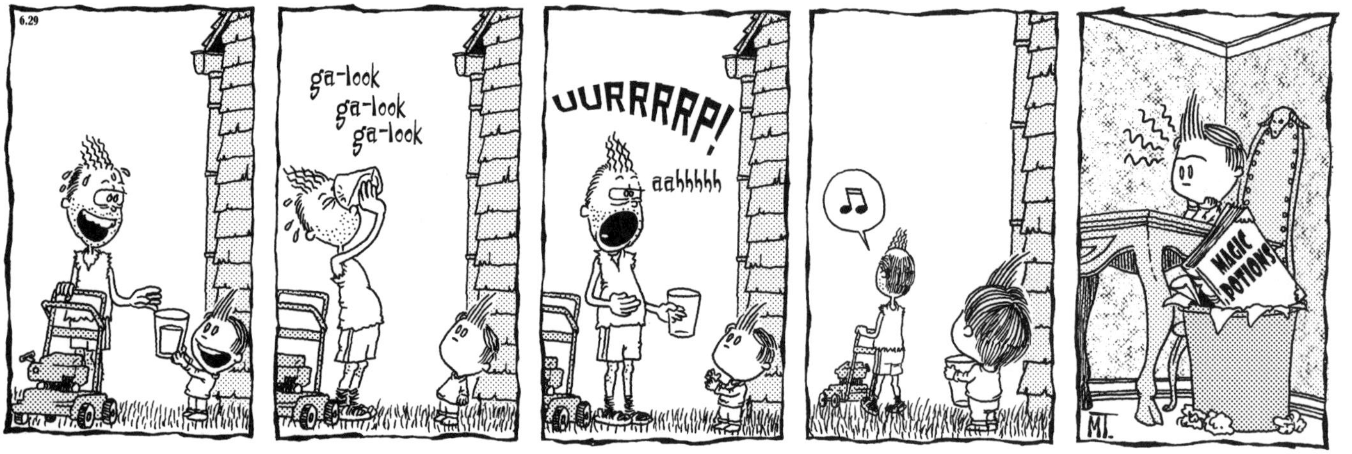
6.29
ga-look
ga-look
ga-look
UURRRRP!
aahhhhh
MAGIC POTIONS

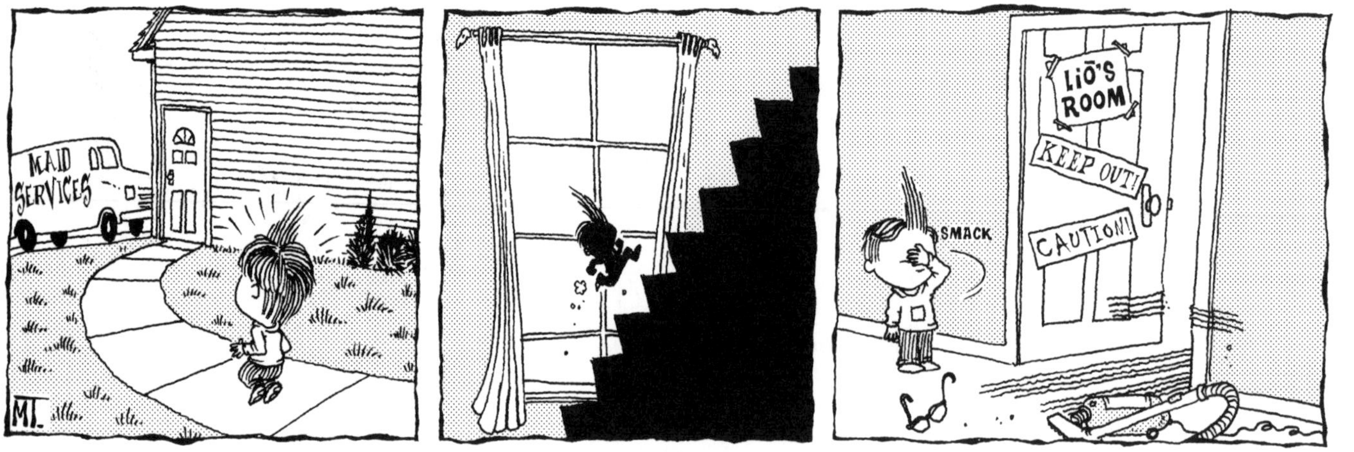
MAID SERVICES
LIO'S ROOM
KEEP OUT!
CAUTION!
SMACK

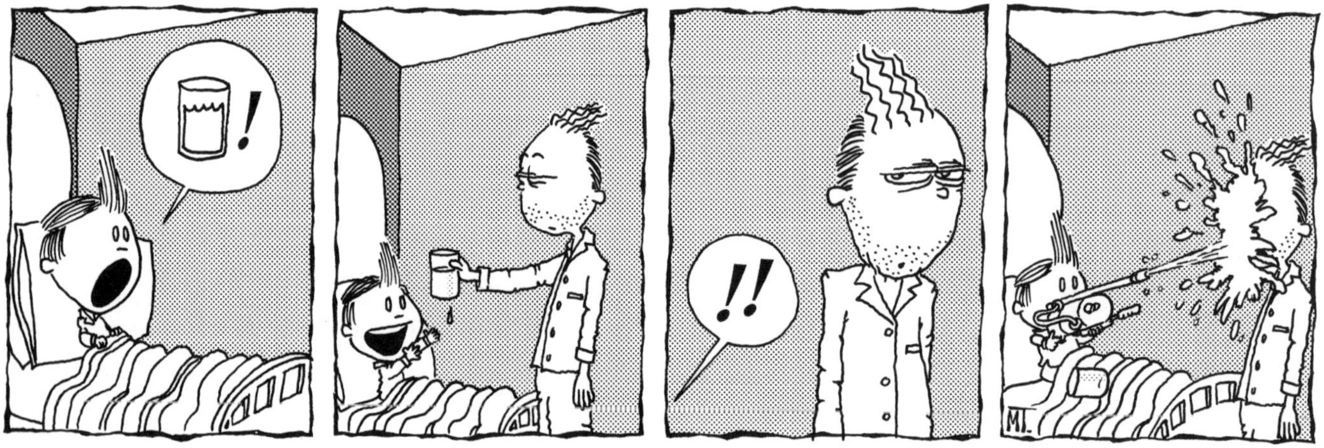
!
!!

COUNTY FAIR
ZUCKERMAN'S FAMOUS PIG
MT.

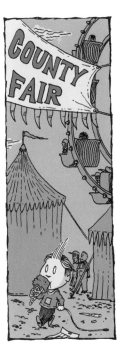

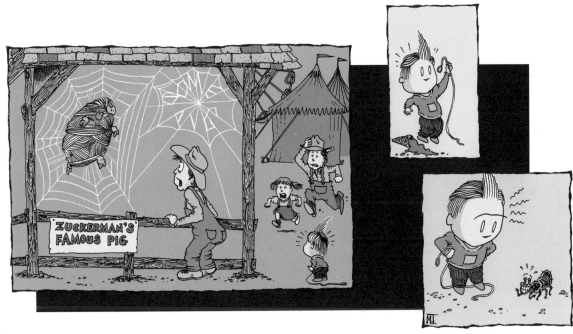

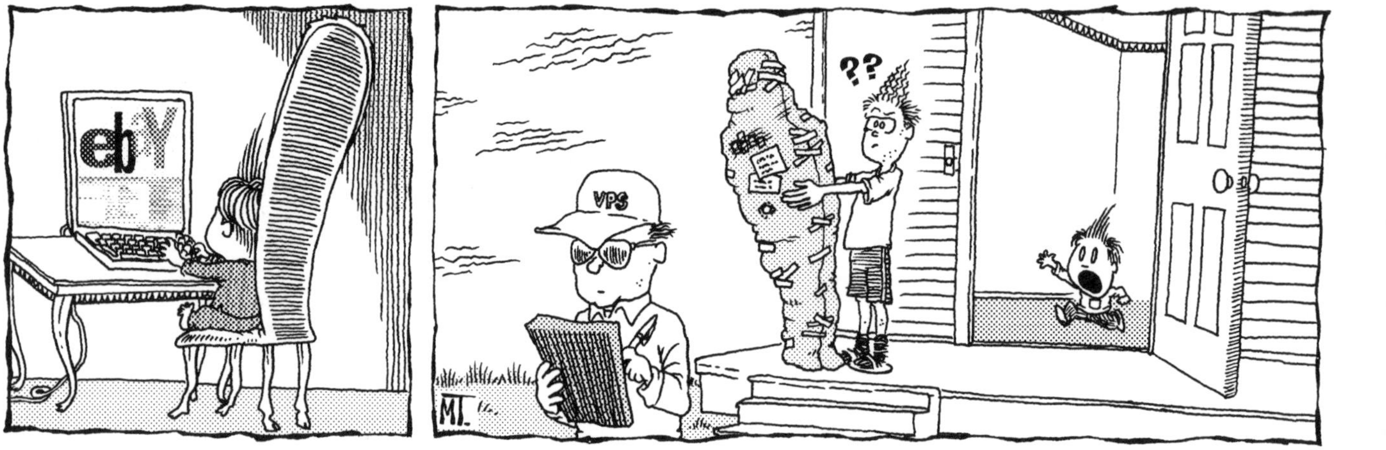
VPS
??

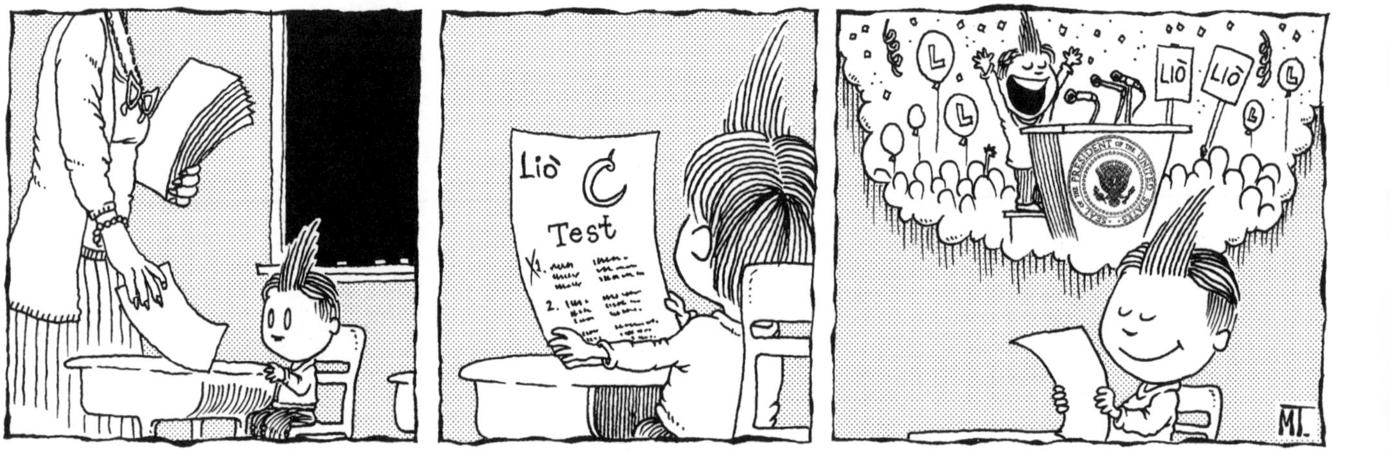
Liò
C
Test
Liò
Liò

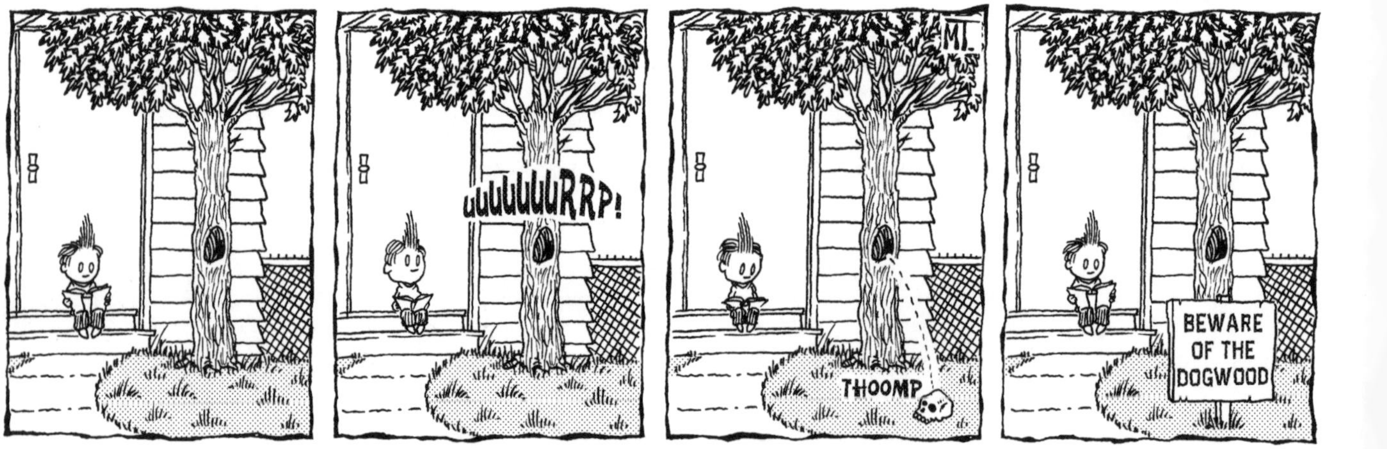
uuuuuuuRRP!
THOOMP
BEWARE OF THE DOGWOOD

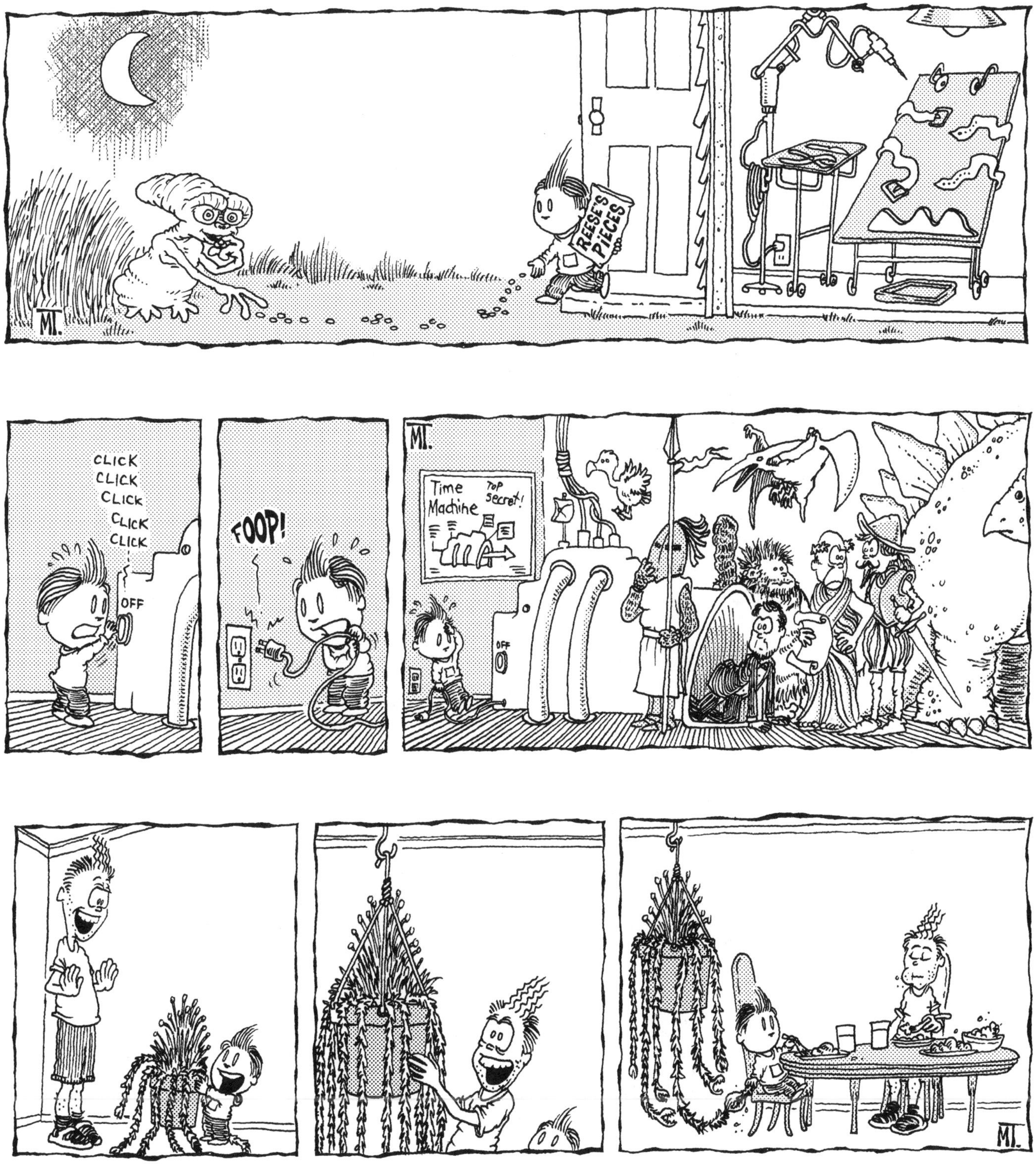
REESE'S PIECES
CLICK
CLICK
CLICK
CLICK
CLICK
OFF
FOOP!
Time Machine
Top Secret!
OFF

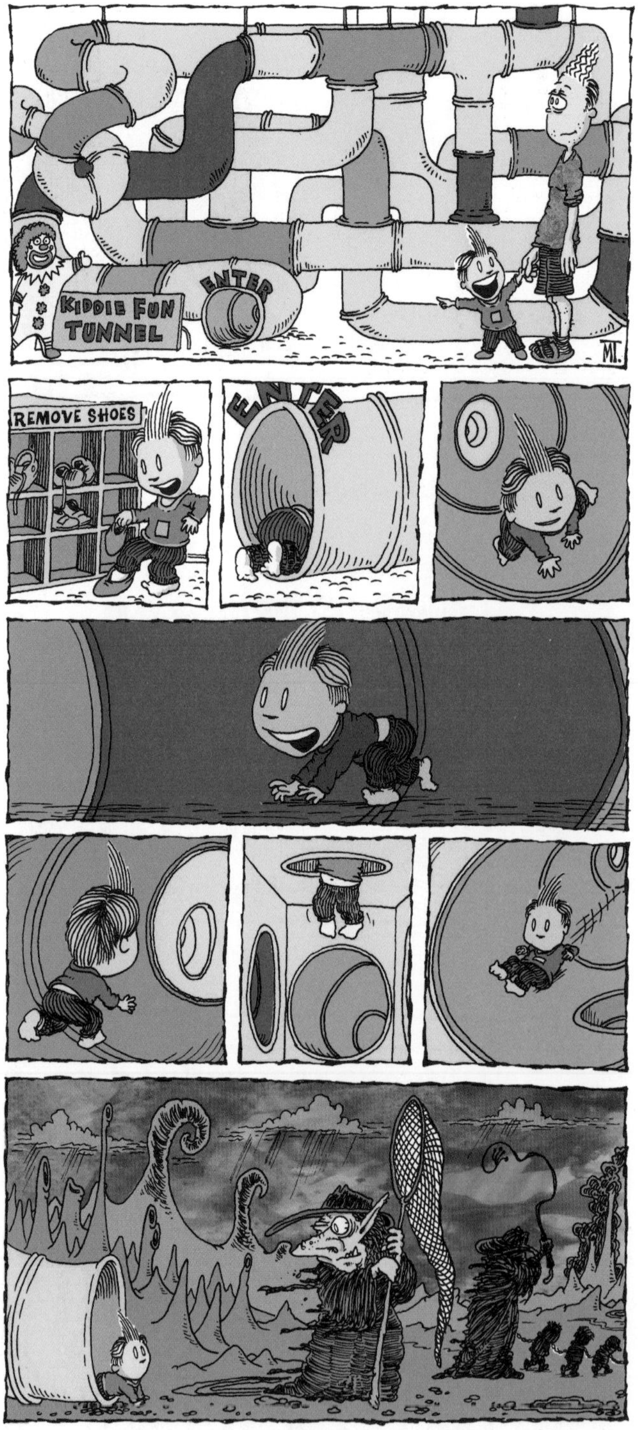
KIDDIE FUN TUNNEL
ENTER
MT.
REMOVE SHOES
ENTER

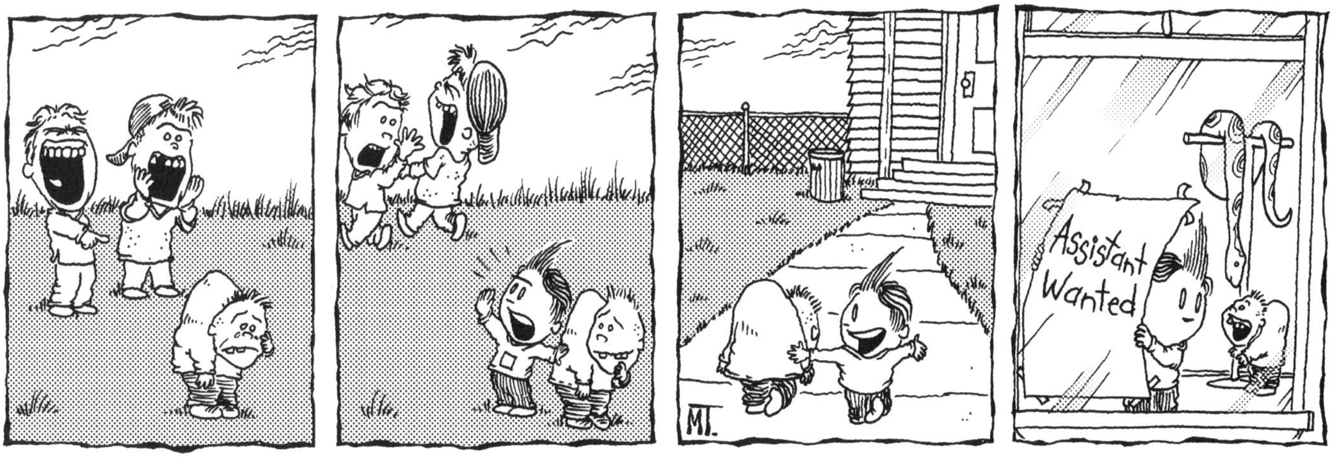
Assistant
Wanted
MT.

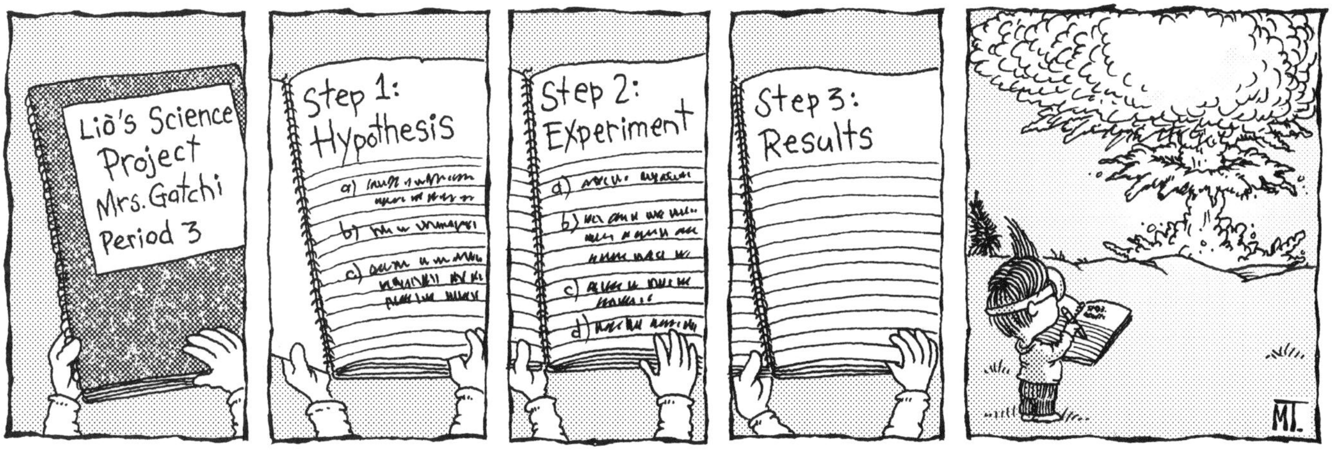
Liò's Science
Project
Mrs. Gatchi
Period 3
Step 1:
Hypothesis
Step 2:
Experiment
Step 3:
Results
MT.

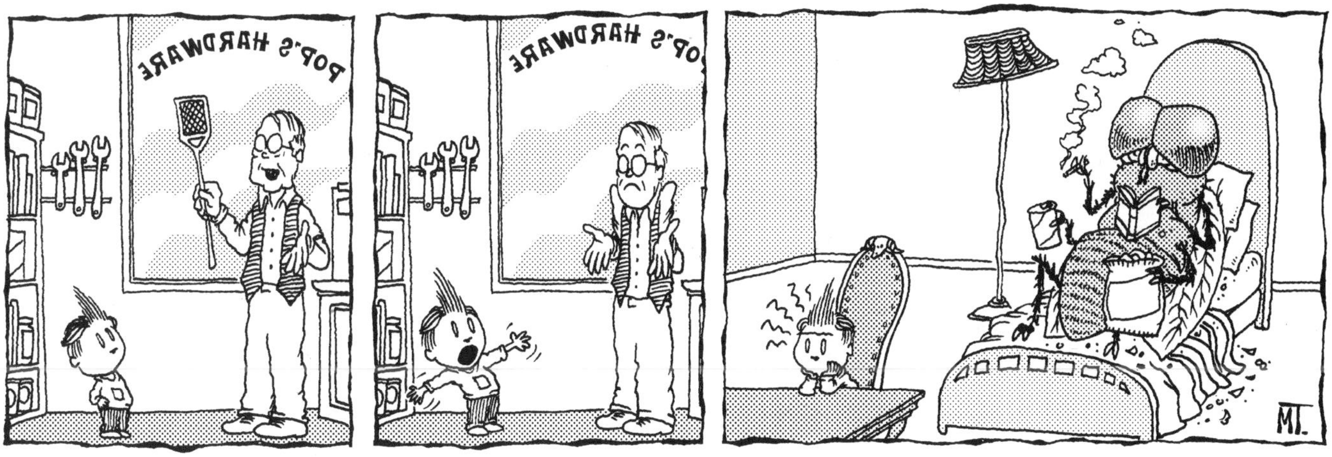
POP'S HARDWARE
OP'S HARDWARE
MT.

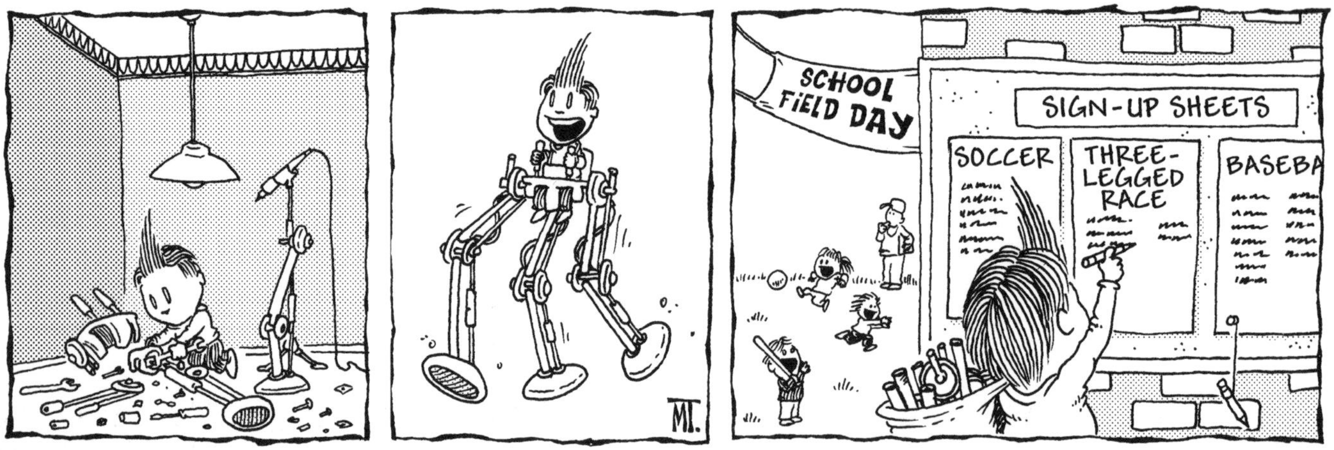
SCHOOL FIELD DAY
SIGN-UP SHEETS
SOCCER
THREE-LEGGED RACE
BASEBA

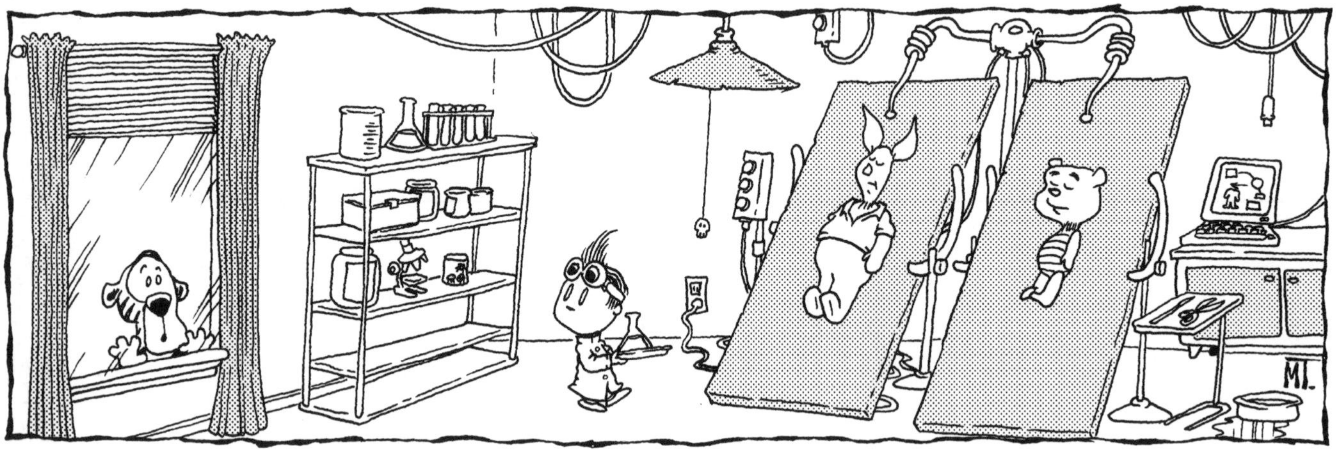

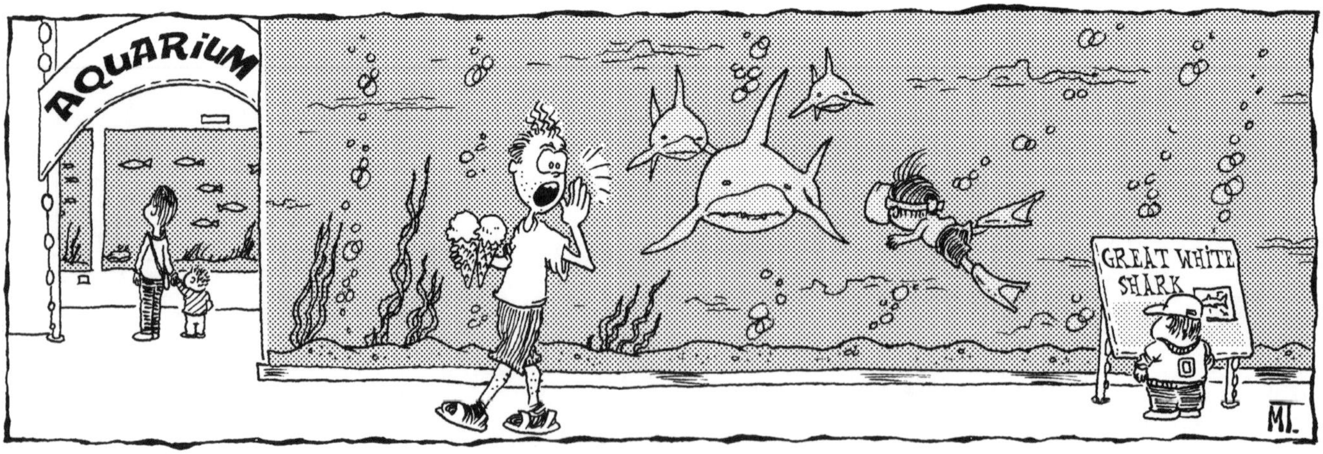
AQUARIUM
GREAT WHITE SHARK

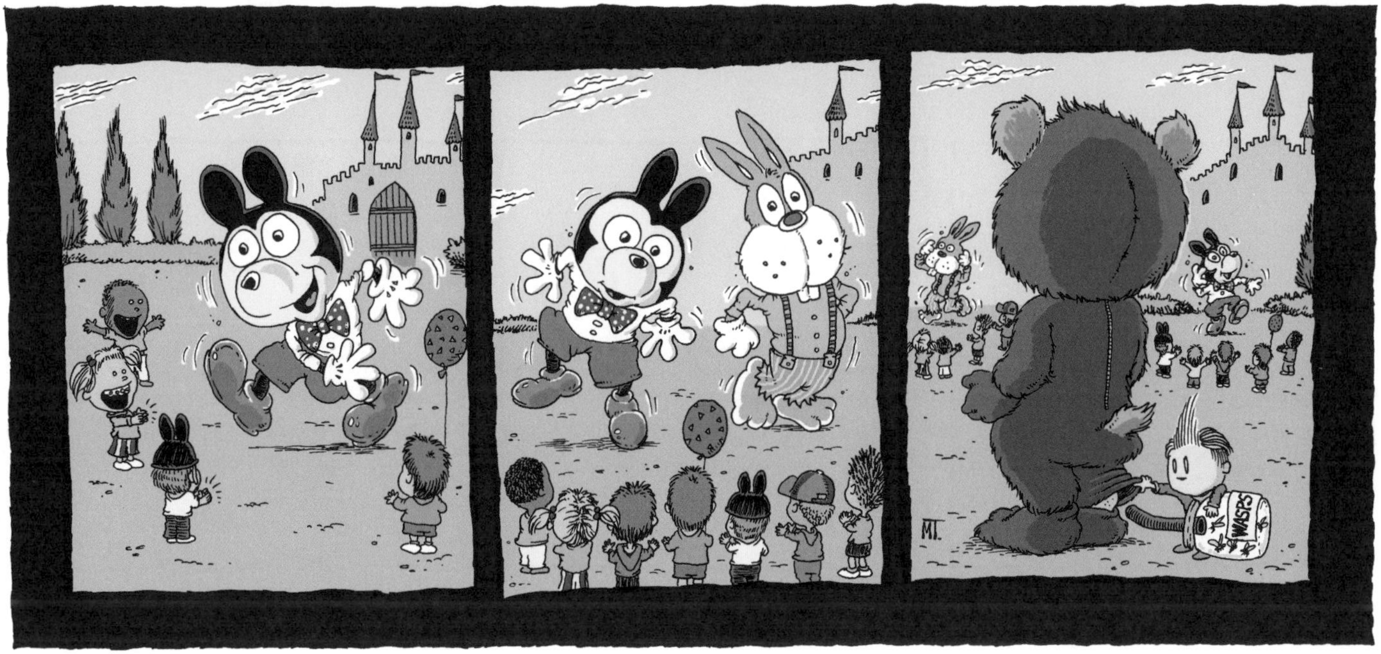
MT.
WASPS

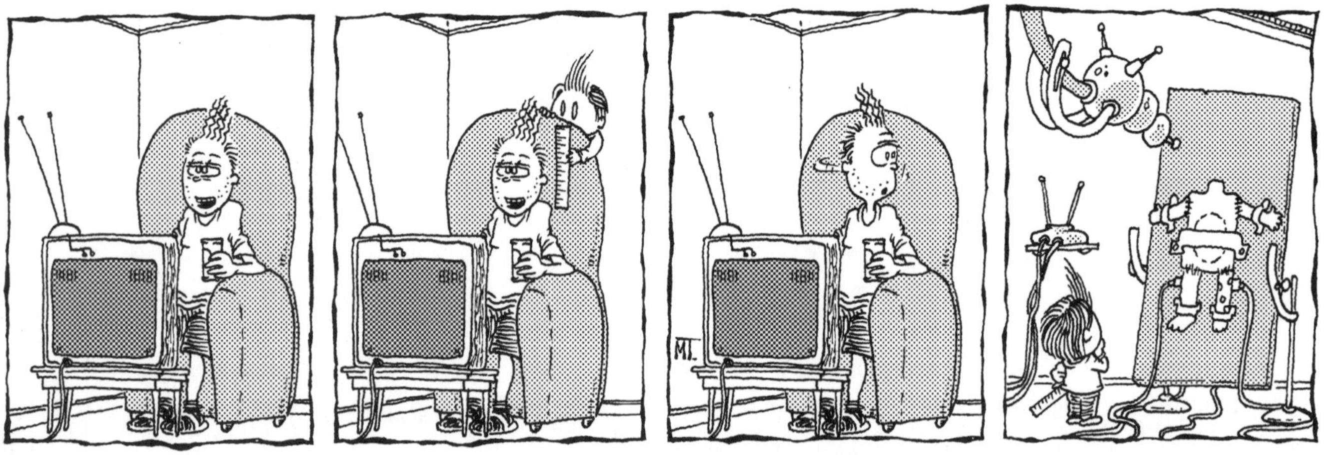

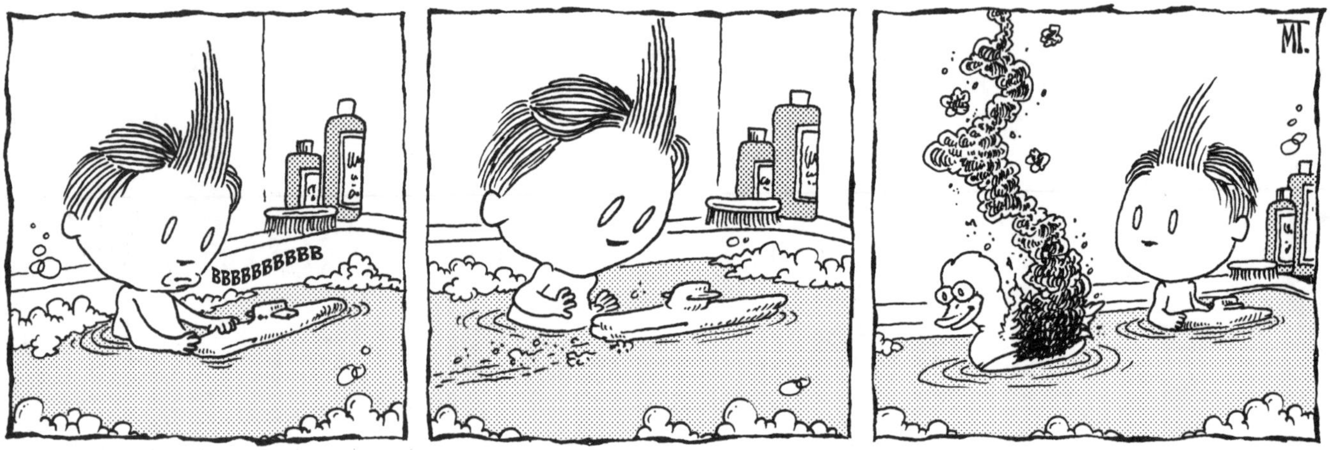
BBBBBBBBBB

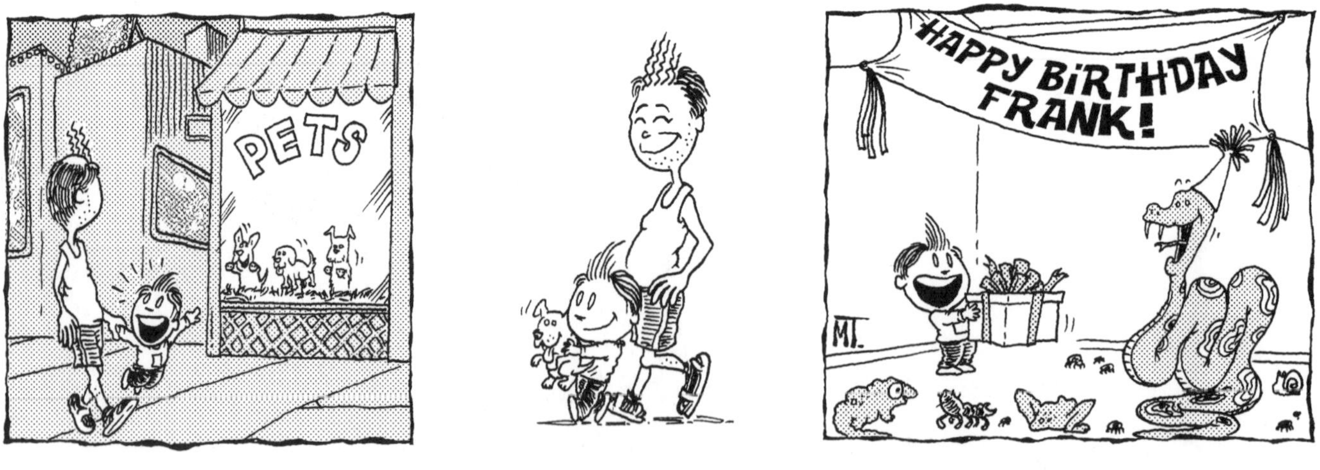
PETS
HAPPY BIRTHDAY FRANK!

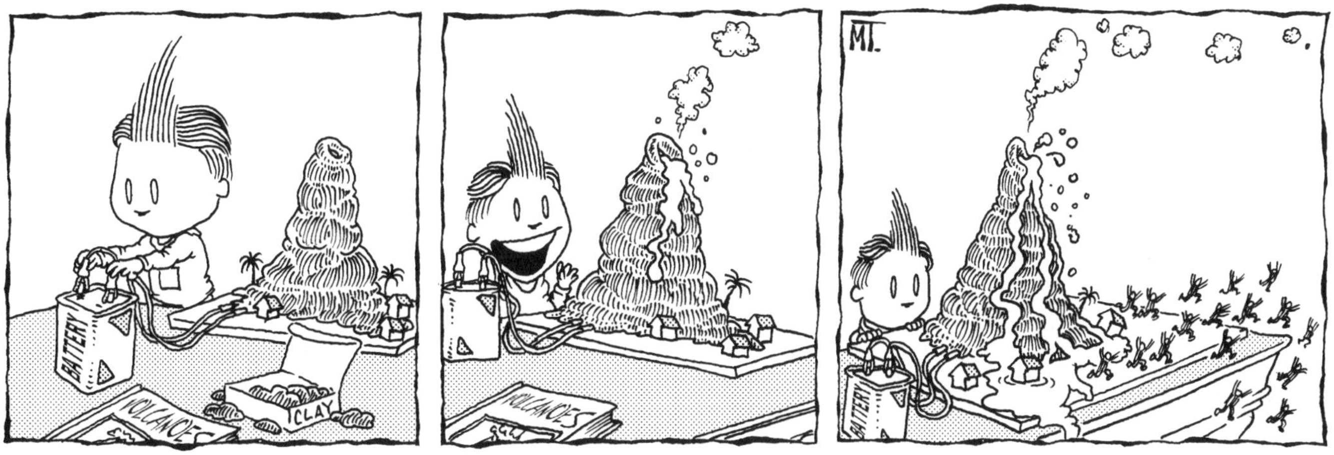
VOLCANOES
CLAY
ML

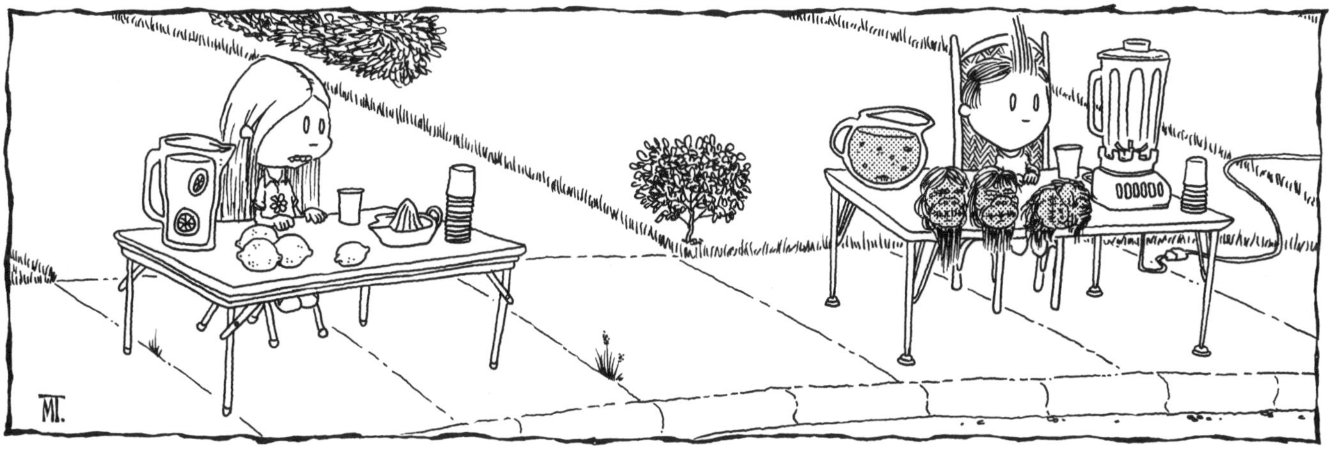
ML

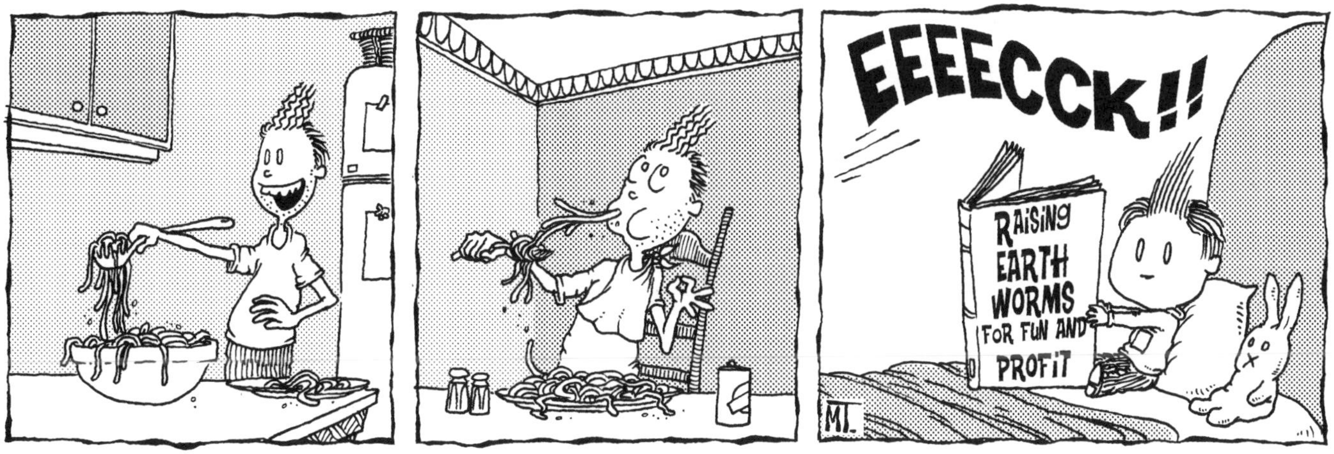
EEEECCK!!
RAISING EARTH WORMS FOR FUN AND PROFIT
ML

INFORMATION
M.C. ESCHER
MT.

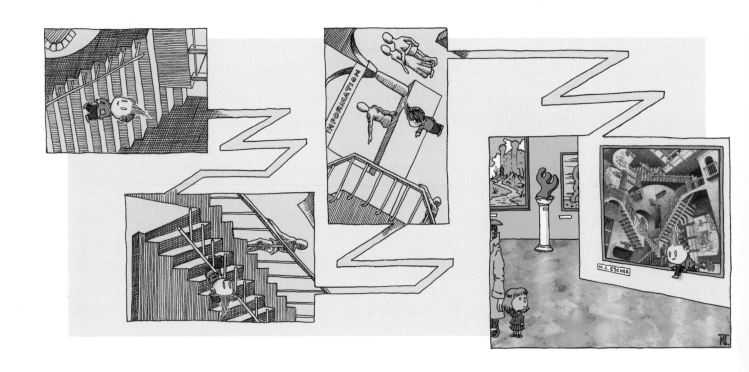

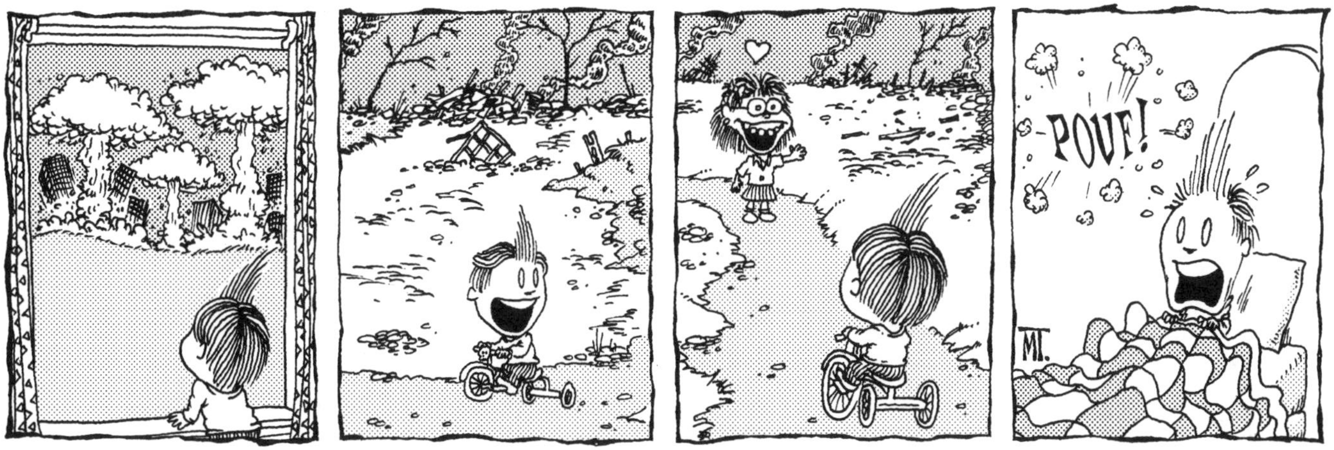
POUF!
MT.

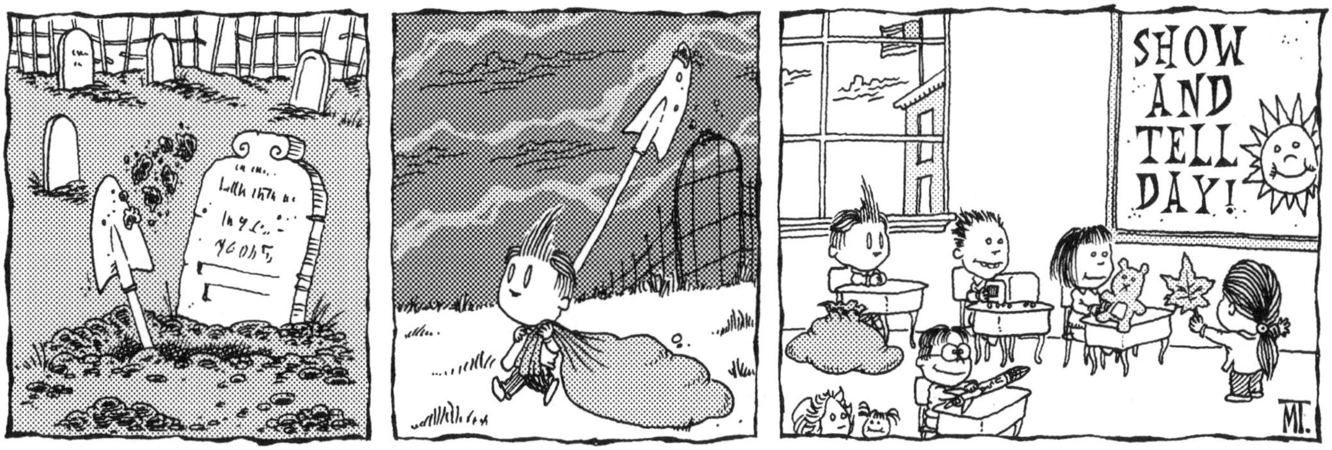
SHOW AND TELL DAY!
MT.

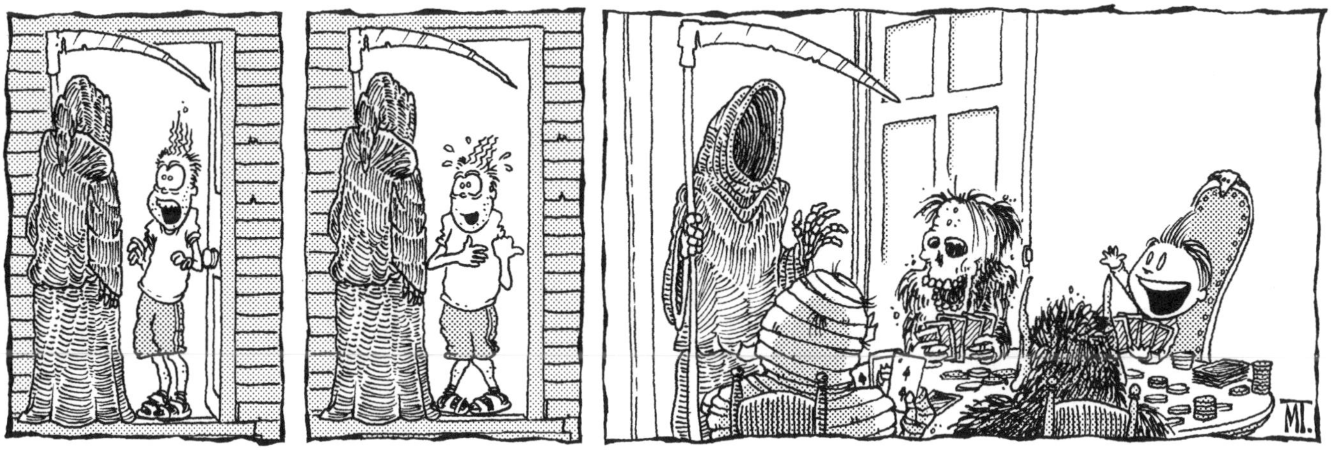
MT.

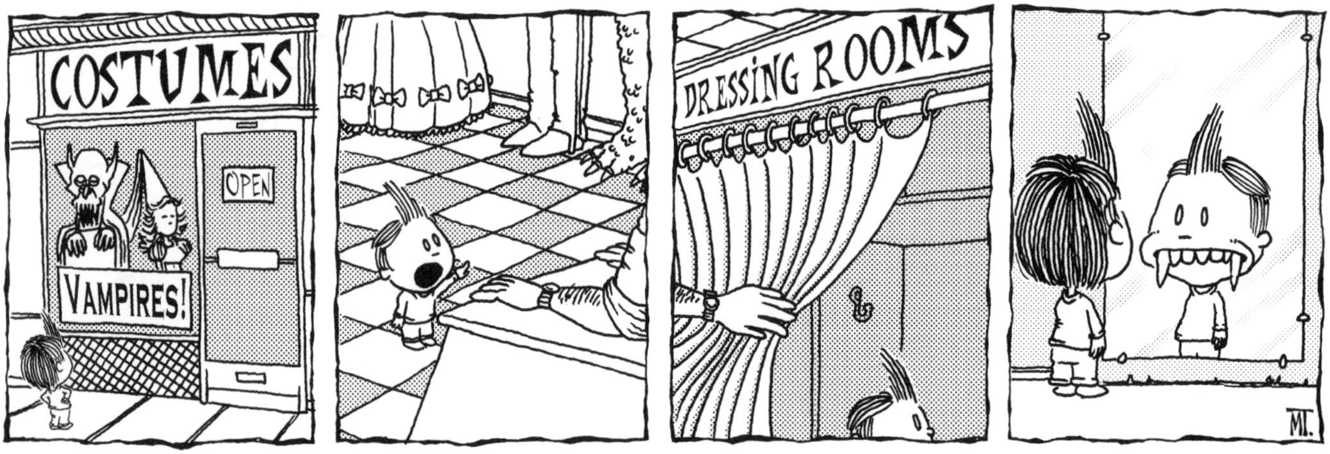
COSTUMES
VAMPIRES!
OPEN
DRESSING ROOMS
MI.

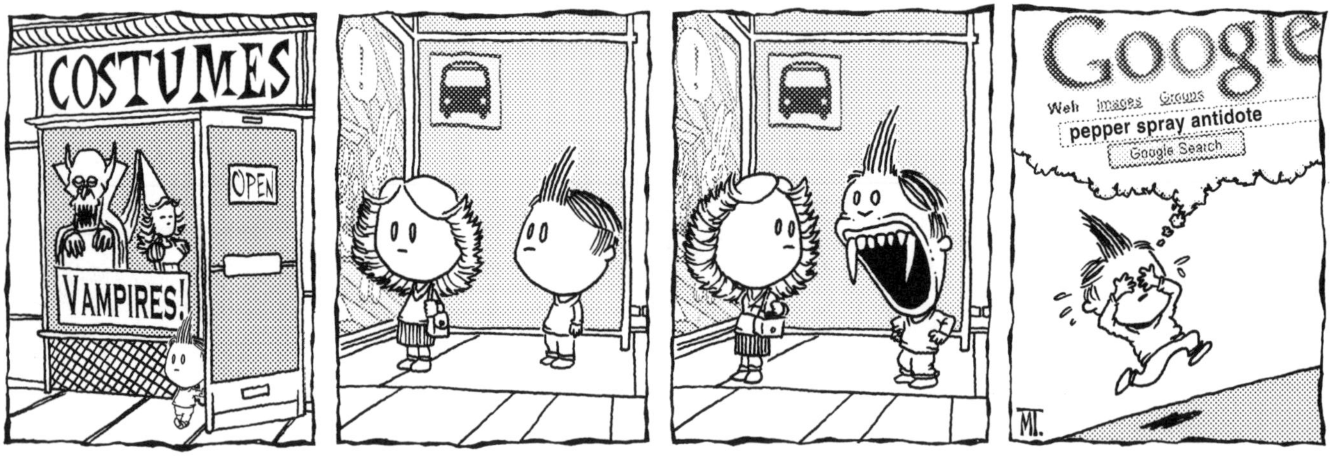
COSTUMES
VAMPIRES!
OPEN
Google
Web Images Groups
pepper spray antidote
Google Search
MI.

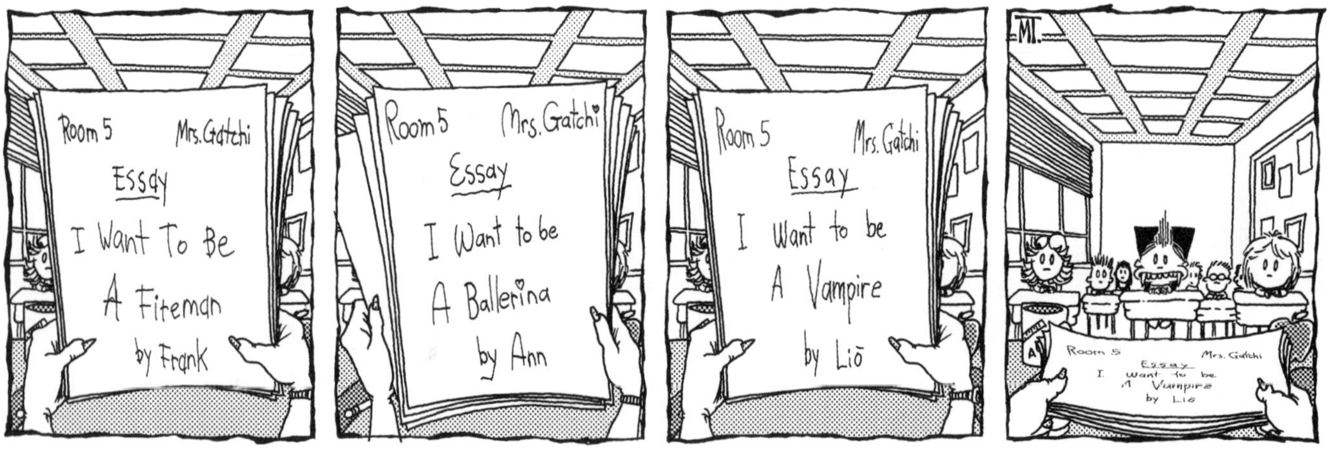
Room 5 Mrs. Gatchi
Essay
I Want To Be
A Fireman
by Frank
Room 5 Mrs. Gatchi
Essay
I Want to be
A Ballerina
by Ann
Room 5 Mrs. Gatchi
Essay
I Want to be
A Vampire
by Liō
MI.
Room 5 Mrs. Gatchi
Essay
I Want to be
A Vampire
by Liō

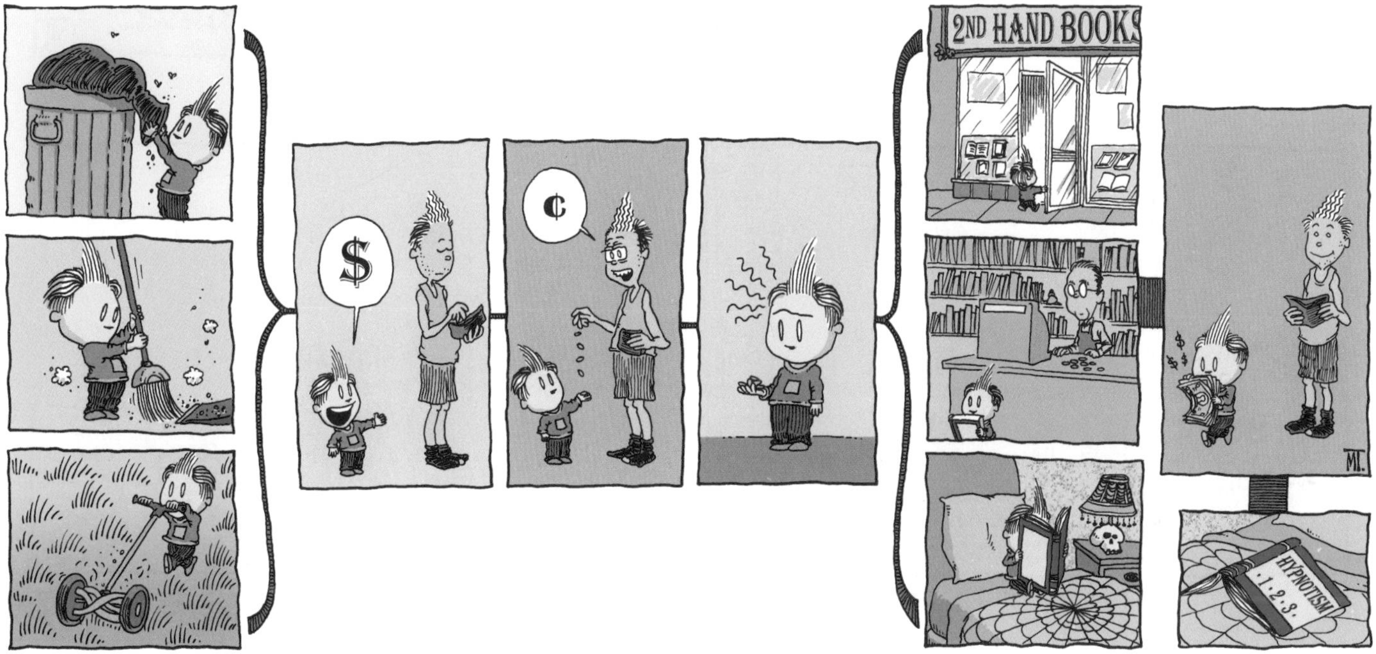
$
¢
2ND HAND BOOKS
HYPNOTISM
1.2.3.

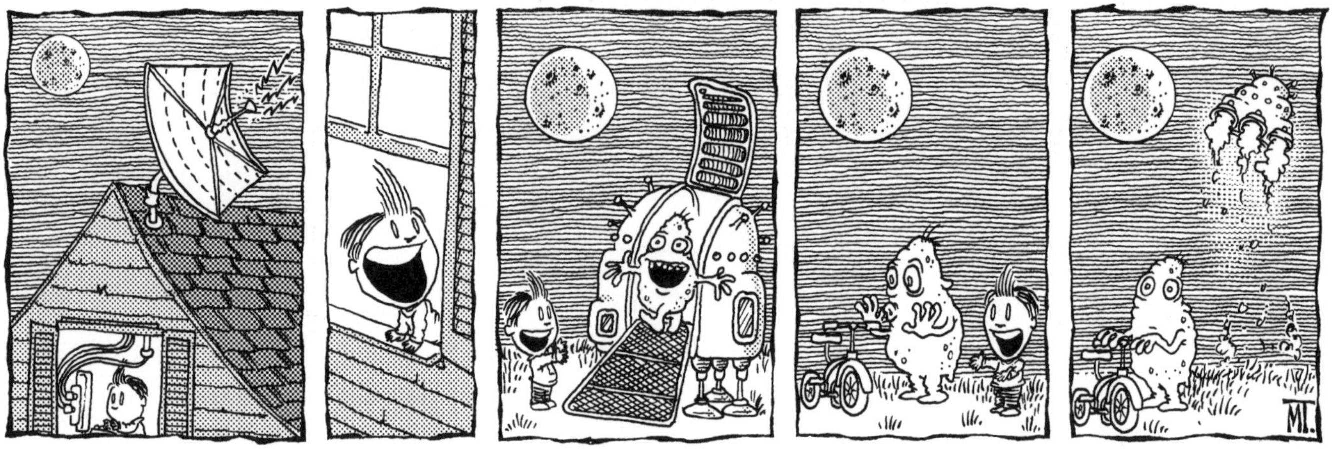

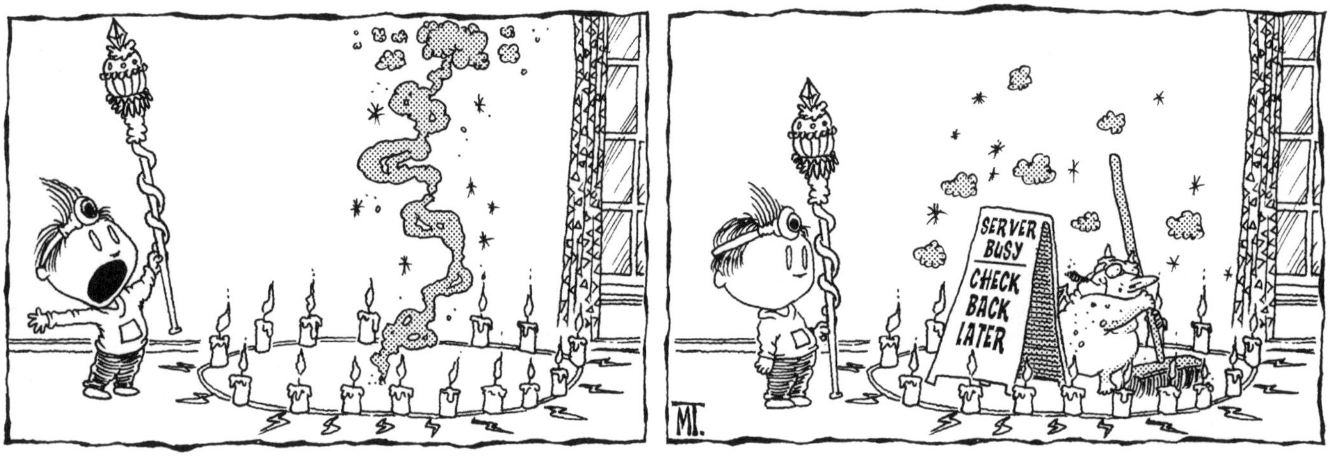
SERVER BUSY
CHECK BACK LATER

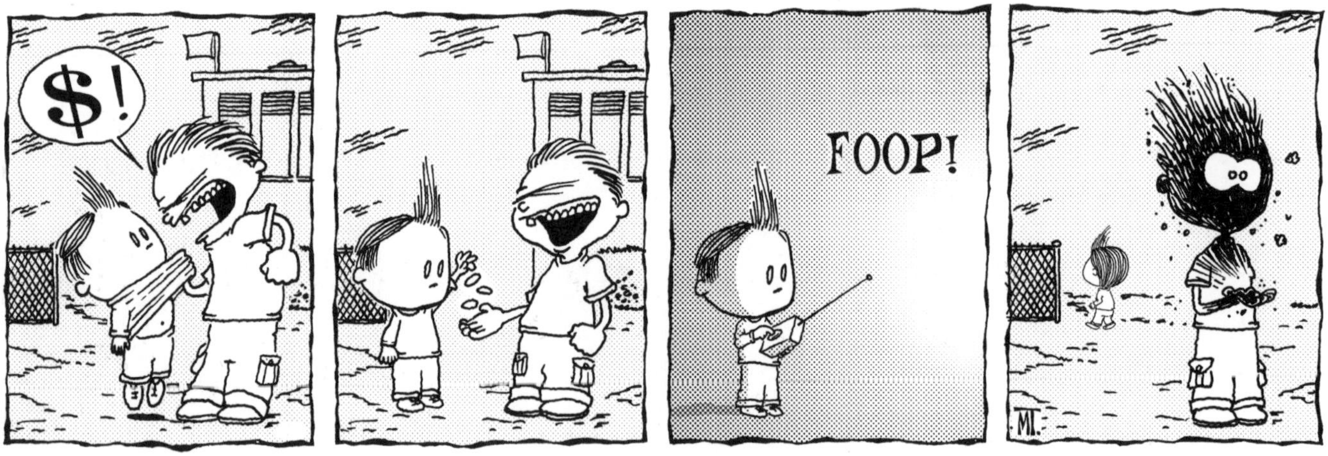
$!
FOOP!

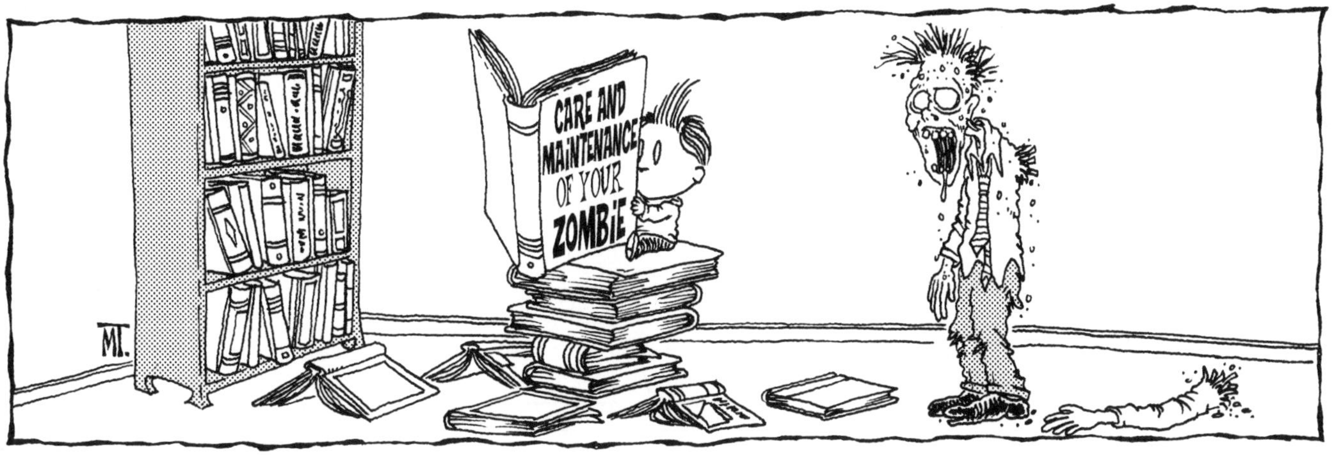
CARE AND MAINTENANCE OF YOUR ZOMBIE
MT.

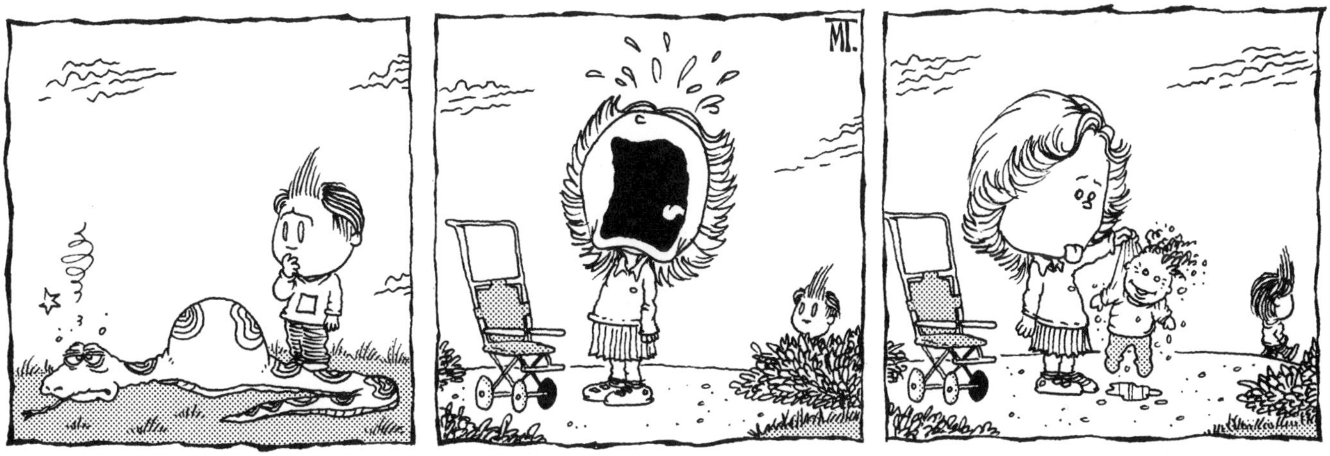
MT.

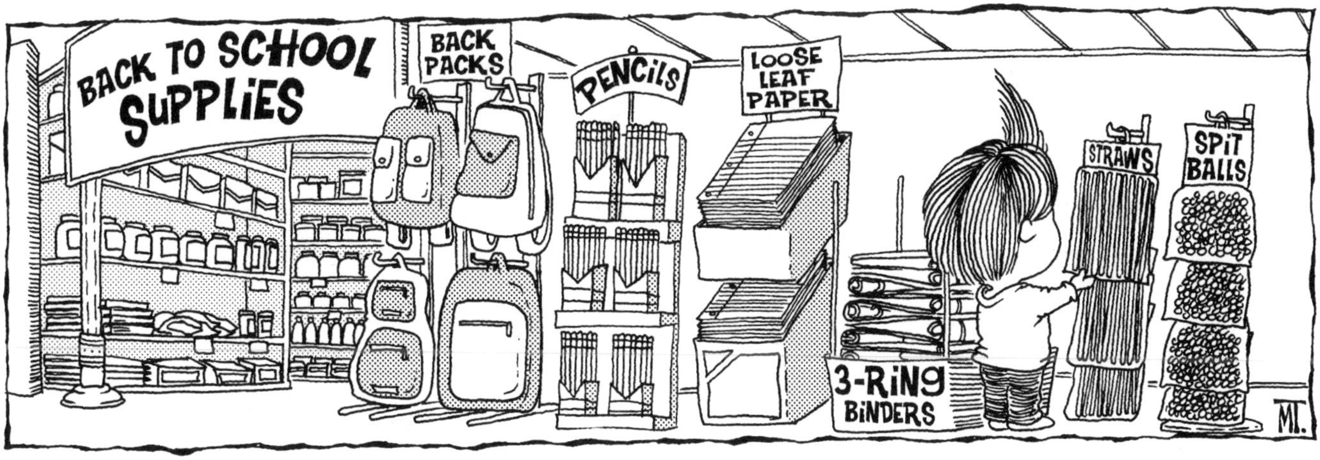
BACK TO SCHOOL SUPPLIES
BACK PACKS
PENCILS
LOOSE LEAF PAPER
3-RING BINDERS
STRAWS
SPIT BALLS
MT.

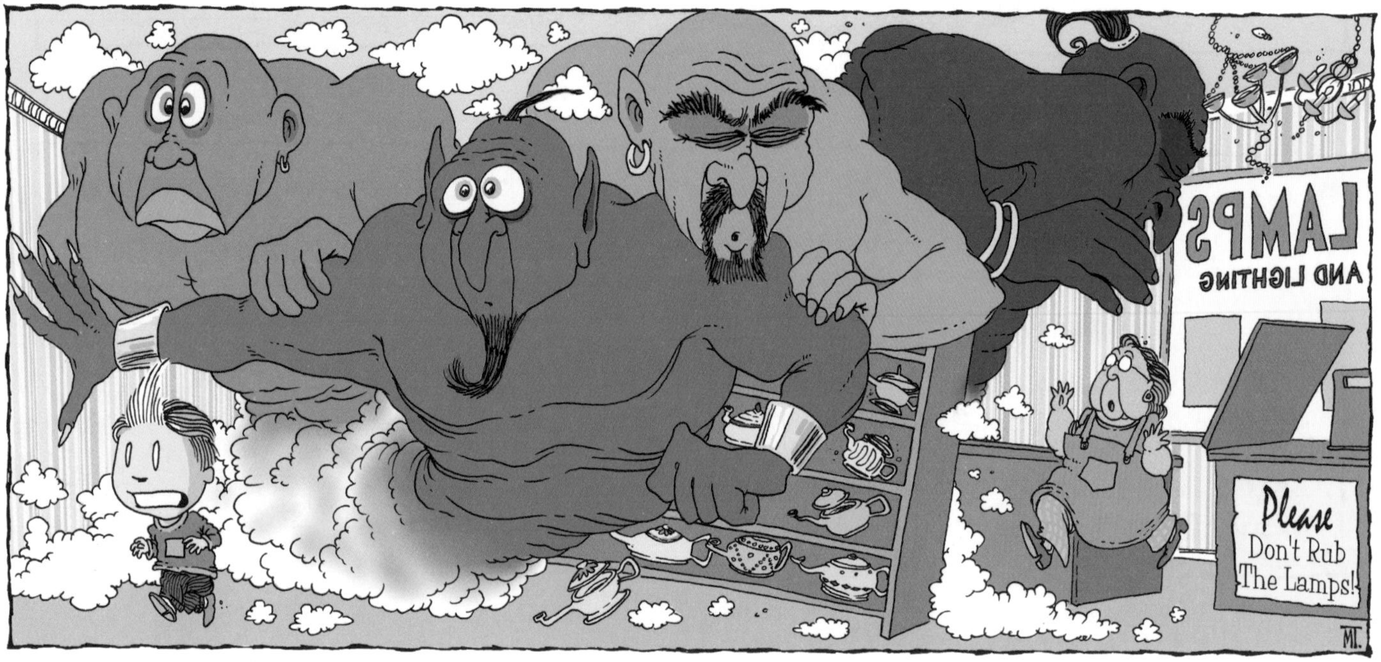
LAMPS
AND LIGHTING
Please
Don't Rub
The Lamps!
ML

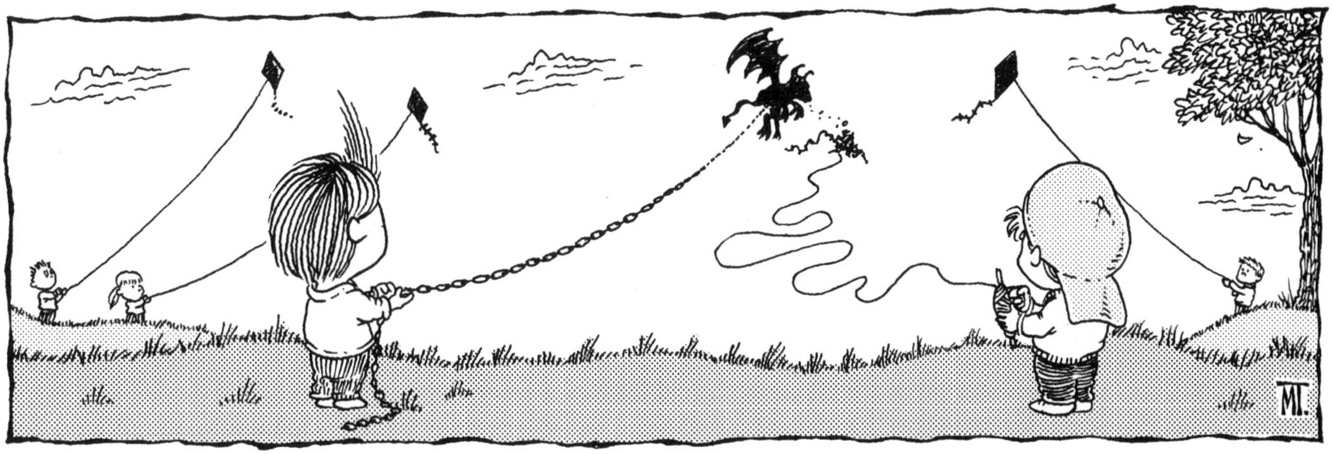

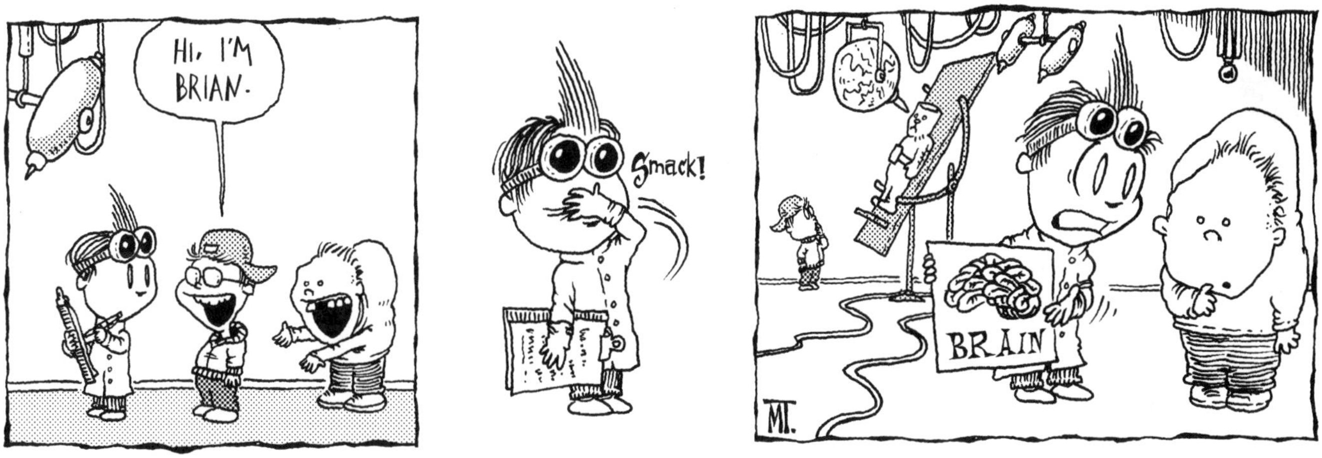
HI, I'M BRIAN.
Smack!
BRAIN

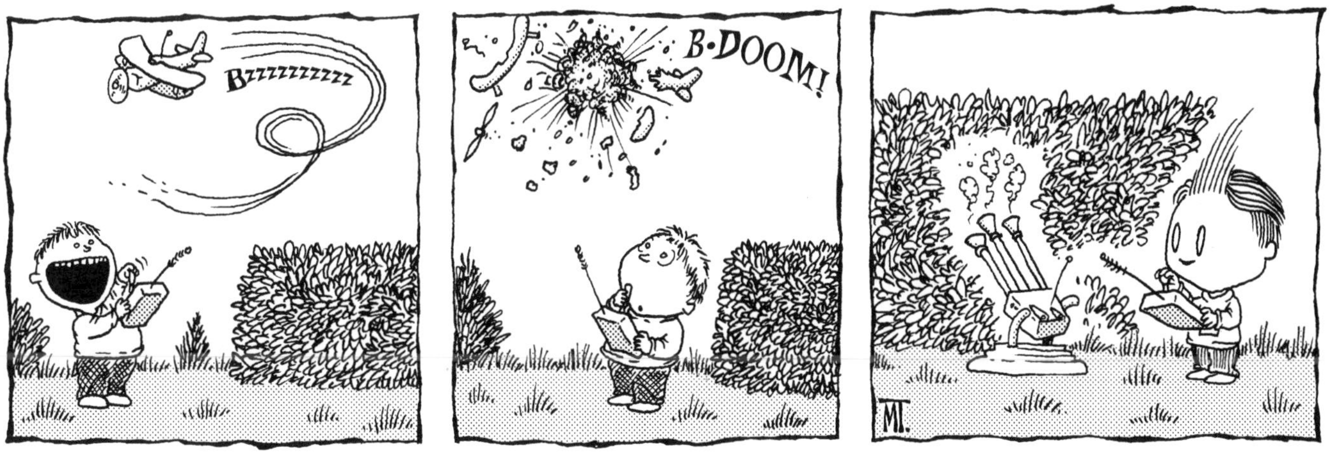
Bzzzzzzzzzz
B·DOOM!

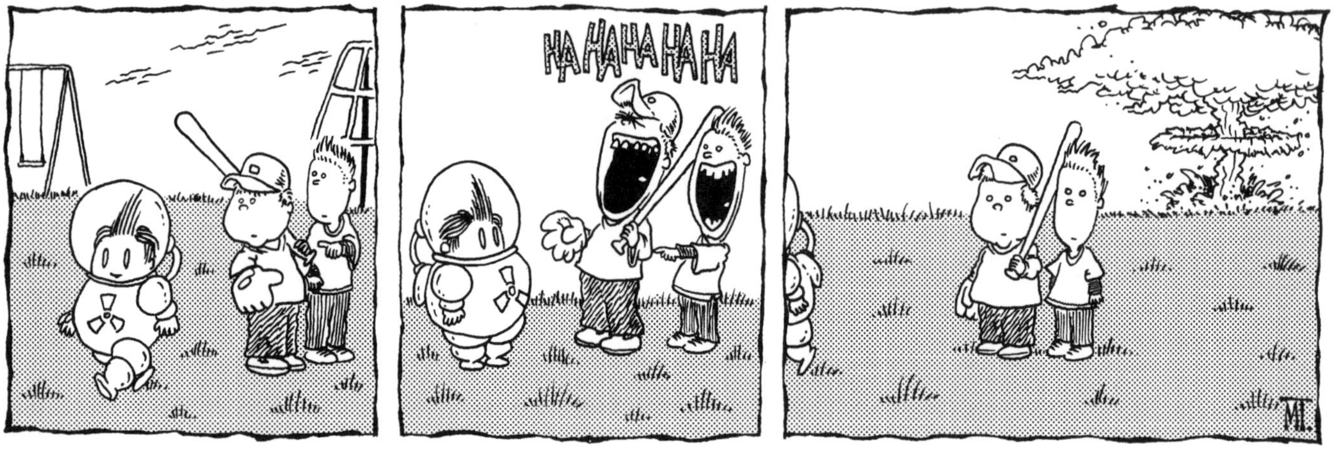
HAHAHAHAHAHA

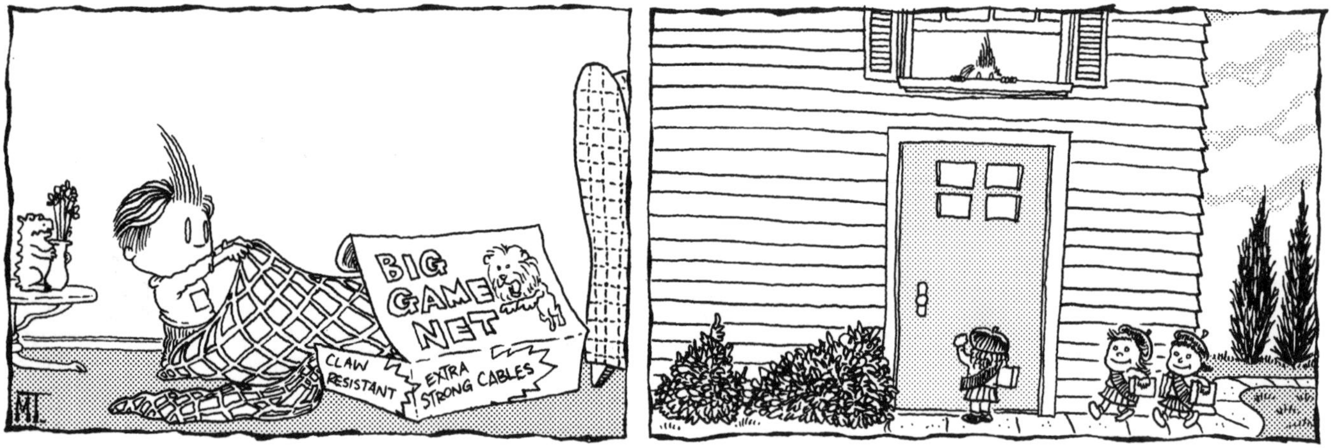
BIG GAME NET
CLAW RESISTANT
EXTRA STRONG CABLES

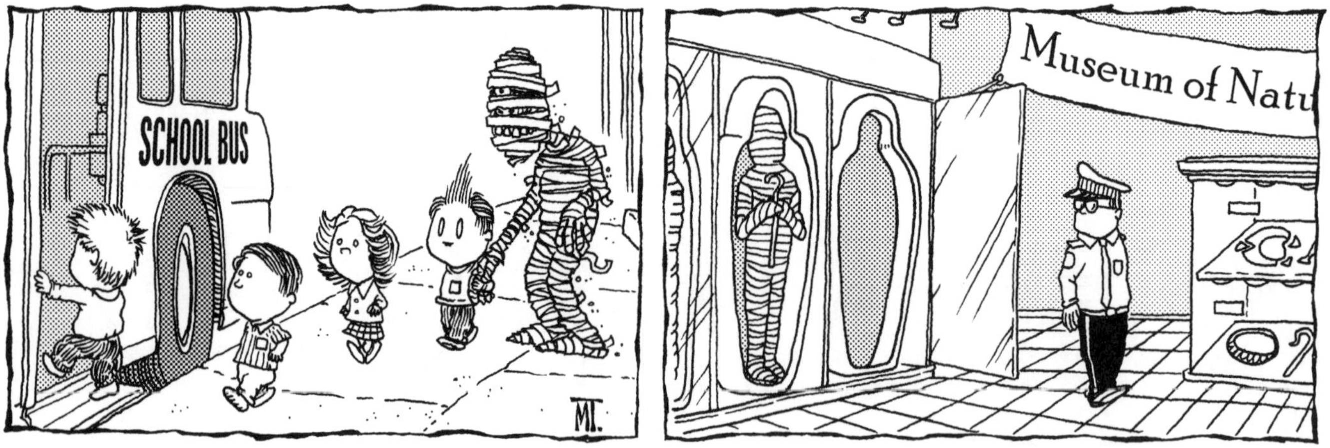
SCHOOL BUS
Museum of Natu

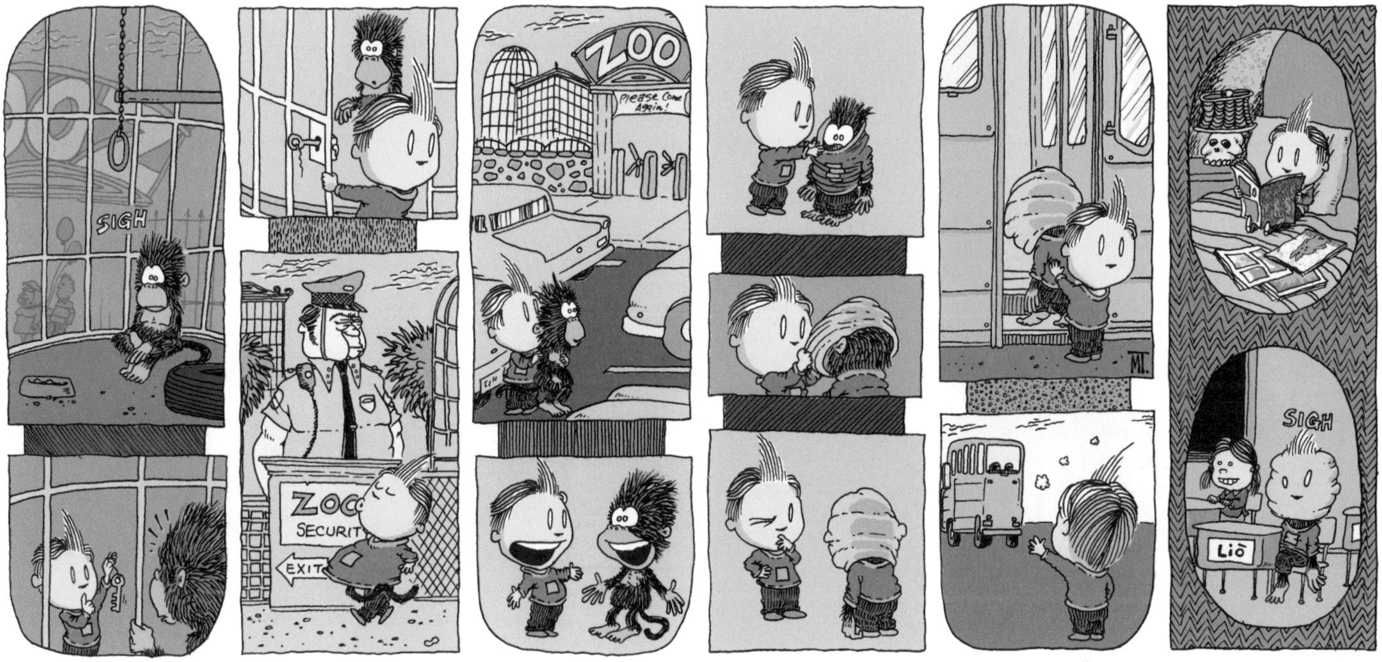
SIGH
ZOO
SECURIT
EXIT
ZOO
Please Come Again!
MI.
SIGH
Liò

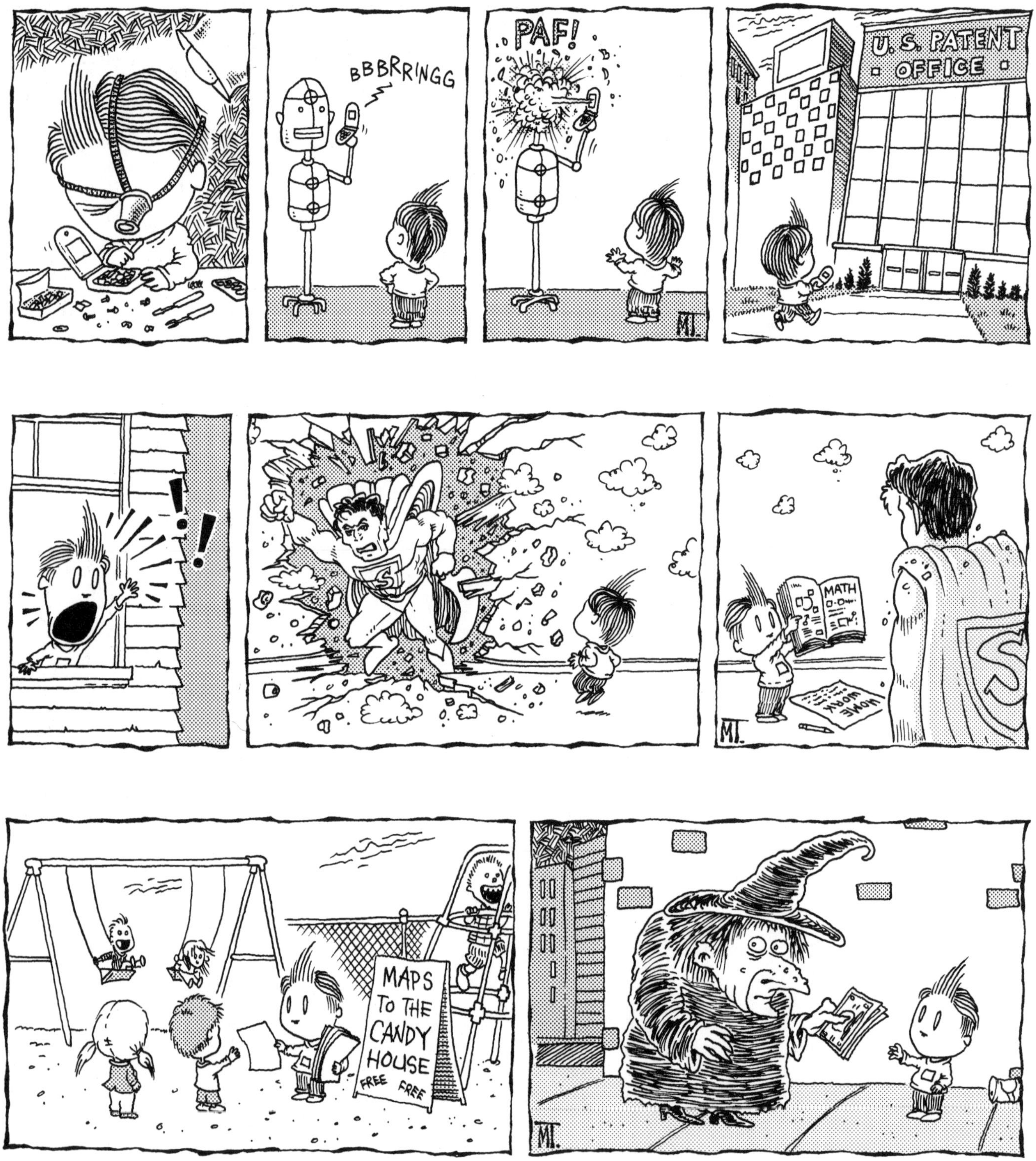
BBBRRINGG
PAF!
U.S. PATENT OFFICE
MATH
HOME WORK
MAPS TO THE CANDY HOUSE
FREE FREE

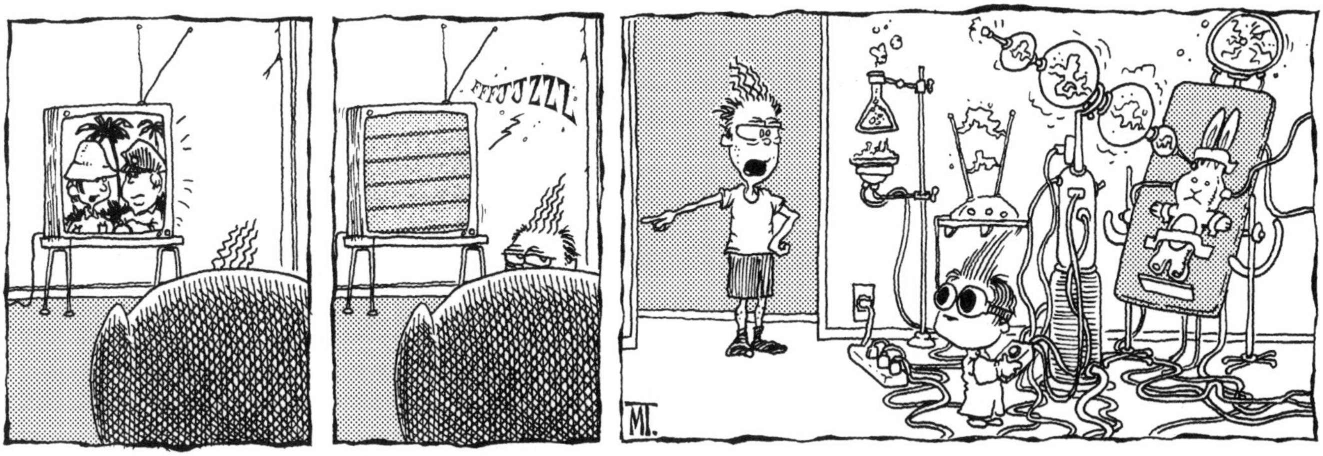
FFFJJZZZ
MI.

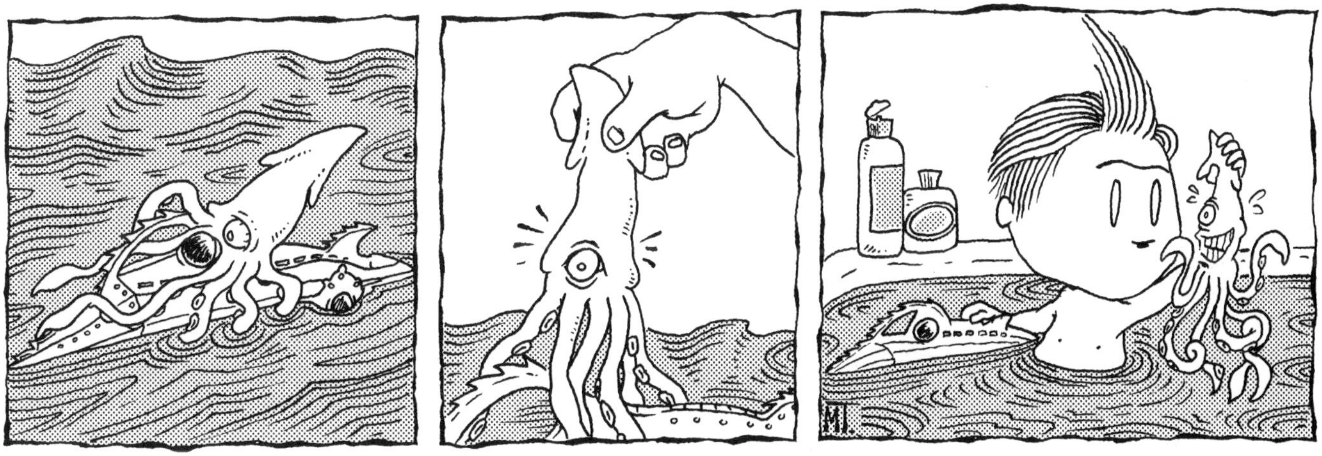
MI.

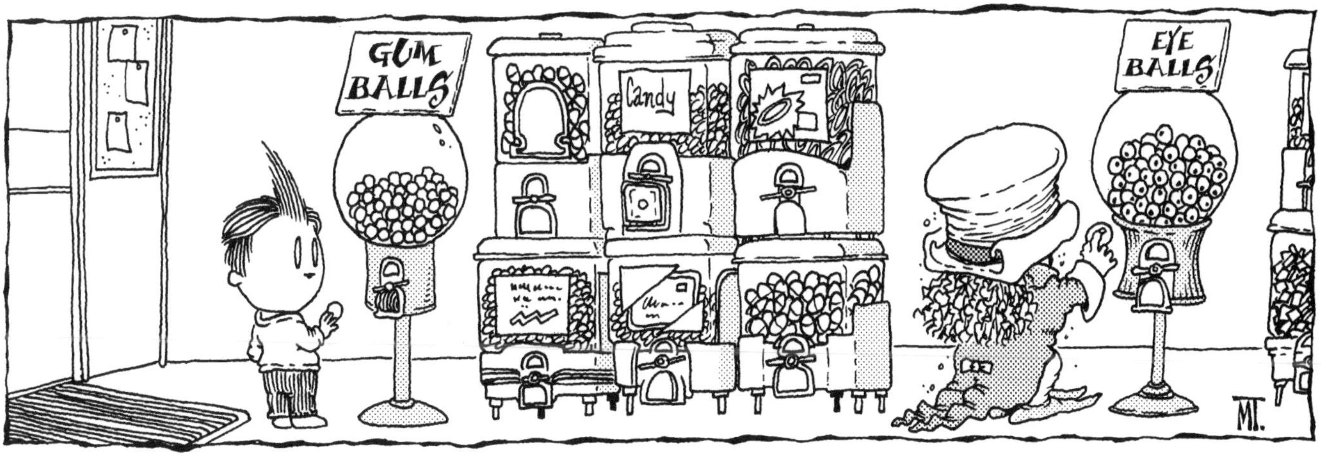
GUM BALLS
Candy
EYE BALLS
MI.

Ditzie Trixie

HONEY, I'M GOING TO TAKE A BATH.

OK!

?

LEAVING YOU A SPECIAL FRIEND DIRK...

AAK!

¼ √3 ·06 90004.7 !

Just Like THE FAR SIDE But Not

Cow pie eating contest

Family From Gehenna

"Mommy left her dance pole out again."

NOTHING LIKE ME BEER.

Brothers Watching Television

YO, SOMETHING BUSTED OUR TV, YA HEARD?

WORD. NOW WHAT WE GONNA TALK ABOUT?

S GOD TO PRAY FOOT.

Mr. Zilch

OK, I GUESS I SHOULD MAKE SOME COMMENT ABOUT HOW LIFE STINKS. I JUST DON'T FEEL SNARKY TODAY.

Bill

Word Fracus

```
G H O P L S G M B D K E W X Z P M G D    X
J Y H F I E H Z A K R S L C T H M P O F  T
V O P F R U H Q A L G D K F O P A        Q
J V D T Z X O H F W E M K L E G P F R E  R
N G B C R T Z L J G Q P C R L P G X R    F T
O Q W H D C K H E A I V R X K D L W      G I
B G D P L T J U X D K F A Z H O V E R K  I N
L F Y I C W L J A Z Y C E D H O S W I    F Q
H G F R I U Y C X L K N M I Q O          F
                                    BOOM
```

BE SO.

Punny Tails

WHAT'RE YOU DOING, PLATYPUS?

SEE THAT ROTTWEILER DOG ON OUR LAWN?

HE'S BEEN DOING HIS BUSINESS IN OUR GARDEN. I WANT TO CATCH HIM IN THE ACT.

YOU STUPID PLATYPUS!

DON'T YOU KNOW A WATCHED ROTT NEVER SOILS?

WHAT'S THIS?

WHAT A YARN!

Liō

MT.

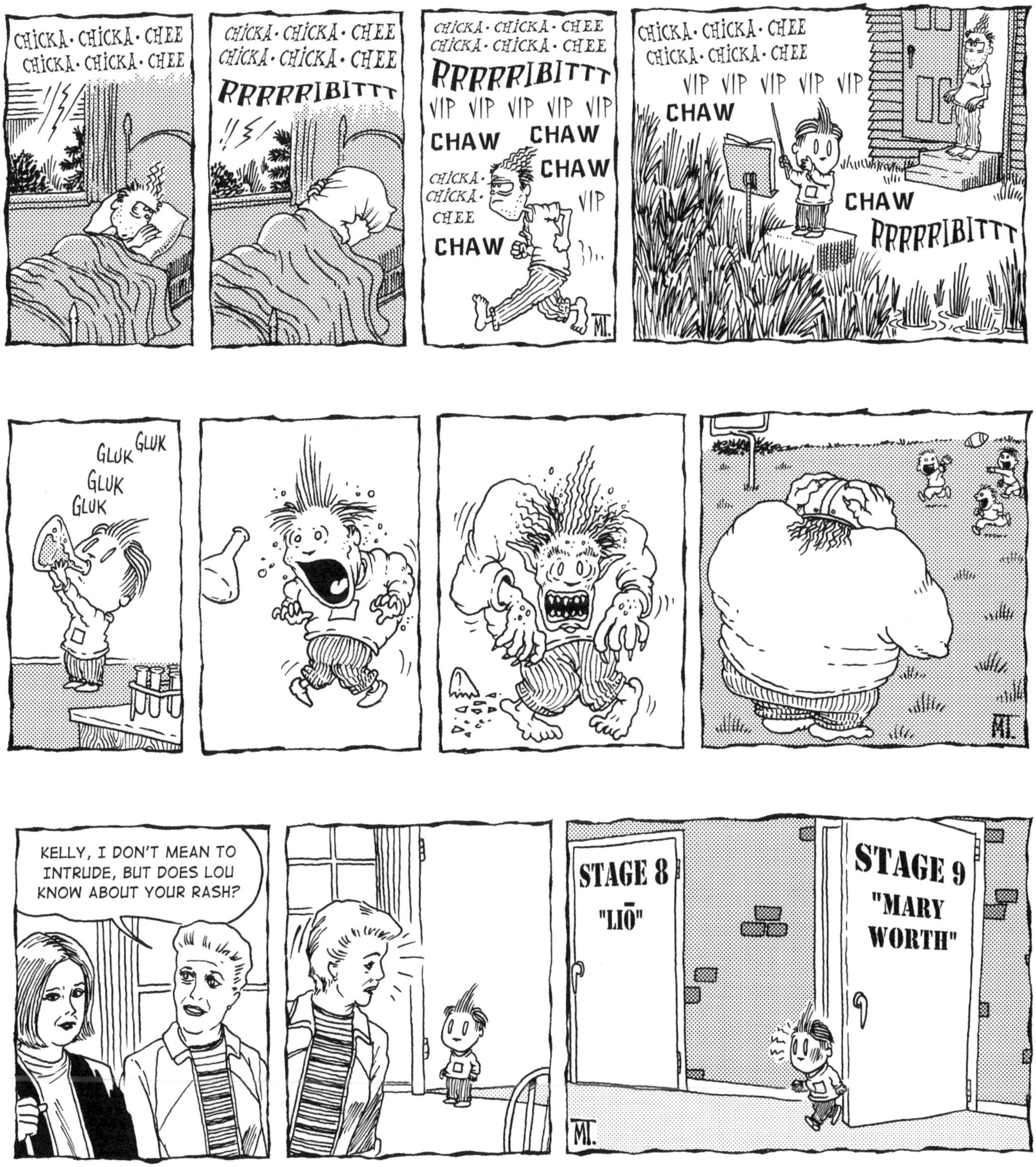
CHICKA · CHICKA · CHEE
CHICKA · CHICKA · CHEE
CHICKA · CHICKA · CHEE
CHICKA · CHICKA · CHEE
RRRRRIBITTT
CHICKA · CHICKA · CHEE
CHICKA · CHICKA · CHEE
RRRRRIBITTT
VIP VIP VIP VIP VIP
CHAW CHAW
CHICKA · CHICKA · CHEE
CHAW
VIP
CHAW
MT.
CHICKA · CHICKA · CHEE
CHICKA · CHICKA · CHEE
VIP VIP VIP VIP VIP
CHAW
CHAW
RRRRRIBITTT
GLUK GLUK
GLUK
GLUK
MT.
KELLY, I DON'T MEAN TO INTRUDE, BUT DOES LOU KNOW ABOUT YOUR RASH?
STAGE 8
"LIŌ"
STAGE 9
"MARY WORTH"
MT.

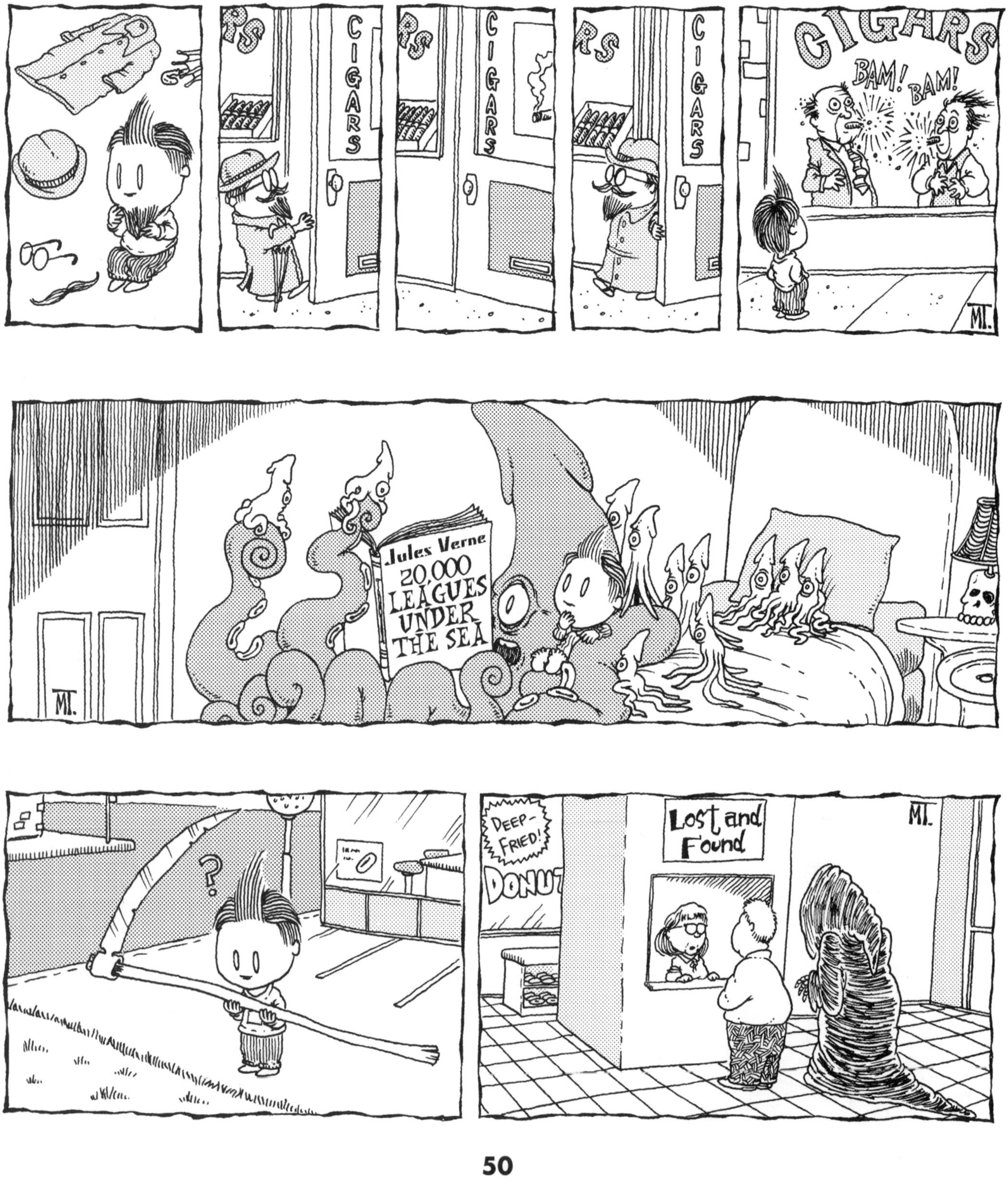
CIGARS
CIGARS
CIGARS
CIGARS
BAM!
BAM!
MT.
Jules Verne
20,000 LEAGUES UNDER THE SEA
MT.
?
DEEP-FRIED!
DONUT
Lost and Found
MT.

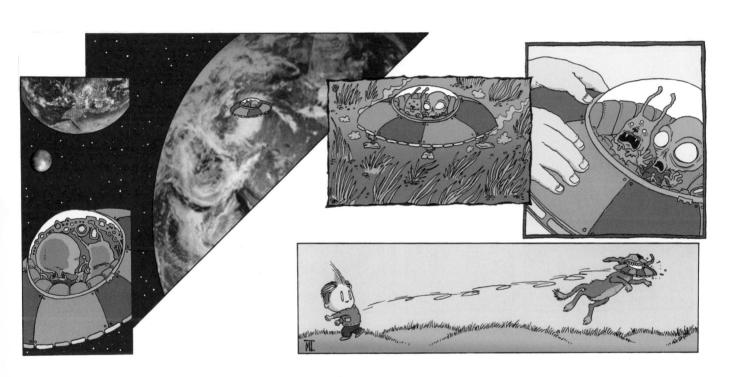

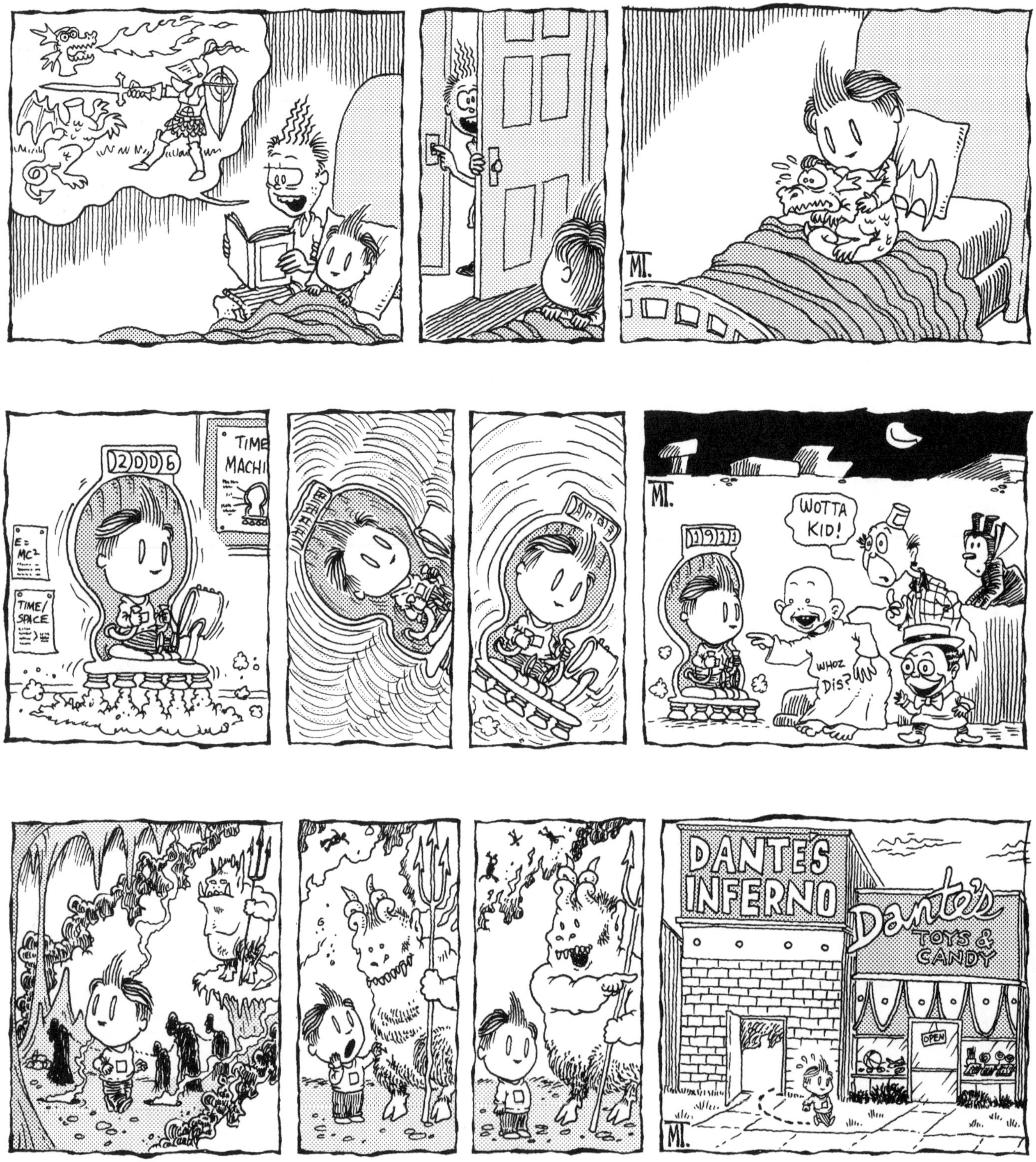
MT.
2006
TIME
MACHI
E=
MC2
TIME/
SPACE
MT.
1911
WOTTA
KID!
WHOZ
DIS?
DANTE'S
INFERNO
Dante's
TOYS &
CANDY
OPEN
MT.

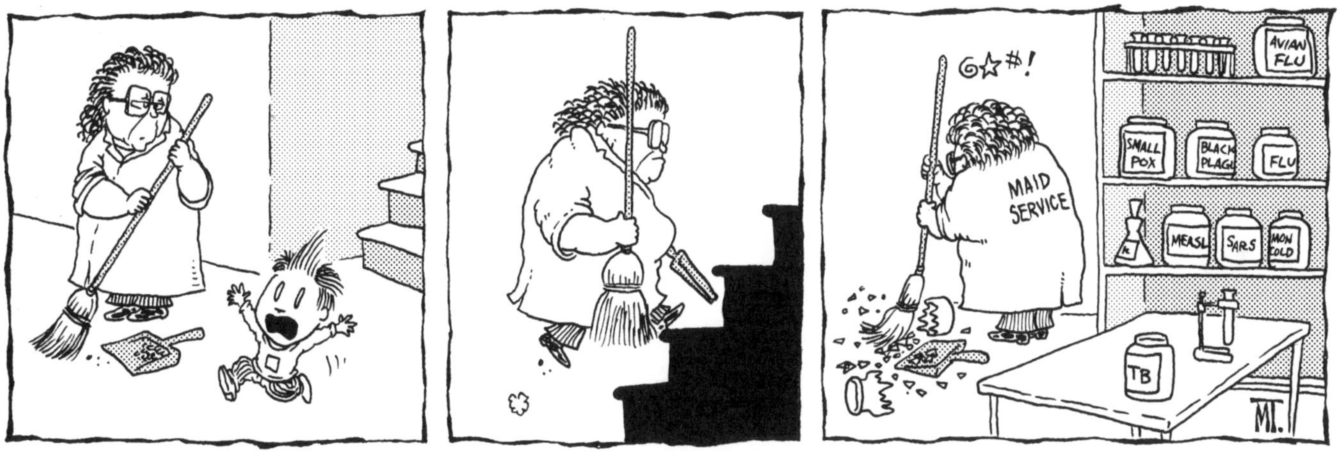
#!
AVIAN FLU
SMALL POX
BLACK PLAGU
FLU
MAID SERVICE
MEASL
SARS
MON COLD
TB

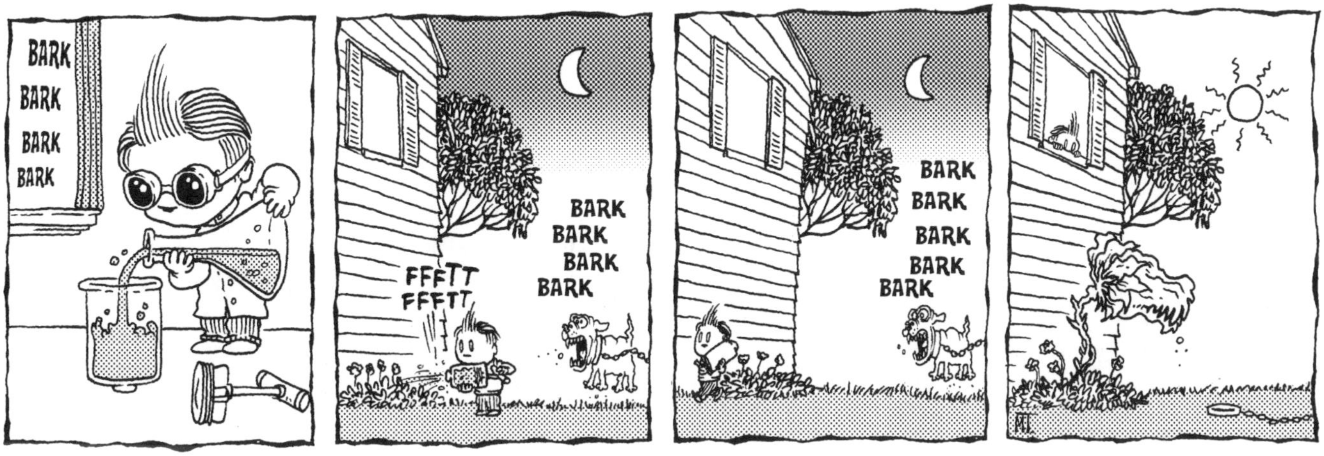
BARK
BARK
BARK
BARK
FFFTT
FFFTT
BARK
BARK
BARK
BARK
BARK
BARK
BARK
BARK
BARK

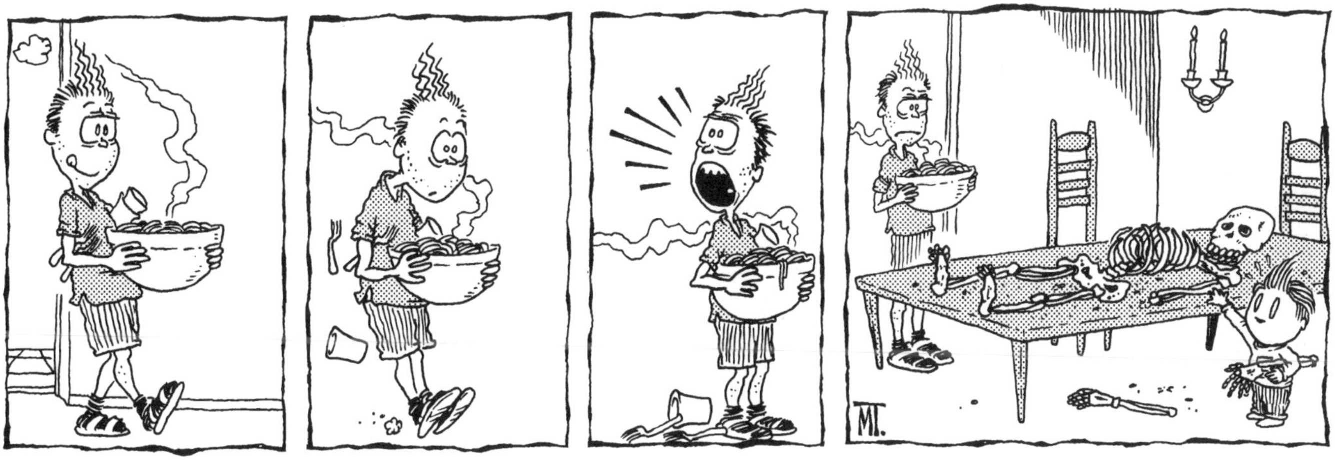

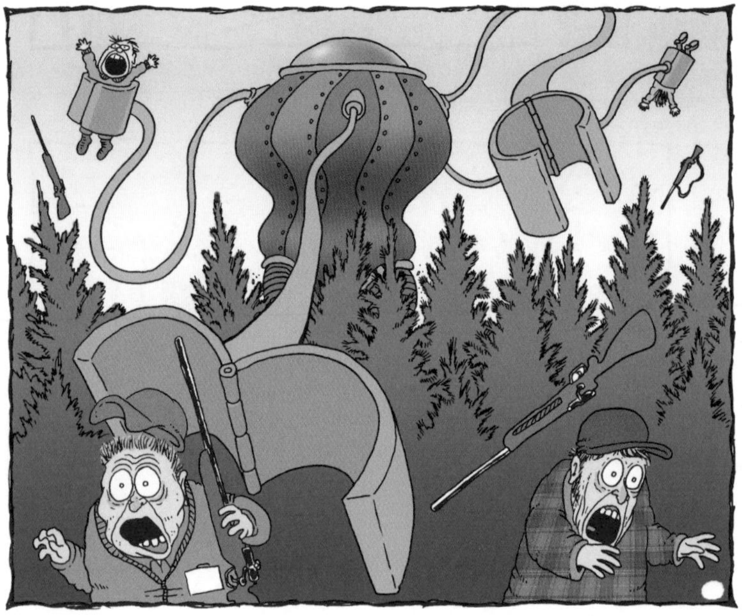

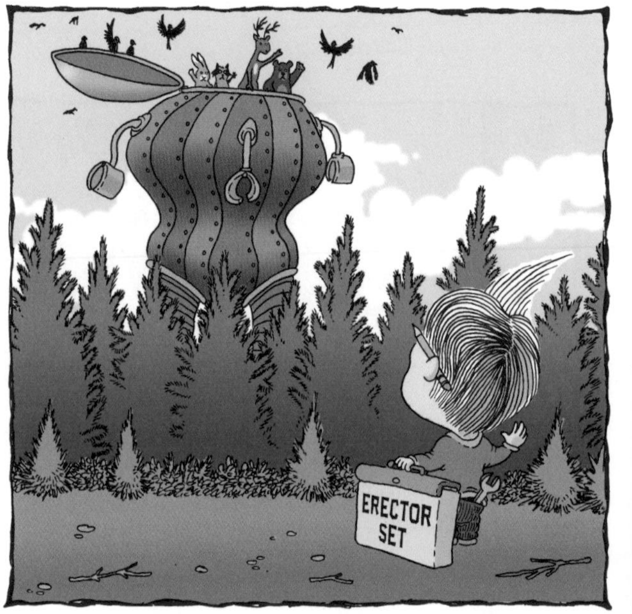
ERECTOR
SET

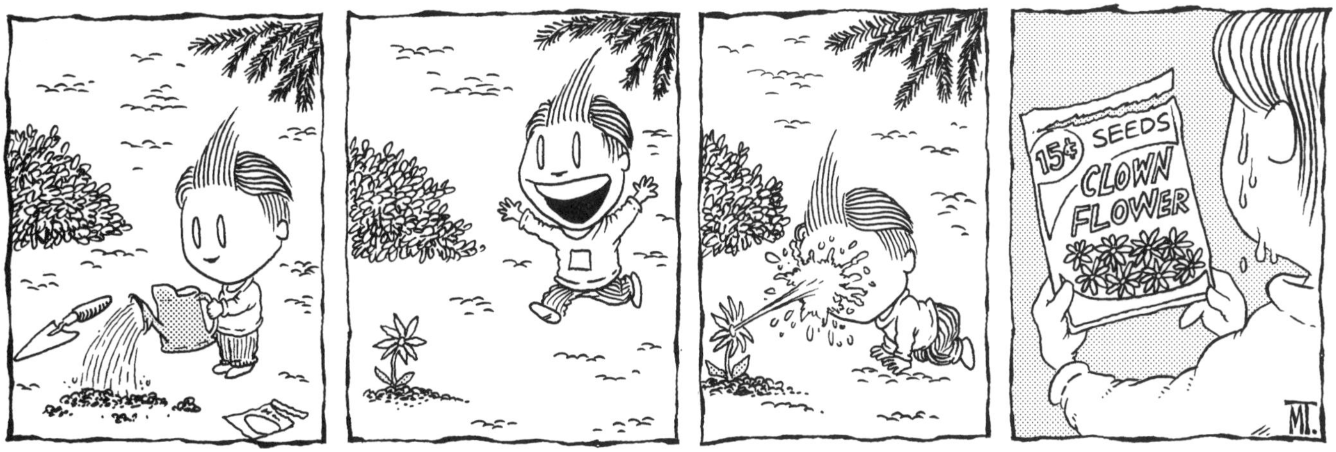
15¢
SEEDS
CLOWN FLOWER
MT.

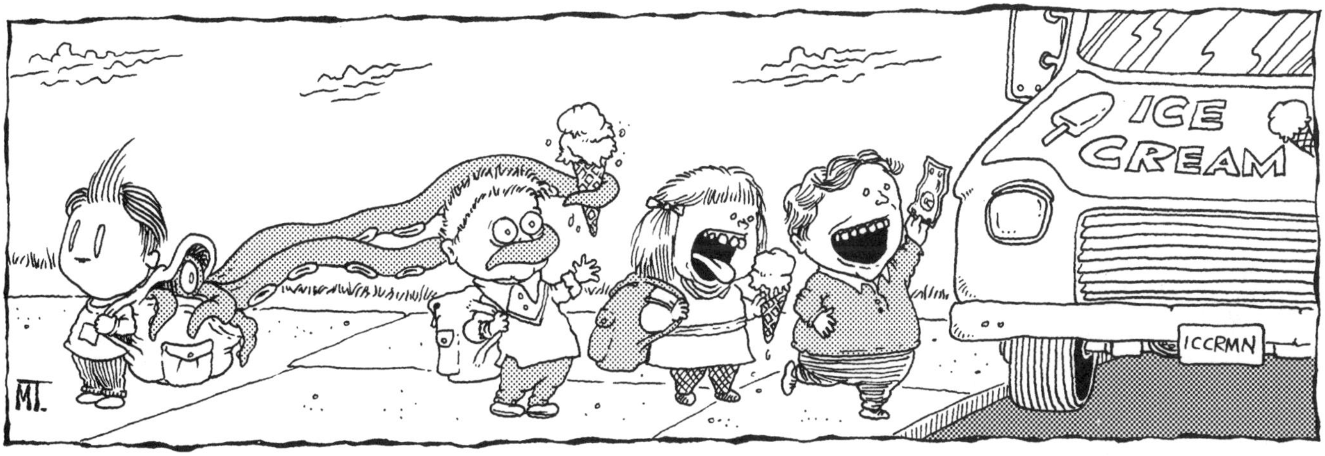
ICE CREAM
ICCRMN
MT.

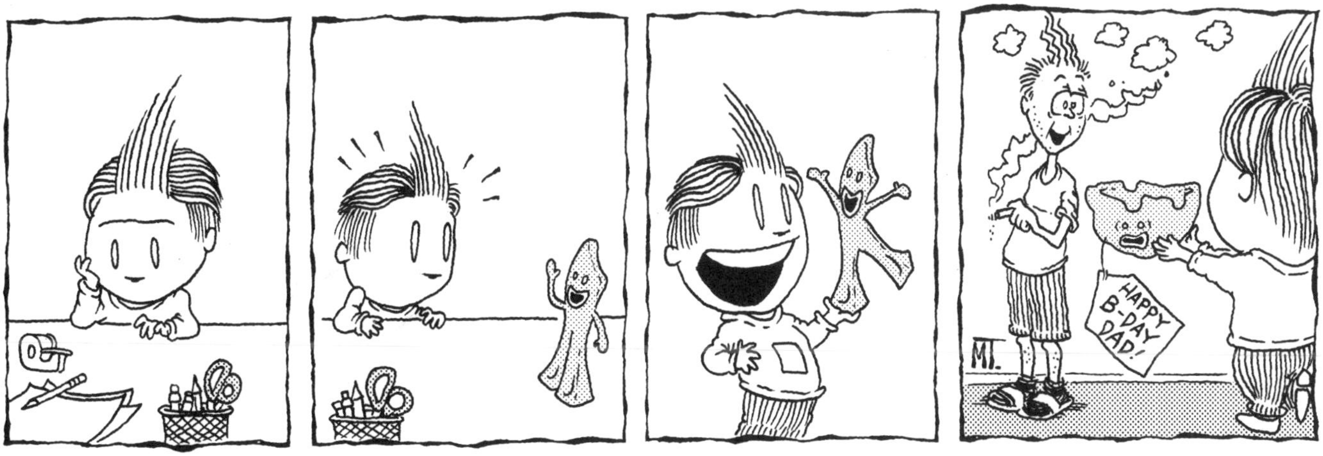
MT.
HAPPY B-DAY DAD!

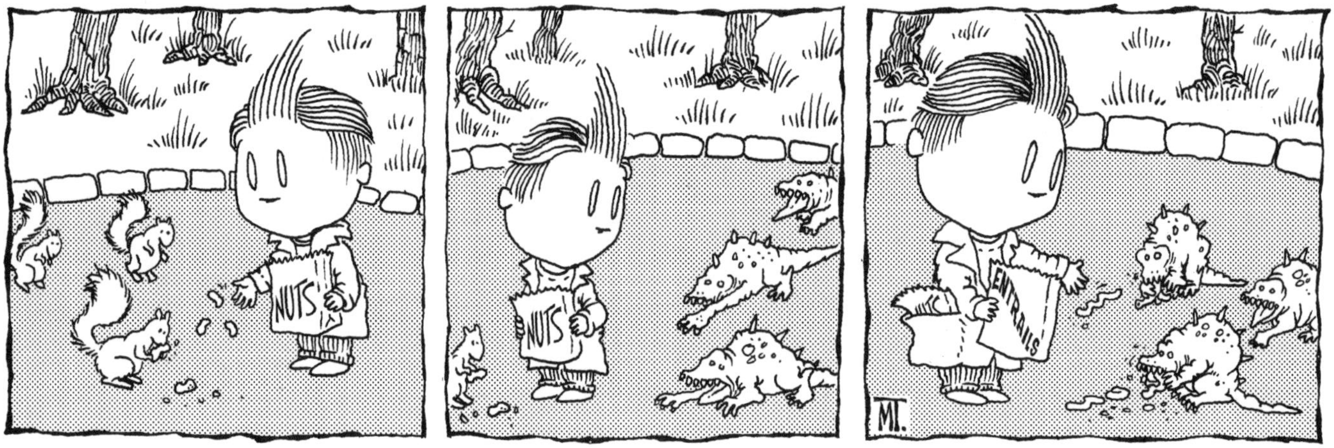
NUTS
NUTS
ENTRAILS

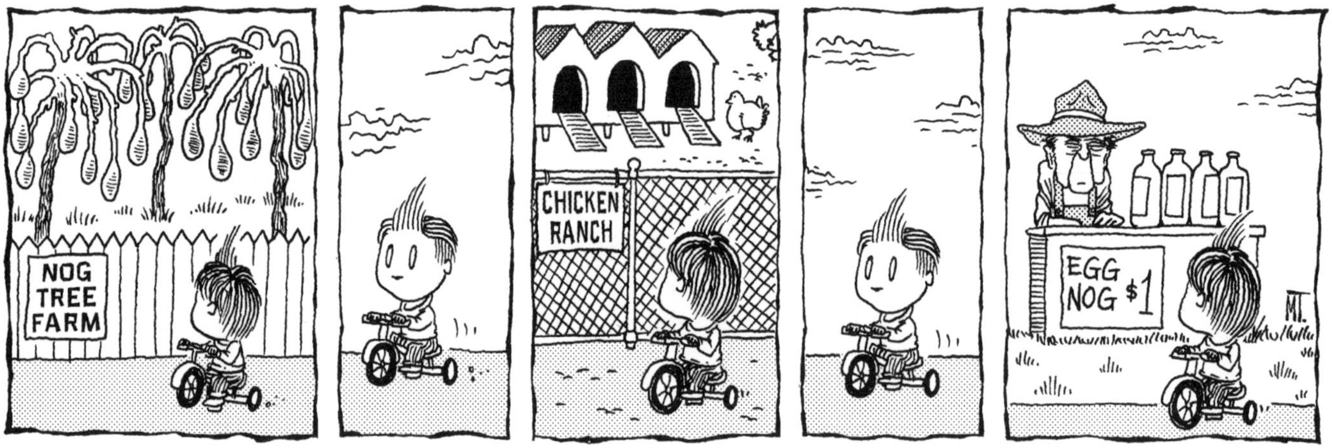
NOG TREE FARM
CHICKEN RANCH
EGG NOG $1

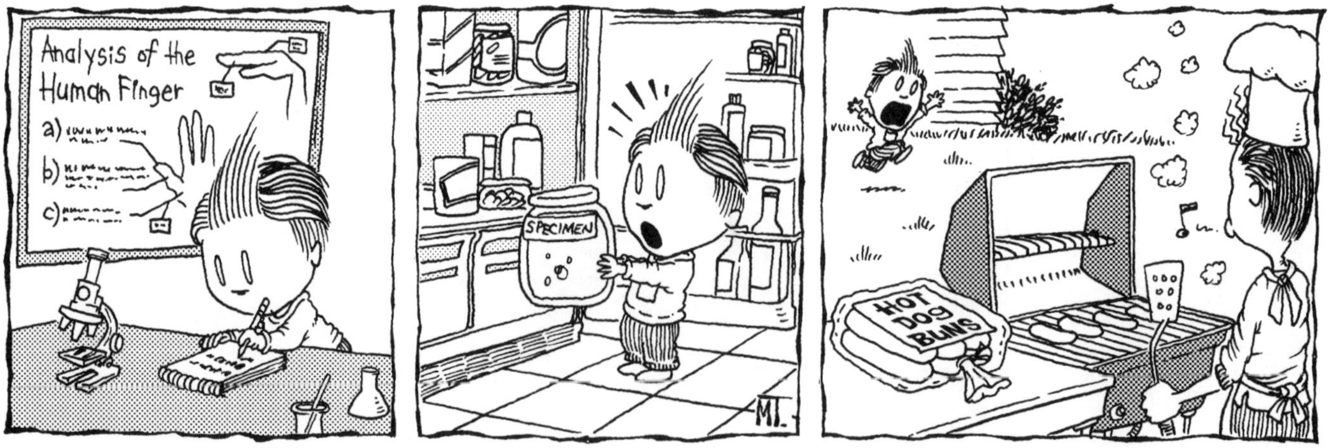
Analysis of the Human Finger
a)
b)
c)
SPECIMEN
HOT DOG BUNS

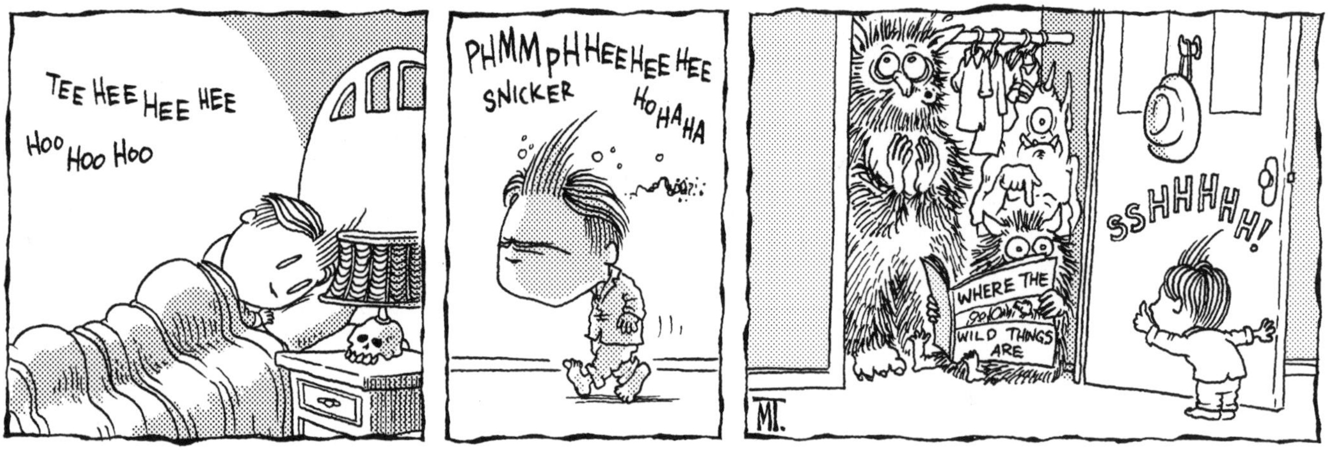
TEE HEE HEE HEE
HOO HOO HOO
PHMM PHHEE HEE HEE
SNICKER
HO HA HA
SSHHHHH!
WHERE THE WILD THINGS ARE
MT.

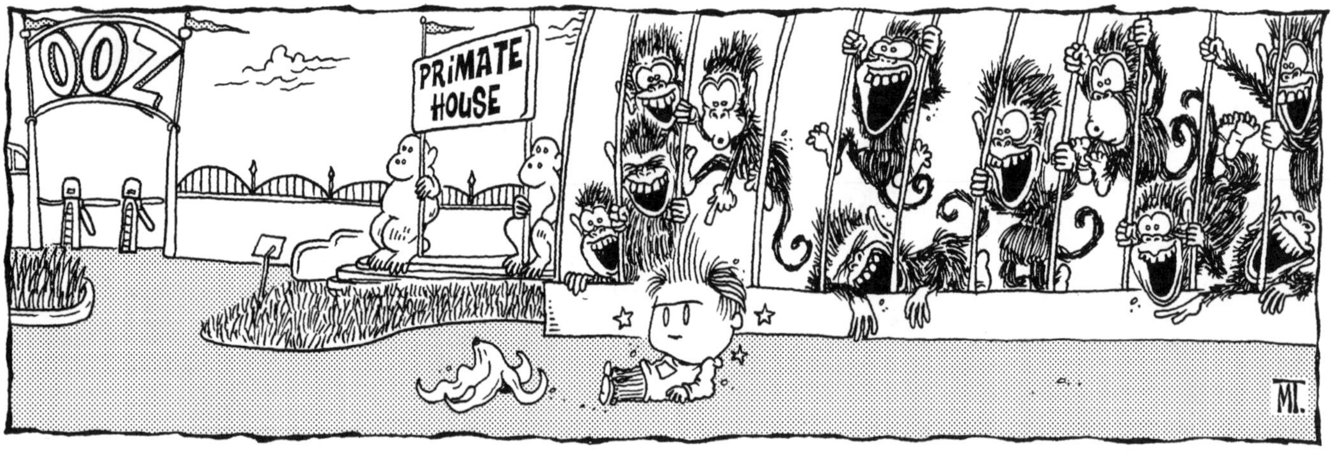
OOZ
PRIMATE HOUSE
MT.

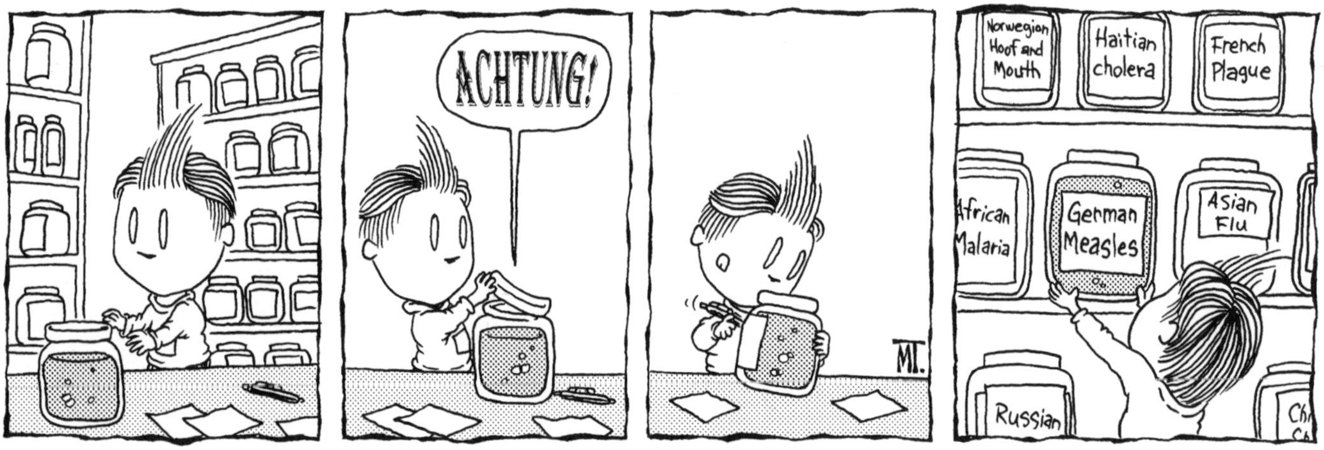
ACHTUNG!
MT.
Norwegian Hoof and Mouth
Haitian cholera
French Plague
African Malaria
German Measles
Asian Flu
Russian

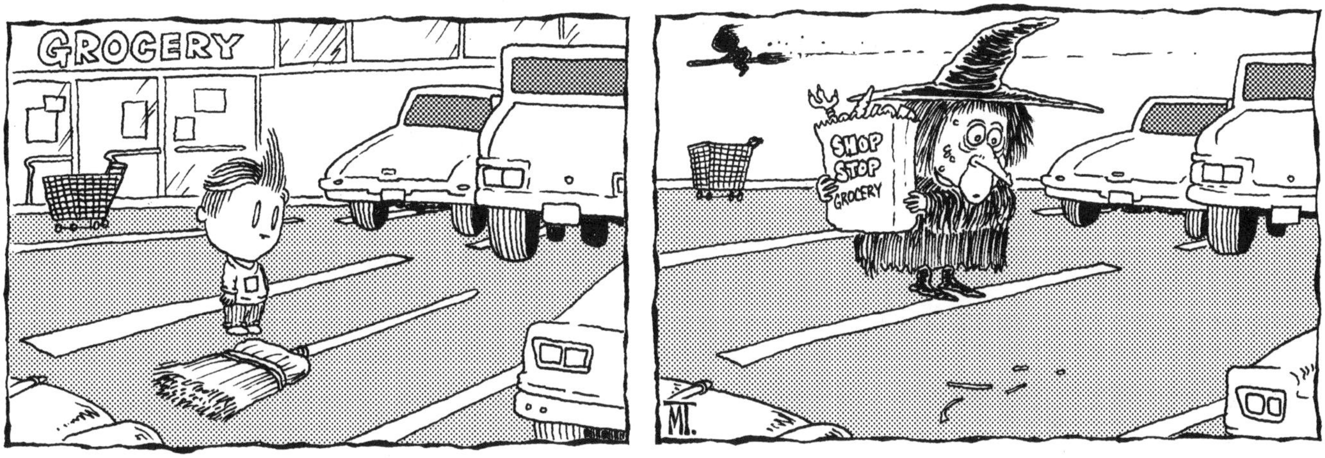
GROCERY
SHOP STOP GROCERY
MI.

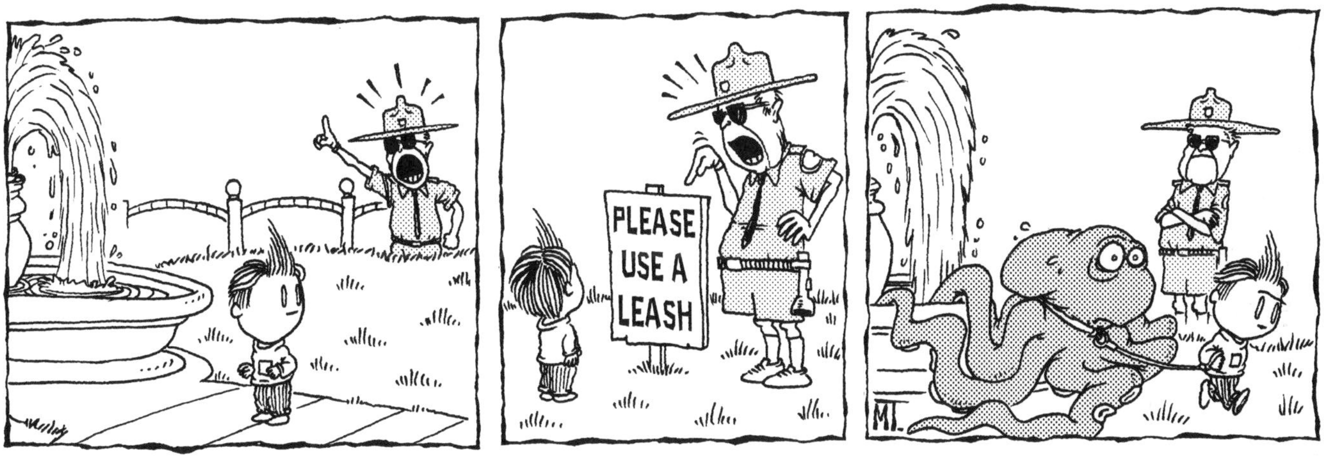
PLEASE USE A LEASH
MI.

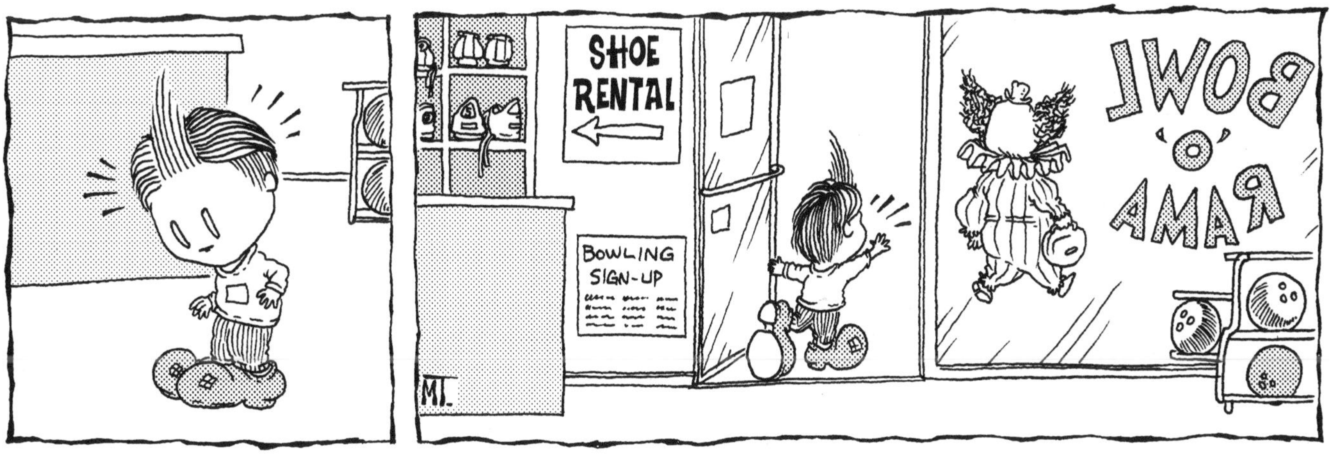
SHOE RENTAL
BOWLING SIGN-UP
BOWL O RAMA
MI.

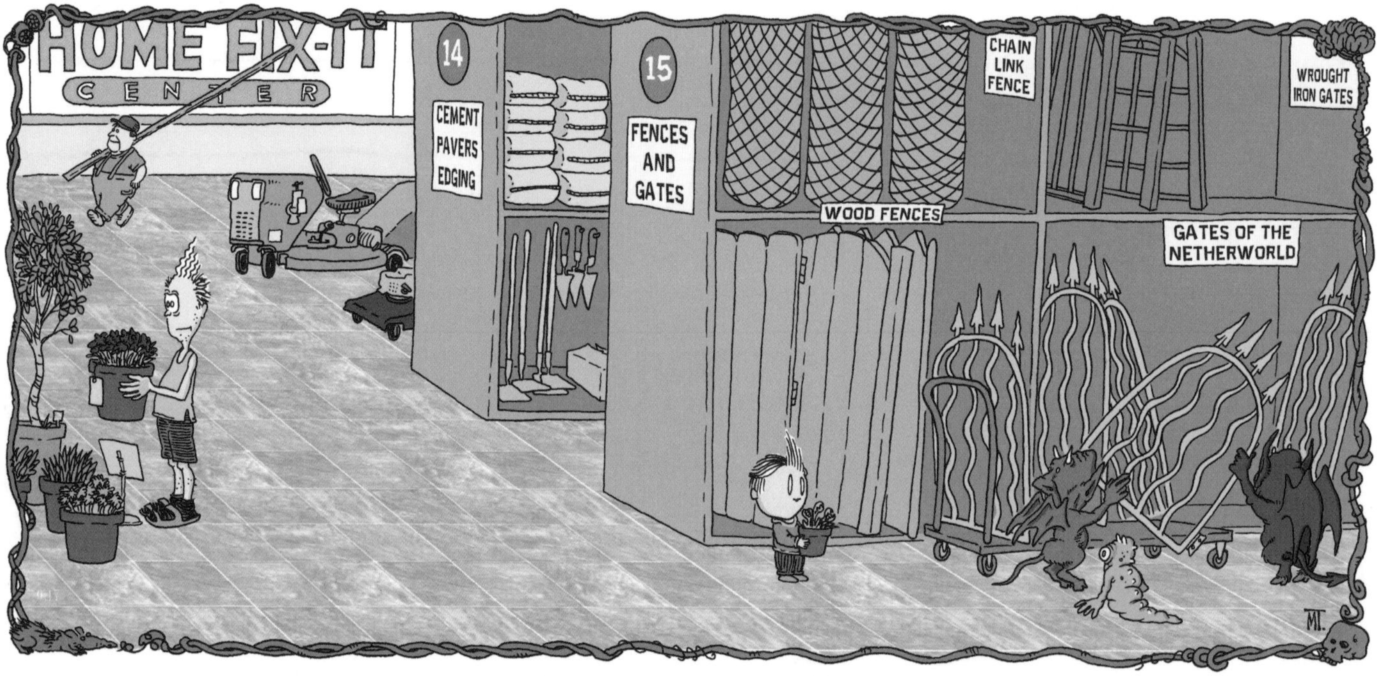
HOME FIX-IT
CENTER
14
CEMENT
PAVERS
EDGING
15
FENCES
AND
GATES
CHAIN
LINK
FENCE
WROUGHT
IRON GATES
WOOD FENCES
GATES OF THE
NETHERWORLD
MT.

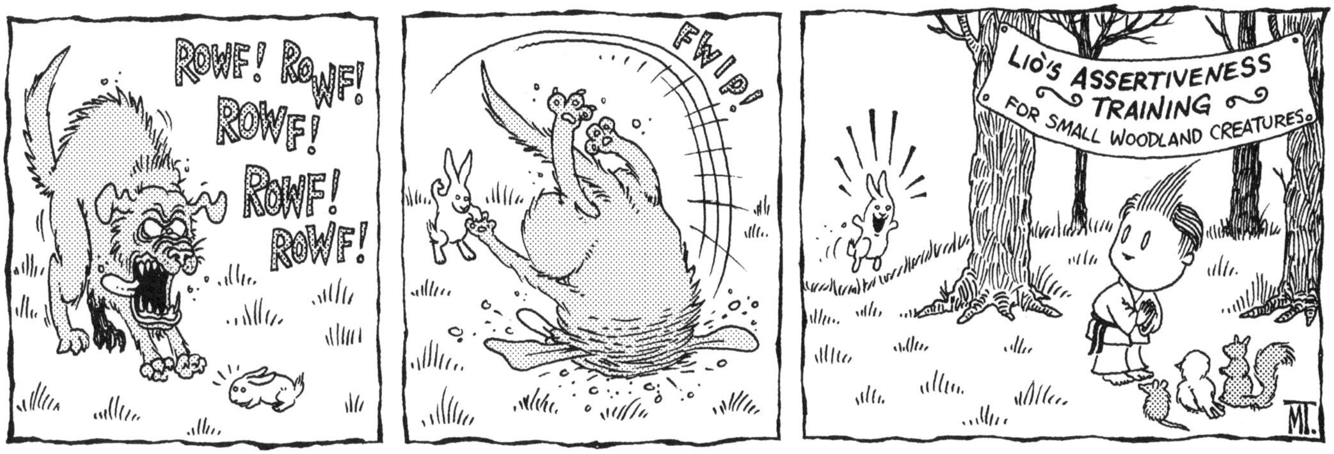
ROWF! ROWF! ROWF! ROWF! ROWF!
FWIP!
LIO'S ASSERTIVENESS TRAINING
FOR SMALL WOODLAND CREATURES
MT.

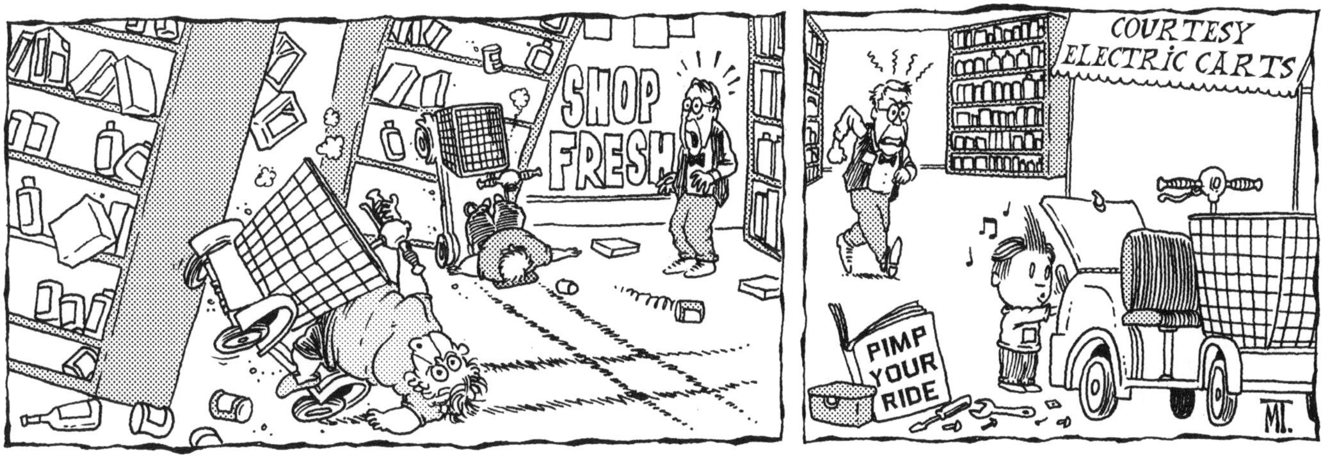
SHOP FRESH
COURTESY ELECTRIC CARTS
10
PIMP YOUR RIDE
MT.

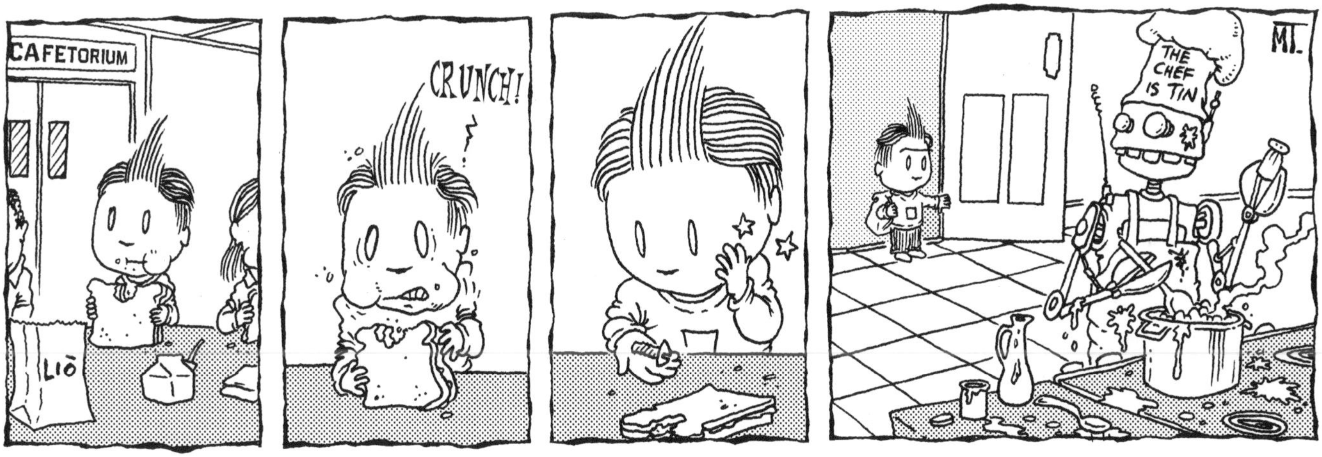
CAFETORIUM
LIO
CRUNCH!
MT.
THE CHEF IS TIN

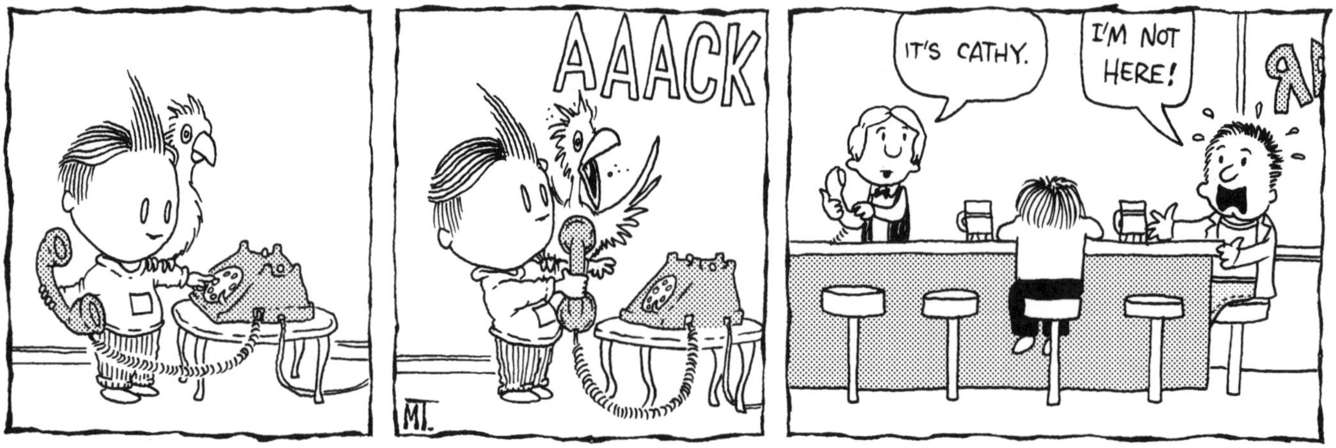
AAACK
IT'S CATHY.
I'M NOT HERE!

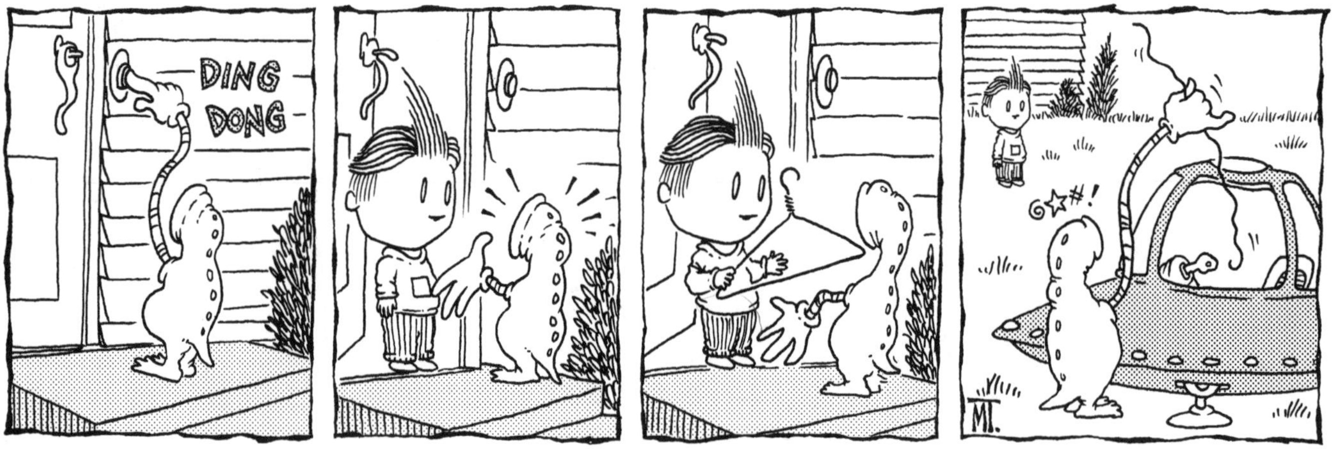
DING DONG

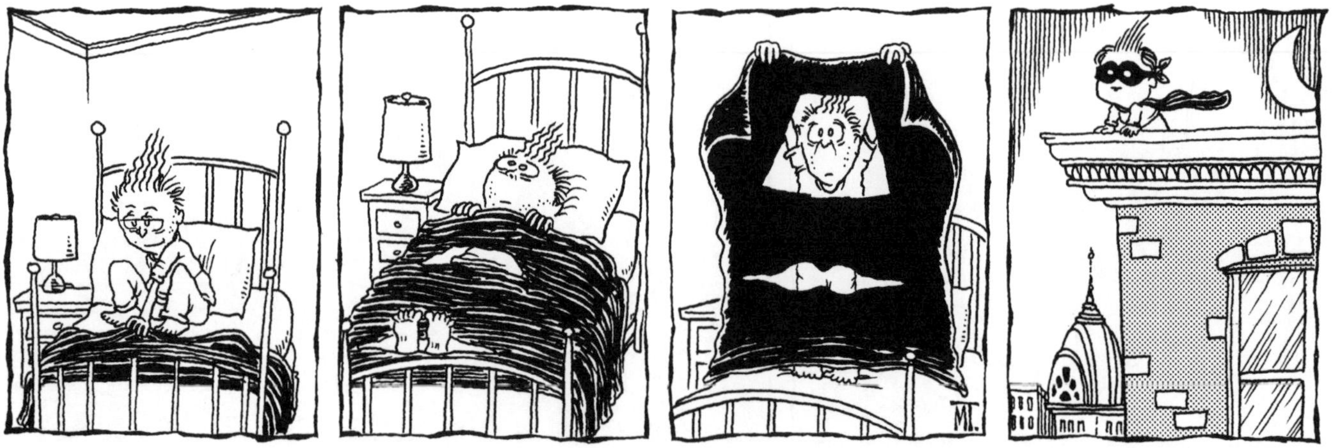

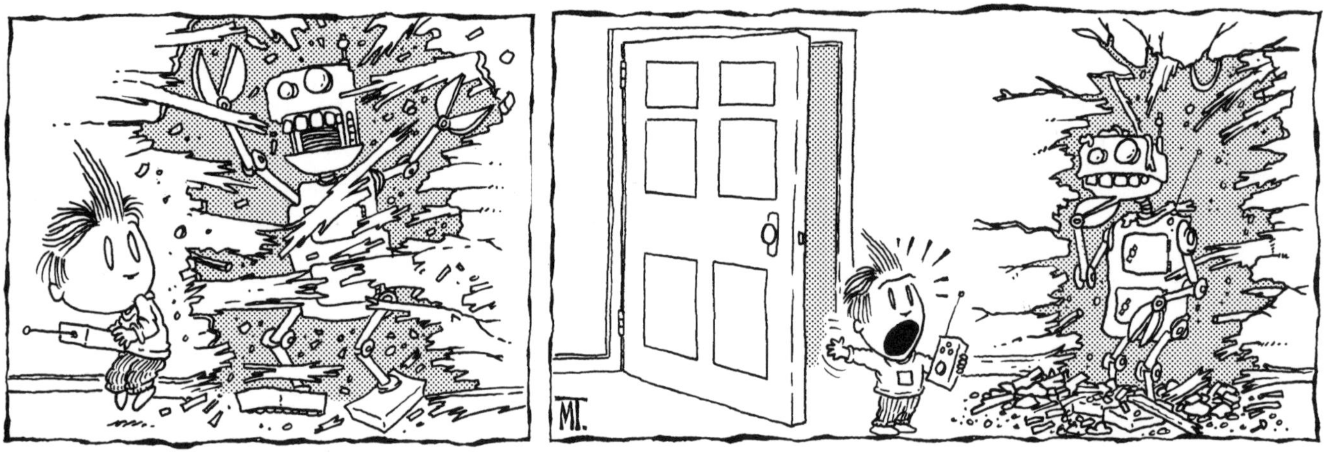

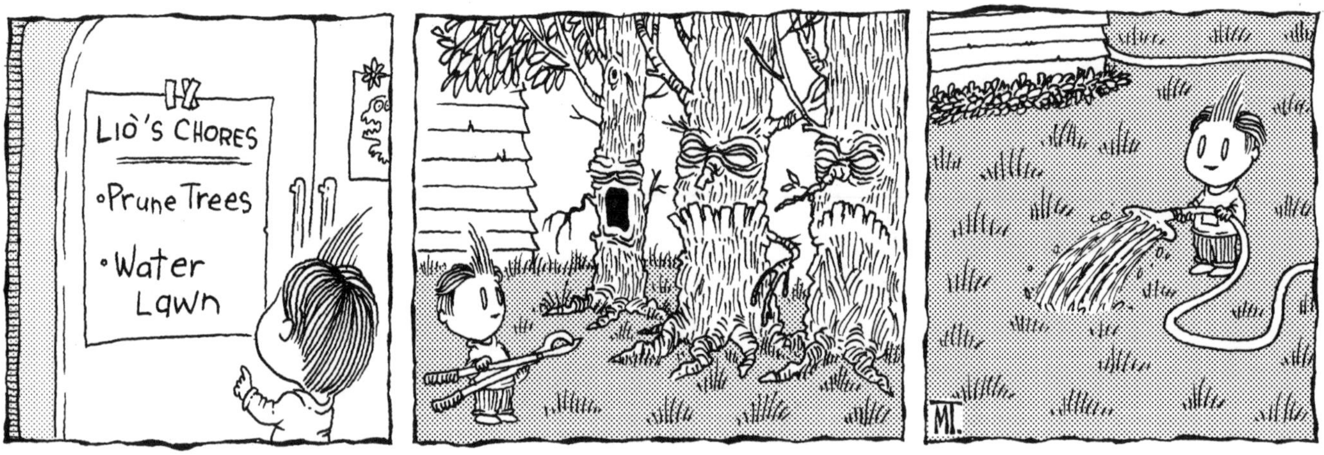
LIO'S CHORES
•Prune Trees
•Water Lawn

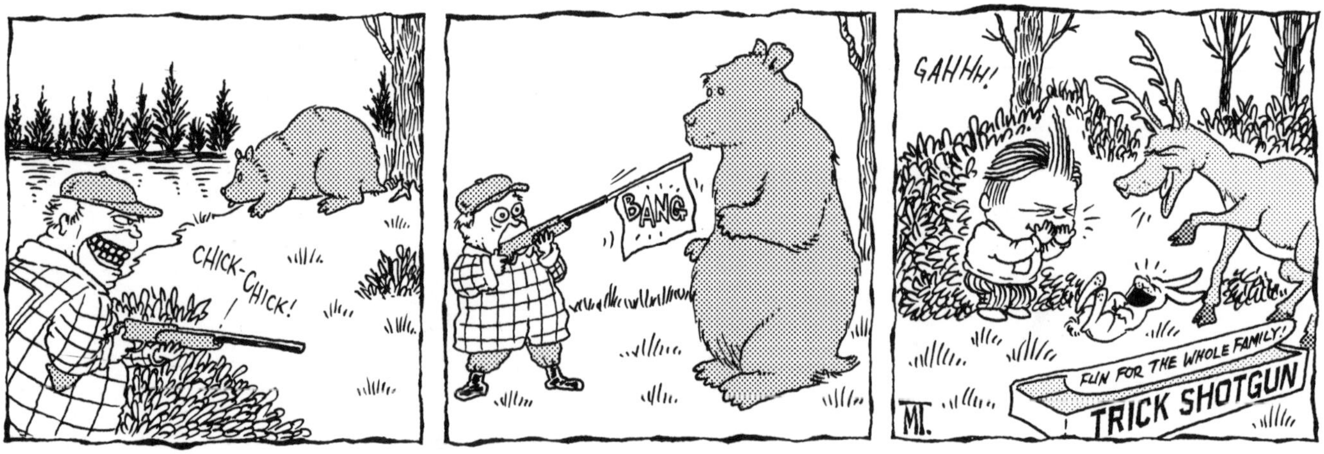
CHICK-CHICK!
BANG
GAHHH!
FUN FOR THE WHOLE FAMILY!
TRICK SHOTGUN

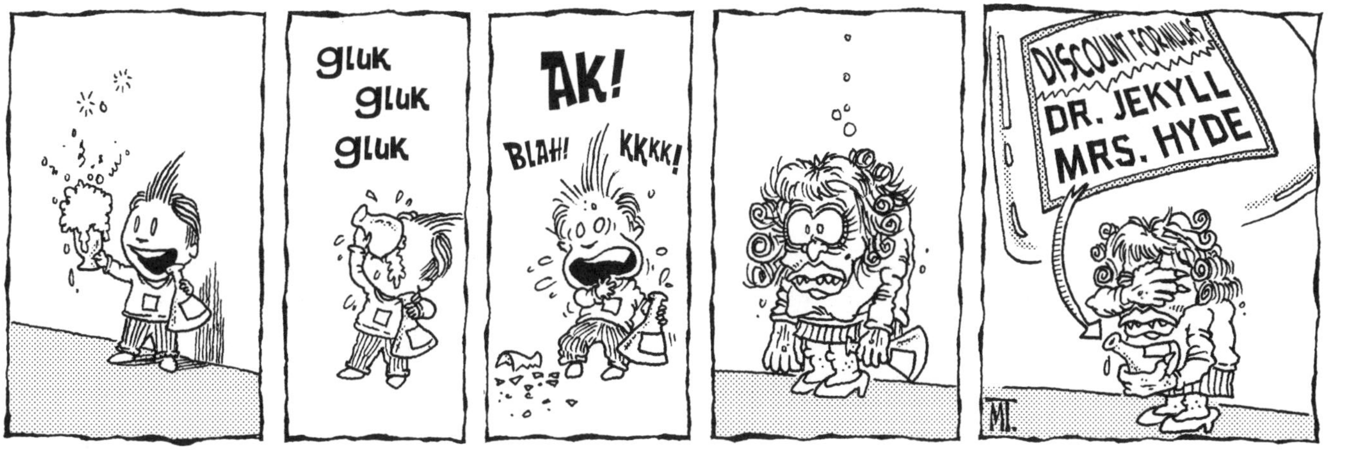
gluk
gluk
gluk
AK!
BLAH!
KKKK!
DISCOUNT FORMULAS
DR. JEKYLL
MRS. HYDE

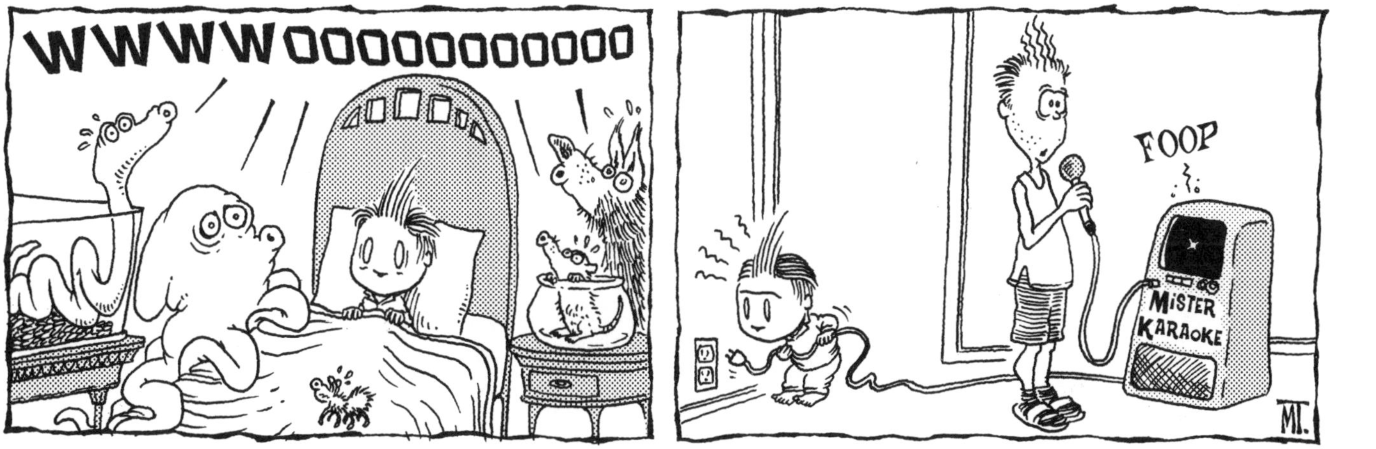
WWWWOOOOOOOOOOO
FOOP
MISTER
KARAOKE

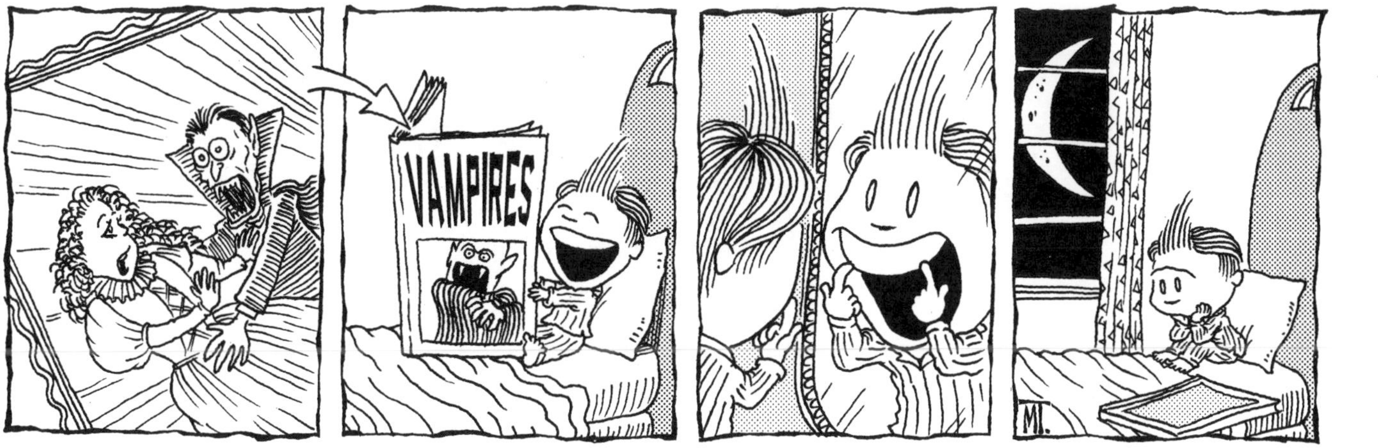
VAMPIRES

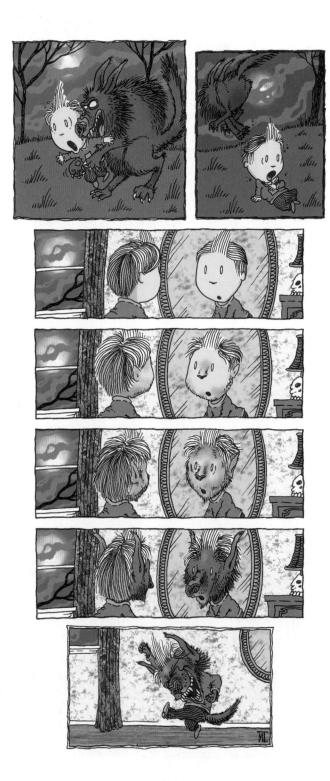

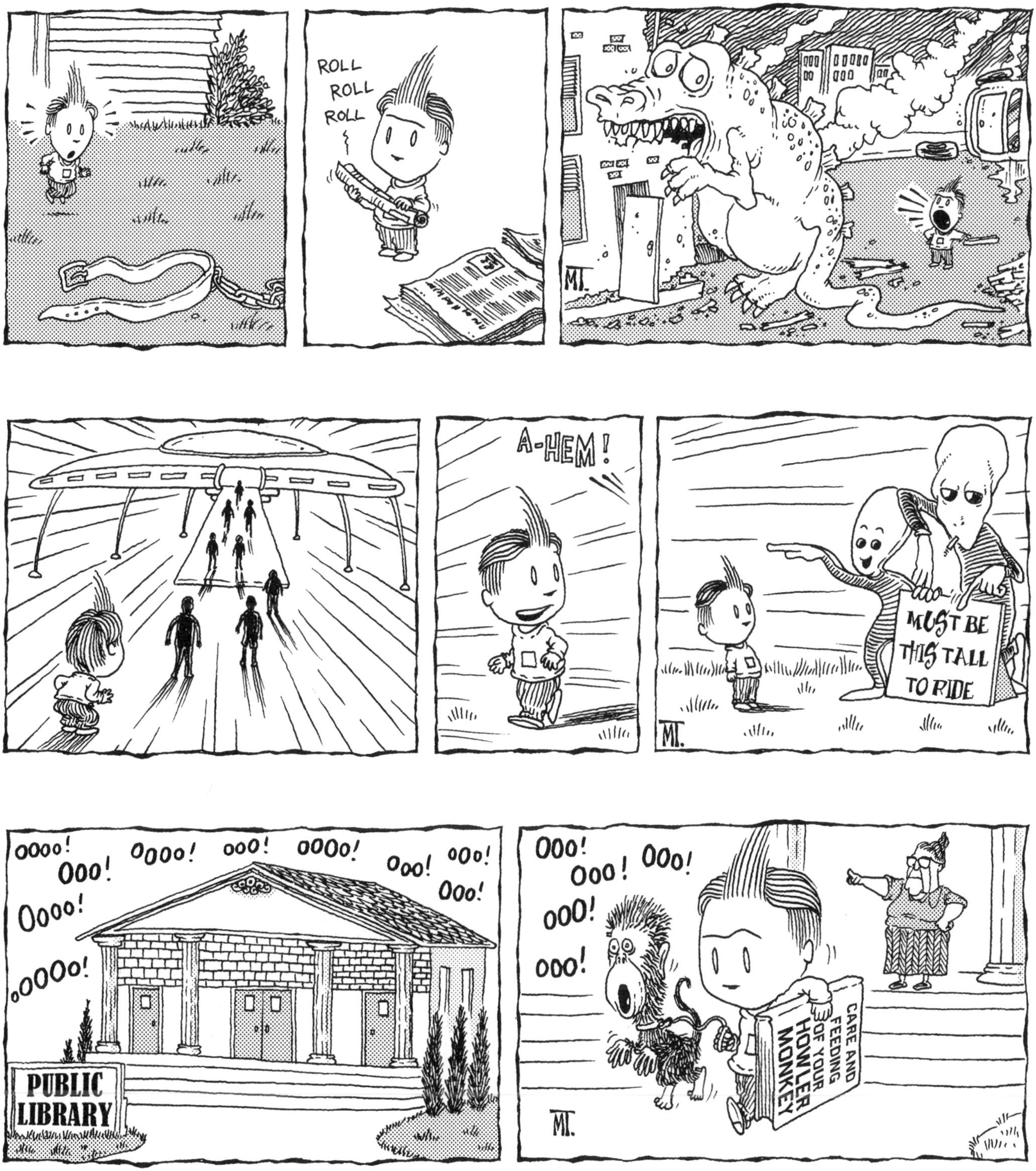
ROLL
ROLL
ROLL
A-HEM!
MUST BE THIS TALL TO RIDE
oooo! ooo! oooo! ooo! oooo! ooo! ooo! ooo! Oooo! oOOOo!
PUBLIC LIBRARY
OOO! OOO! OOO! OOO! OOO!
CARE AND FEEDING OF YOUR HOWLER MONKEY

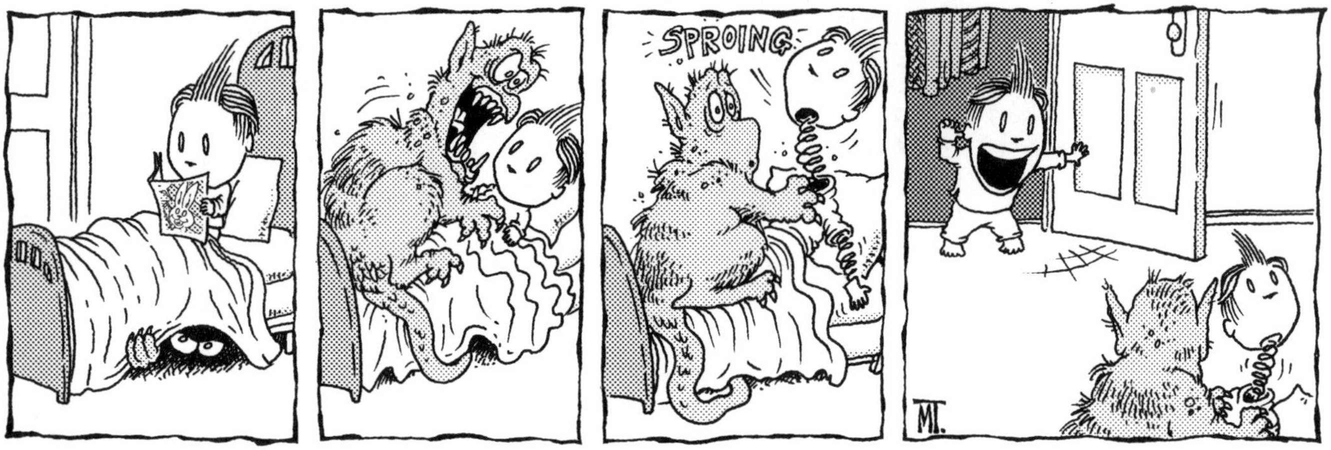
SPROING

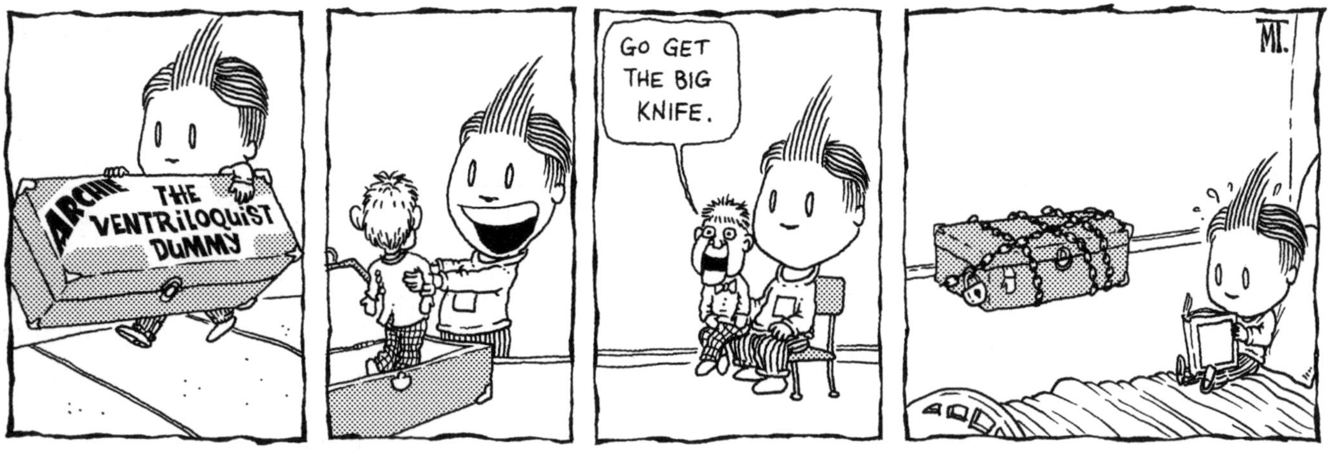
ARCHIE THE VENTRILOQUIST DUMMY
GO GET THE BIG KNIFE.

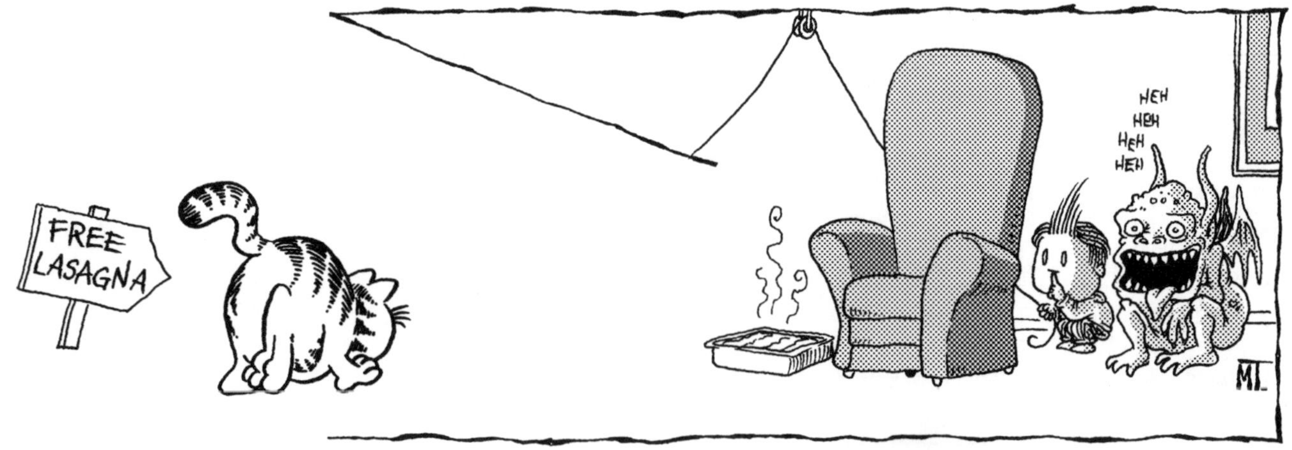
FREE LASAGNA
HEH HEH HEH HEH

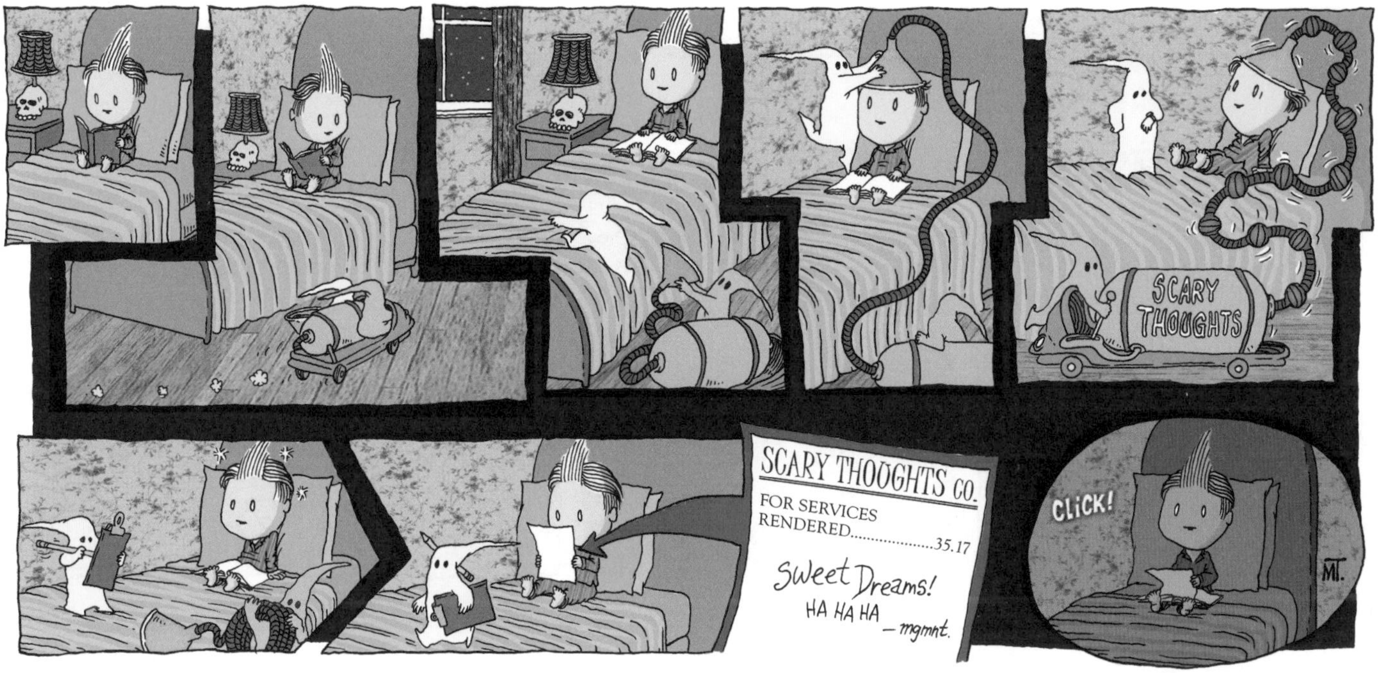
SCARY
THOUGHTS
SCARY THOUGHTS CO.
FOR SERVICES
RENDERED....................35.17
Sweet Dreams!
HA HA HA — mgmnt.
CLICK!
MT.

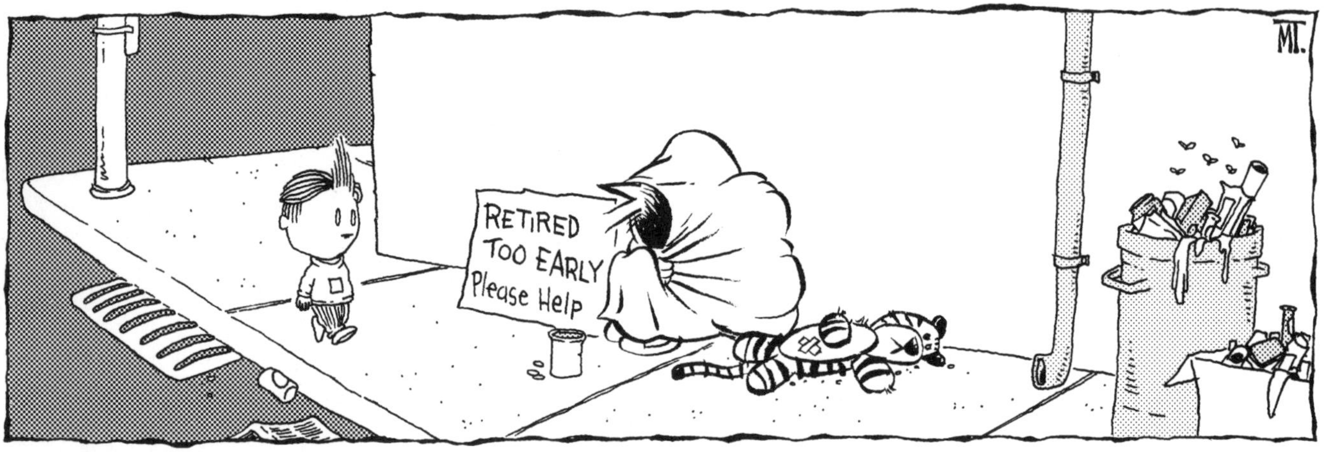
MT.
RETIRED
TOO EARLY
Please Help

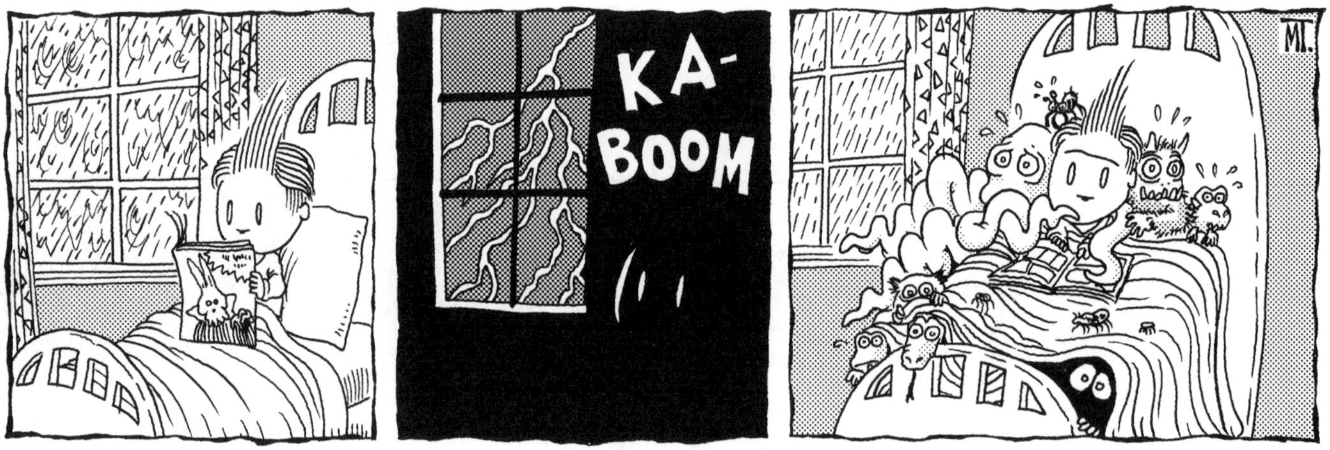
KA-
BOOM
MT.

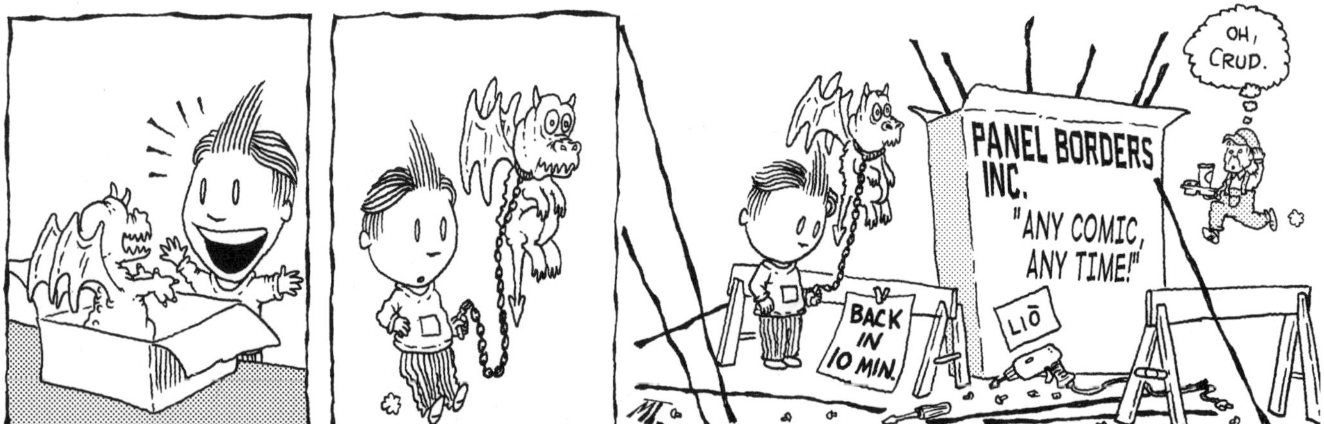
OH,
CRUD.
PANEL BORDERS
INC.
"ANY COMIC,
ANY TIME!"
BACK
IN
10 MIN.
LIŌ
MT.

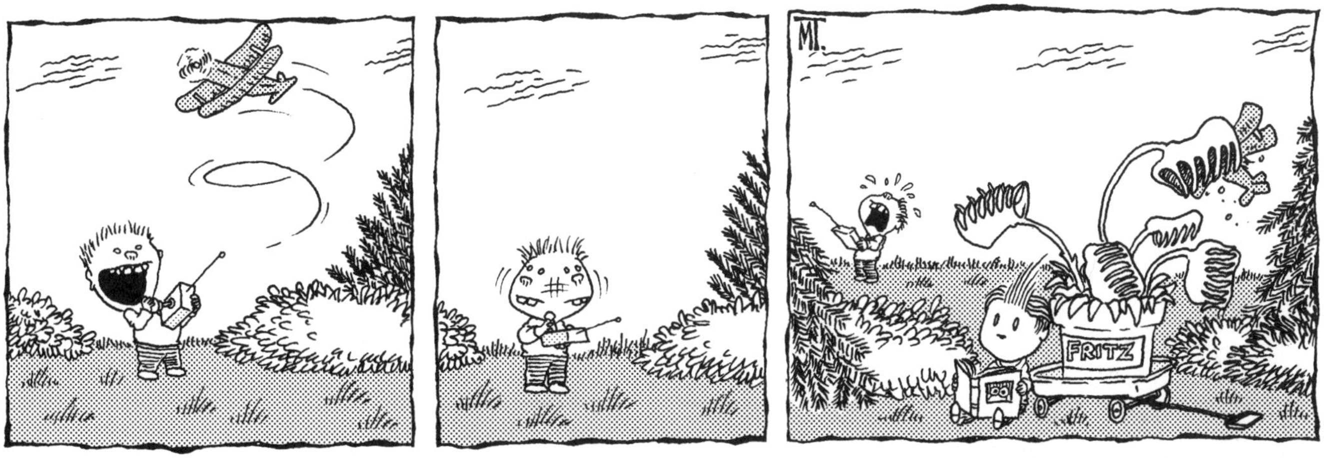
FRITZ

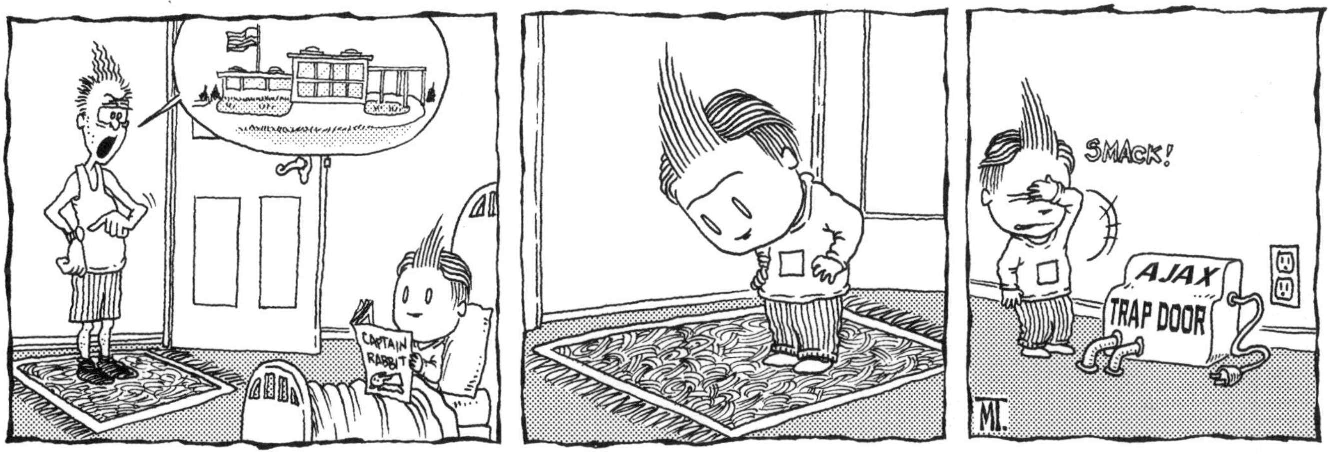
CAPTAIN RABBIT
SMACK!
AJAX
TRAP DOOR

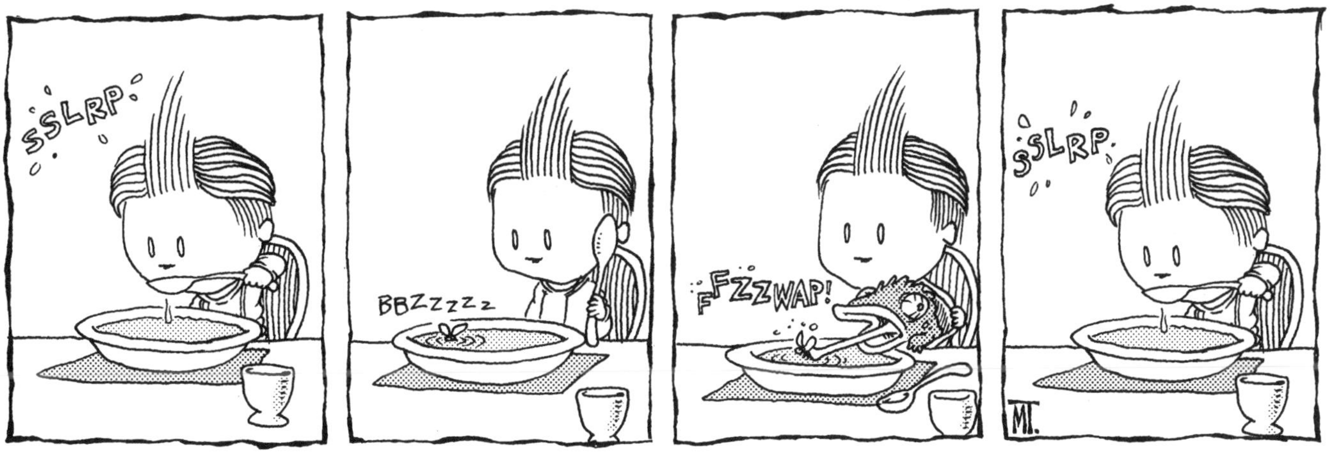
SSLRP
BBZZZZZ
FFZZWAP!
SSLRP

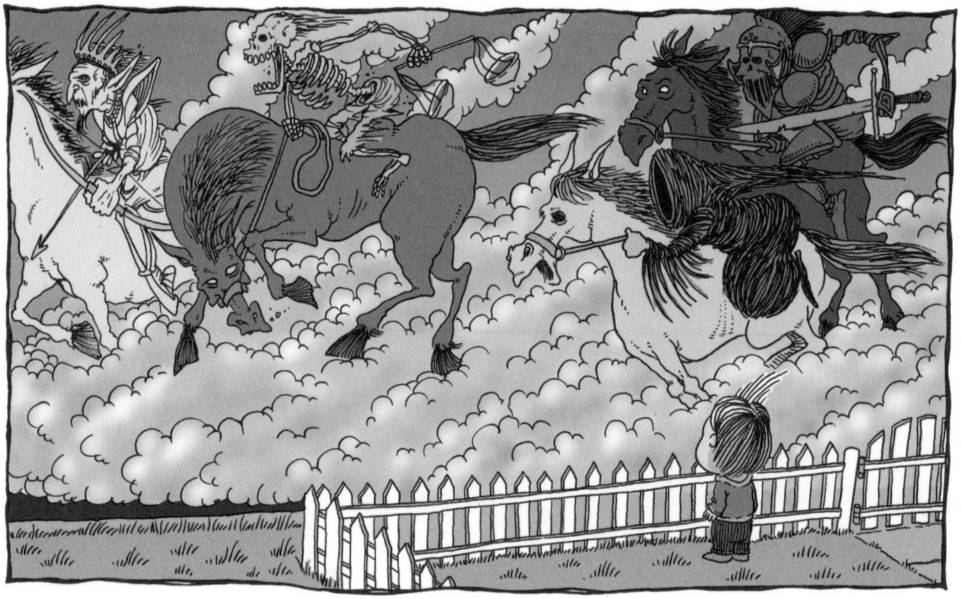

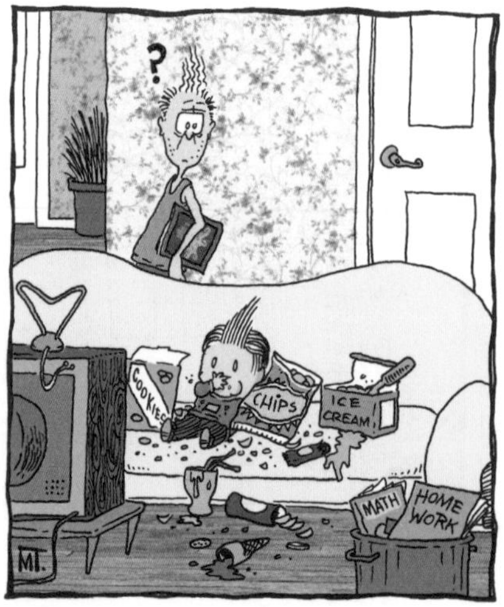
?
COOKIES
CHIPS
ICE CREAM
MATH
HOME WORK
MI.

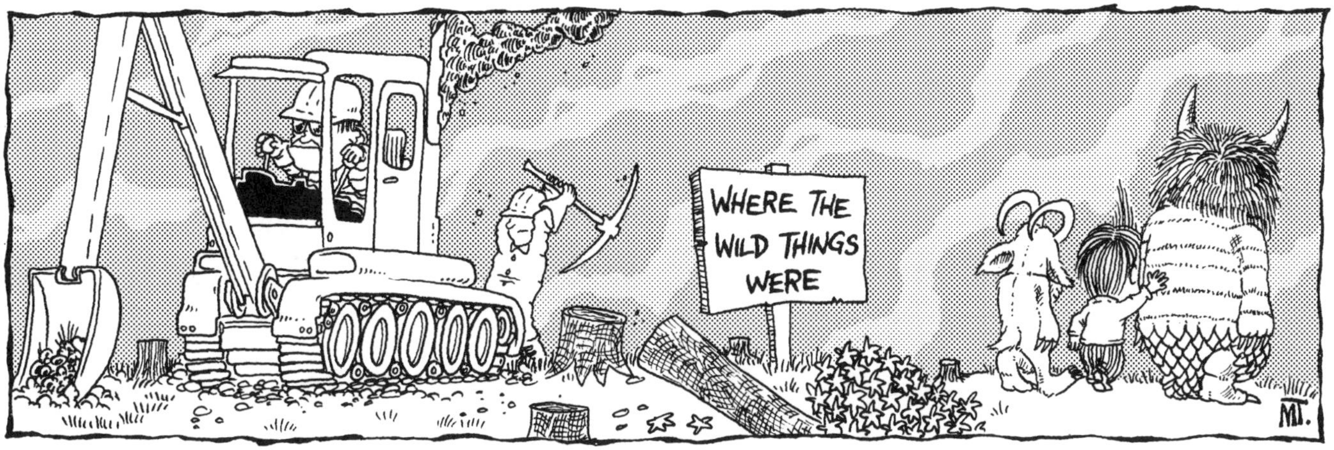
WHERE THE WILD THINGS WERE
MT.

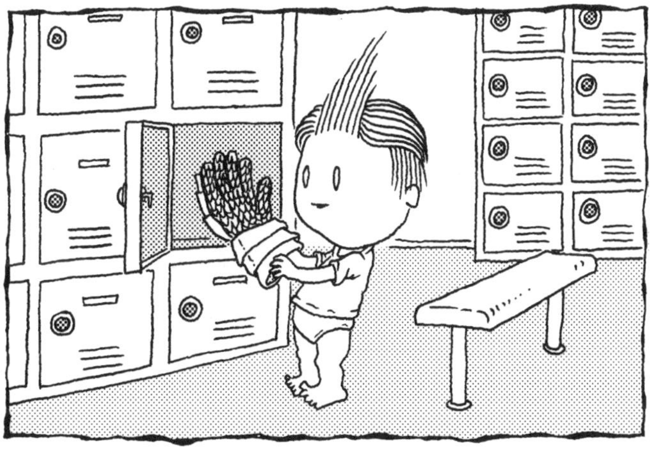

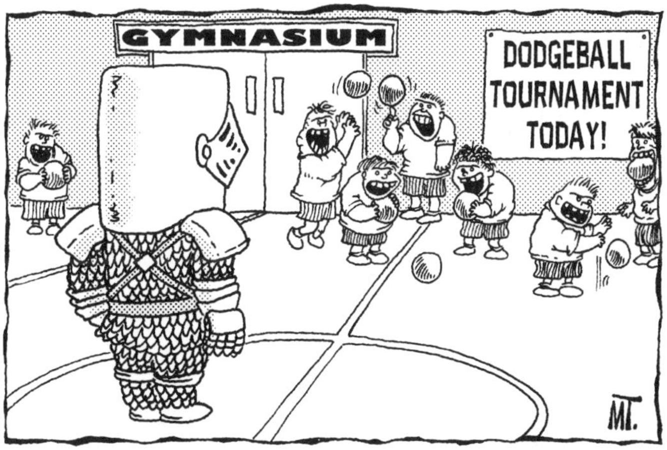
GYMNASIUM
DODGEBALL TOURNAMENT TODAY!
MT.

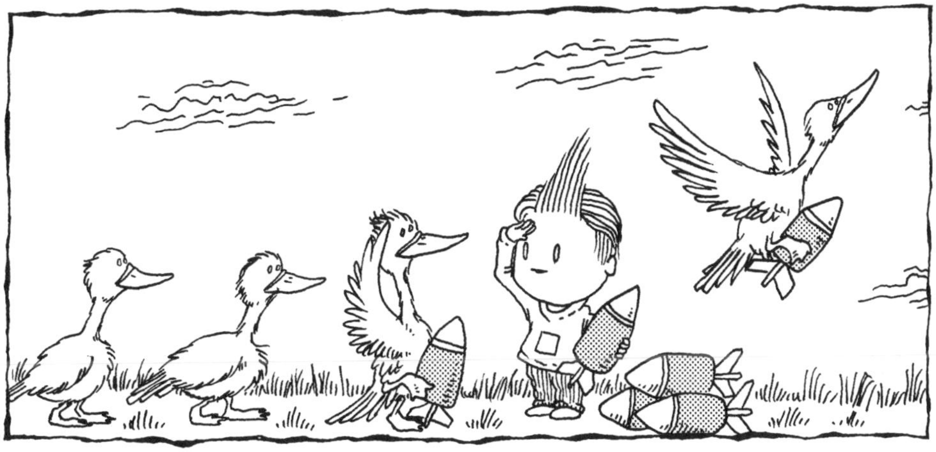

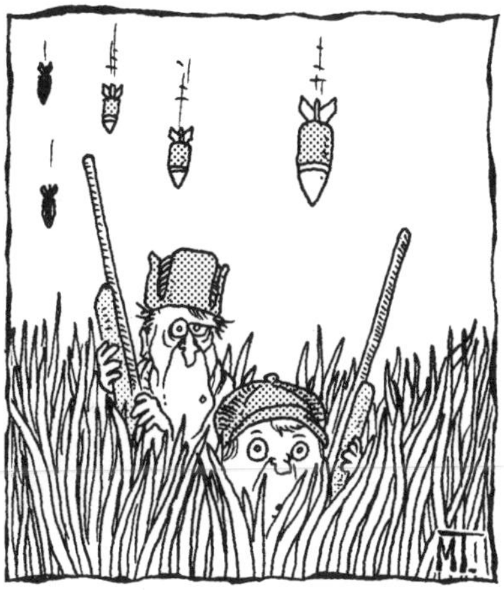
MT.

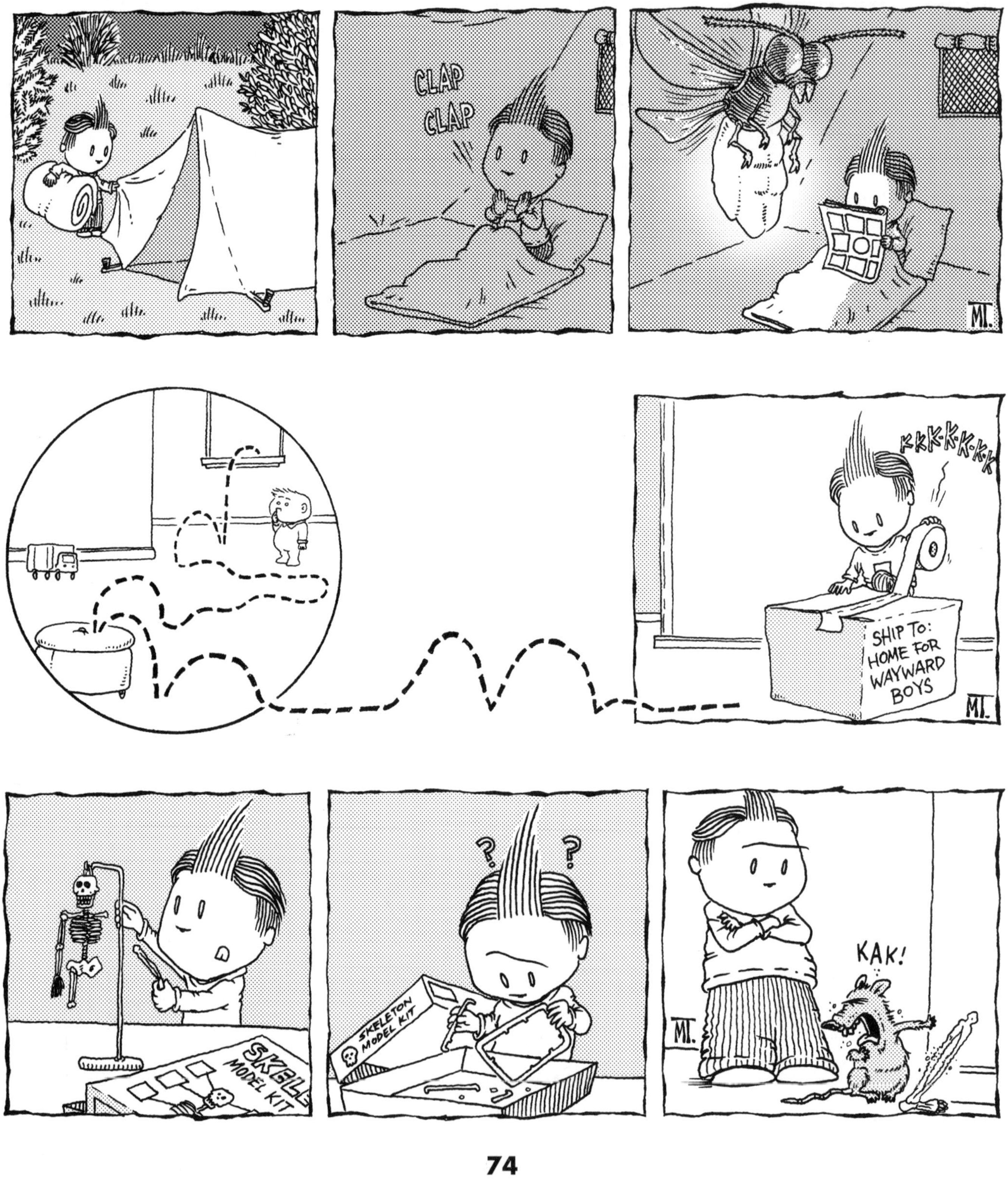
CLAP
CLAP
MI.
KKK-K-K-K-K
SHIP TO: HOME FOR WAYWARD BOYS
MI.
MODEL KIT
? ?
SKELETON MODEL KIT
MI.
KAK!

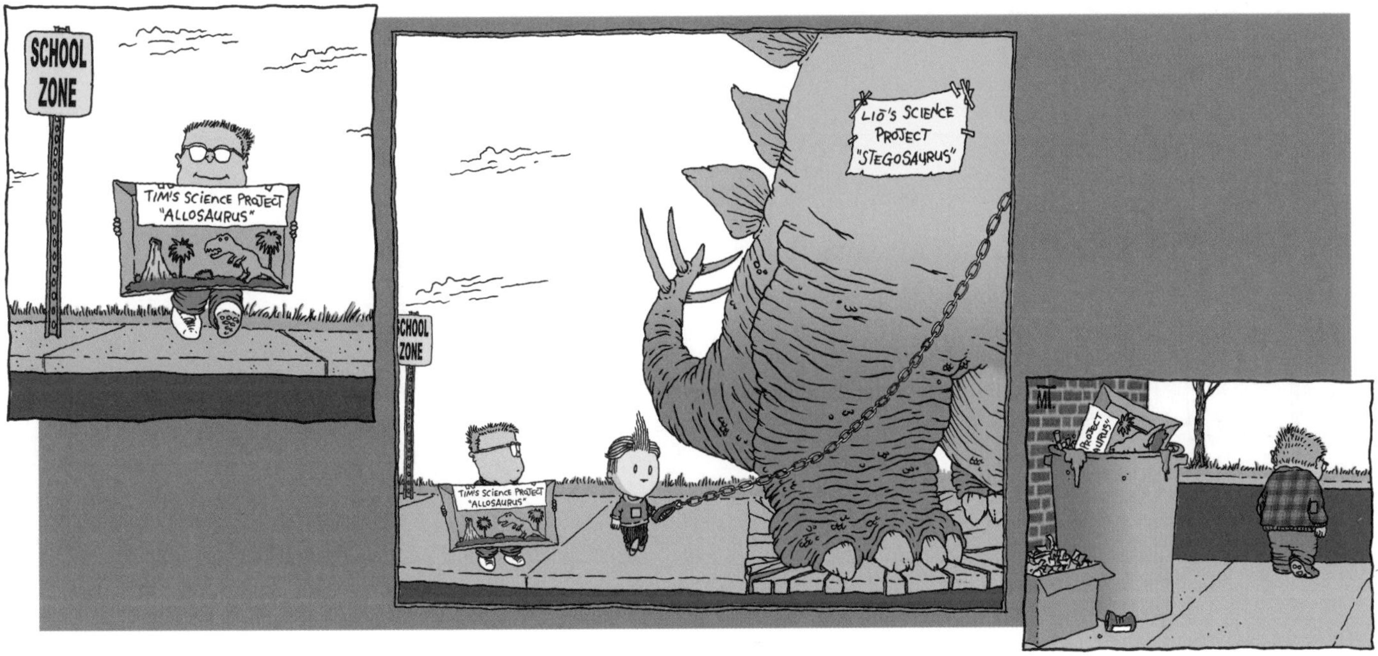
SCHOOL ZONE
TIM'S SCIENCE PROJECT "ALLOSAURUS"
LIŌ'S SCIENCE PROJECT "STEGOSAURUS"

THINGS THAT GO BUMP IN THE NIGHT
BUMP BUMP BUMPITY
BUMP
BUMP
BUMP
THINGS THAT GO
LOST
Bulging Eyes, Eight Legs, Answers to "ISHMAEL"
LOST
BOYS
BRING YOUR PET TO SCHOOL DAY!
SMACK!
MS. ROBBINS

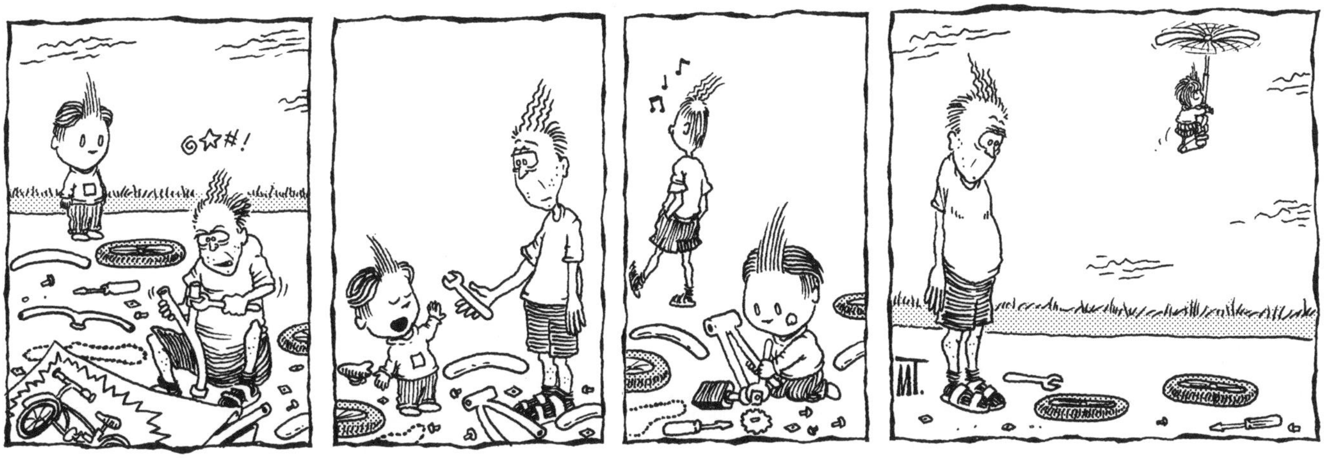

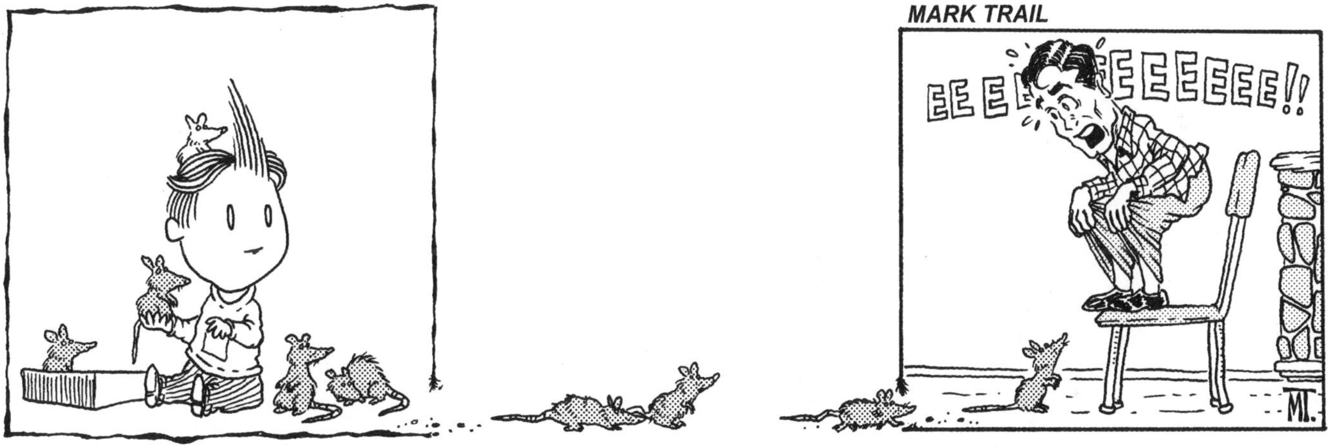
MARK TRAIL
EE EE EEEEEEE!!

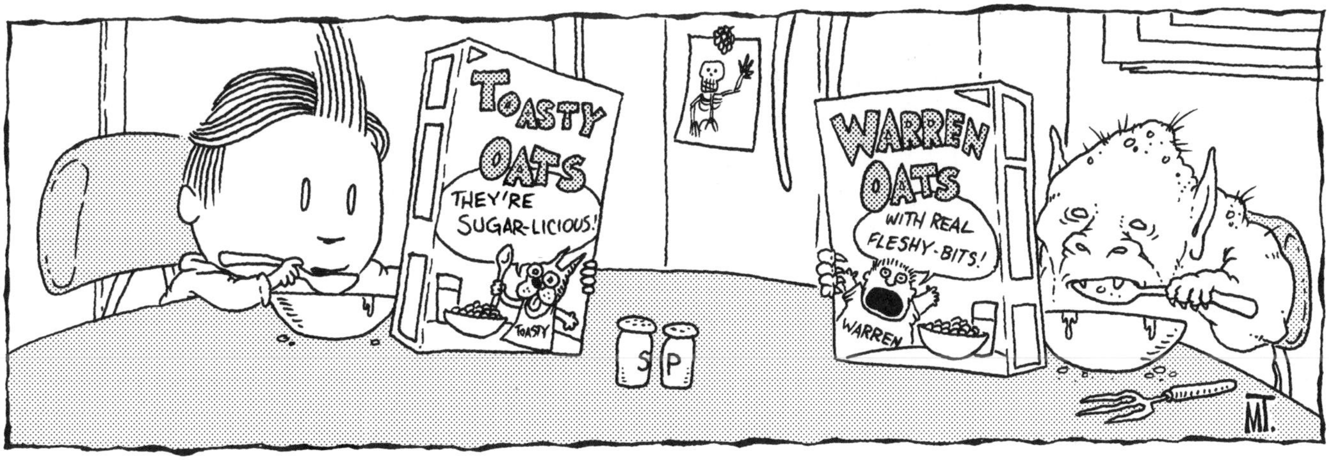
TOASTY OATS
THEY'RE SUGAR-LICIOUS!
TOASTY
WARREN OATS
WITH REAL FLESHY-BITS!
WARREN
S
P

MT.

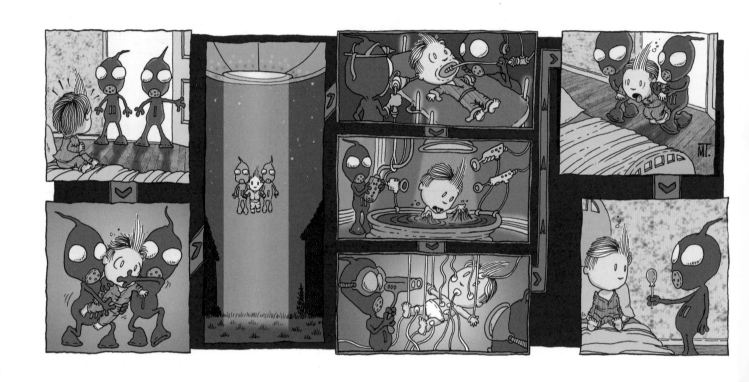

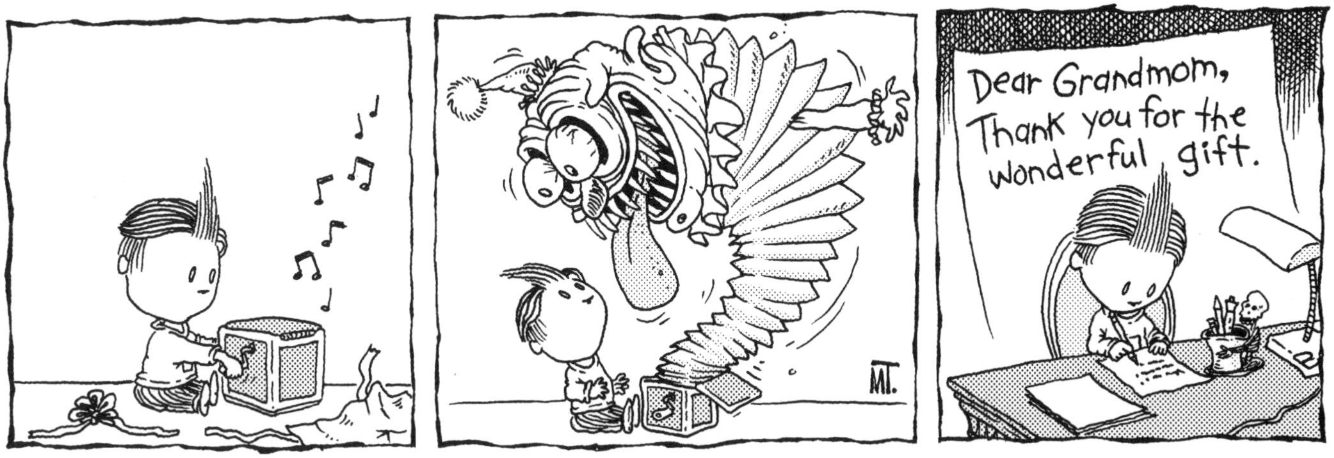
Dear Grandmom,
Thank you for the wonderful gift.

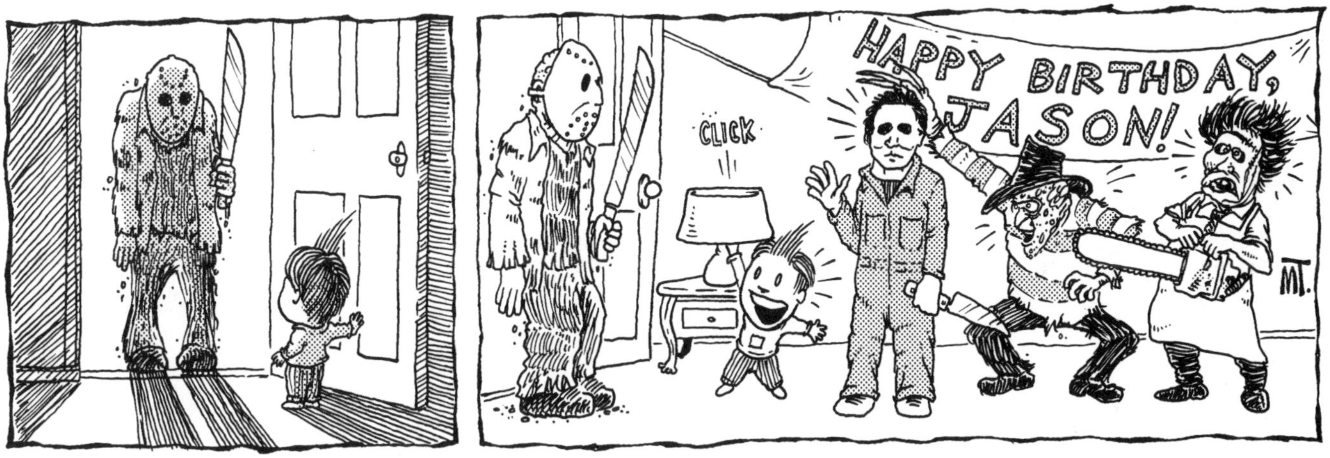
CLICK
HAPPY BIRTHDAY, JASON!

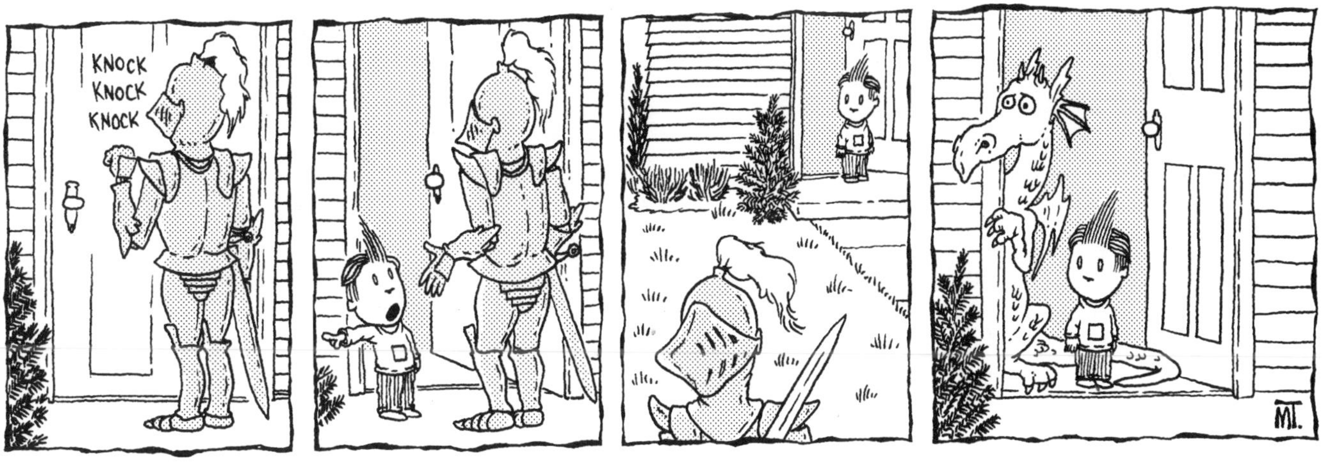
KNOCK
KNOCK
KNOCK

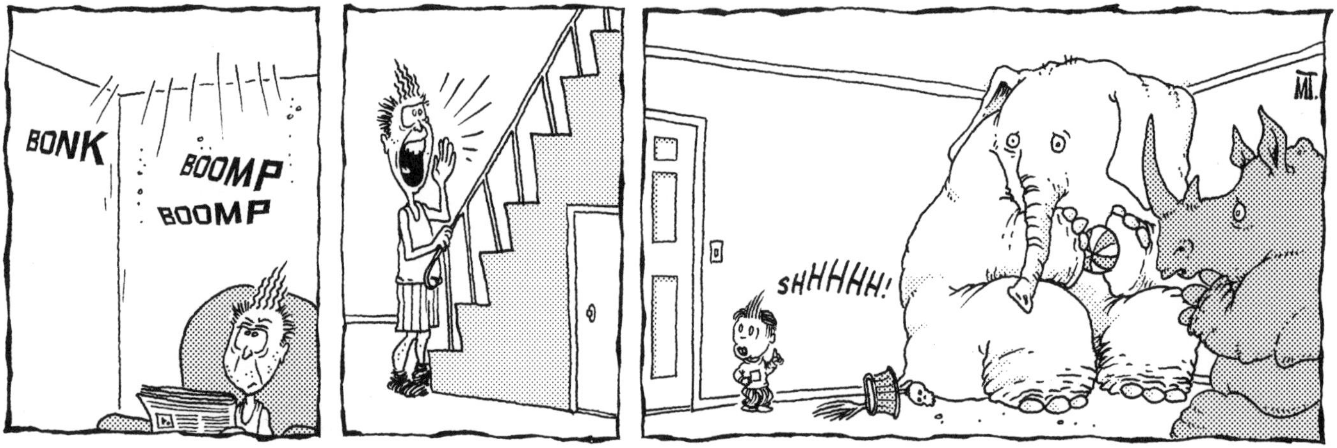
BONK
BOOMP
BOOMP
SHHHHH!
MT.

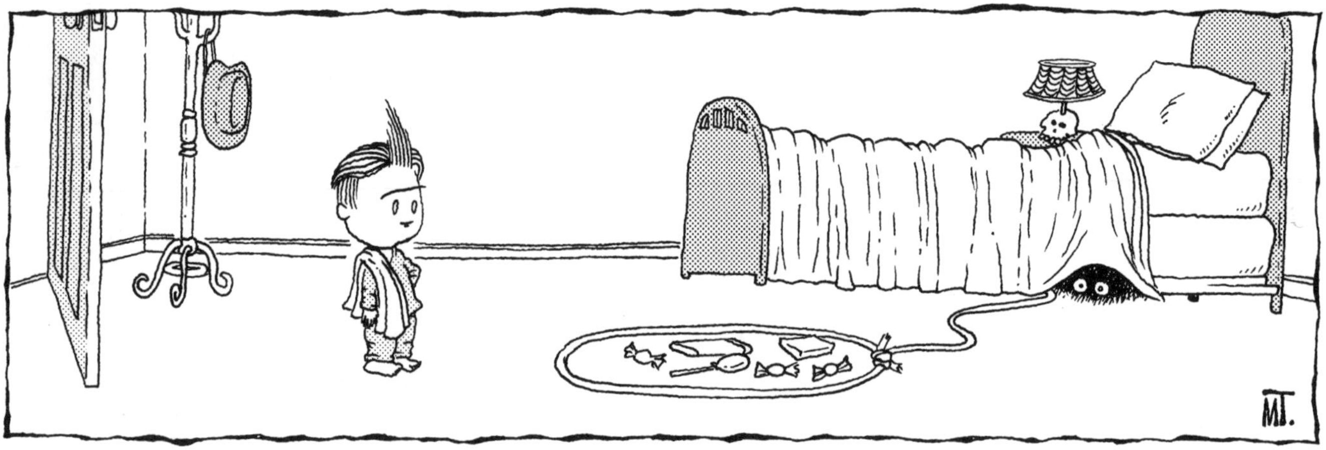
MT.

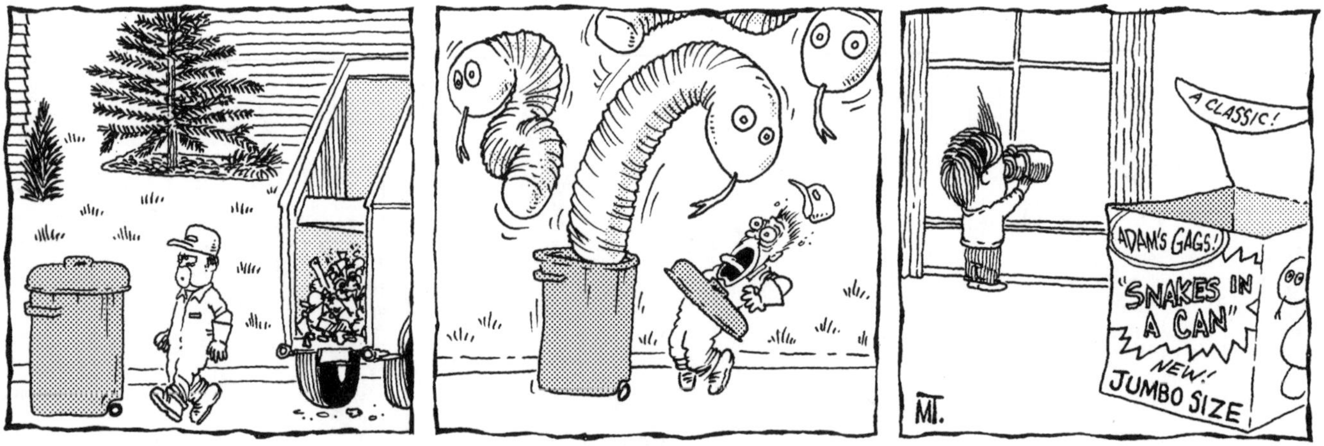
A CLASSIC!
ADAM'S GAGS!
"SNAKES IN A CAN"
NEW!
JUMBO SIZE
MT.

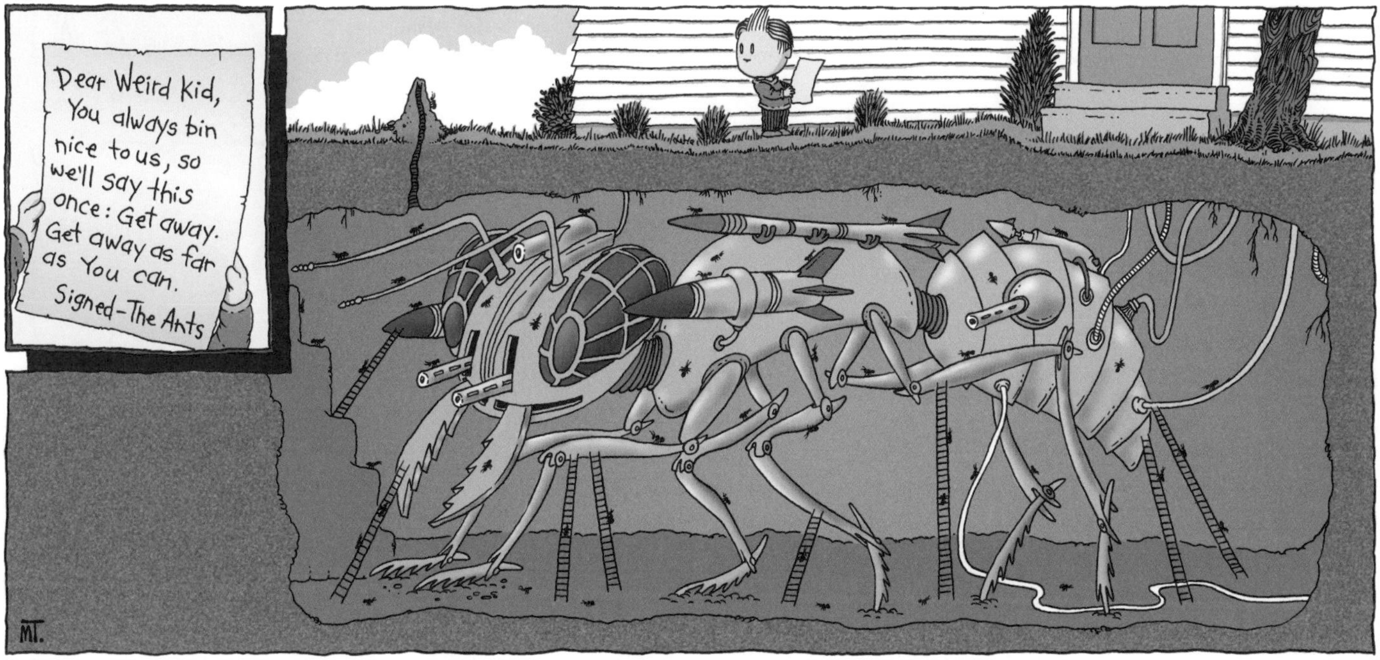
Dear Weird Kid,
You always bin nice to us, so we'll say this once: Get away. Get away as far as You can.
Signed-The Ants
MT.

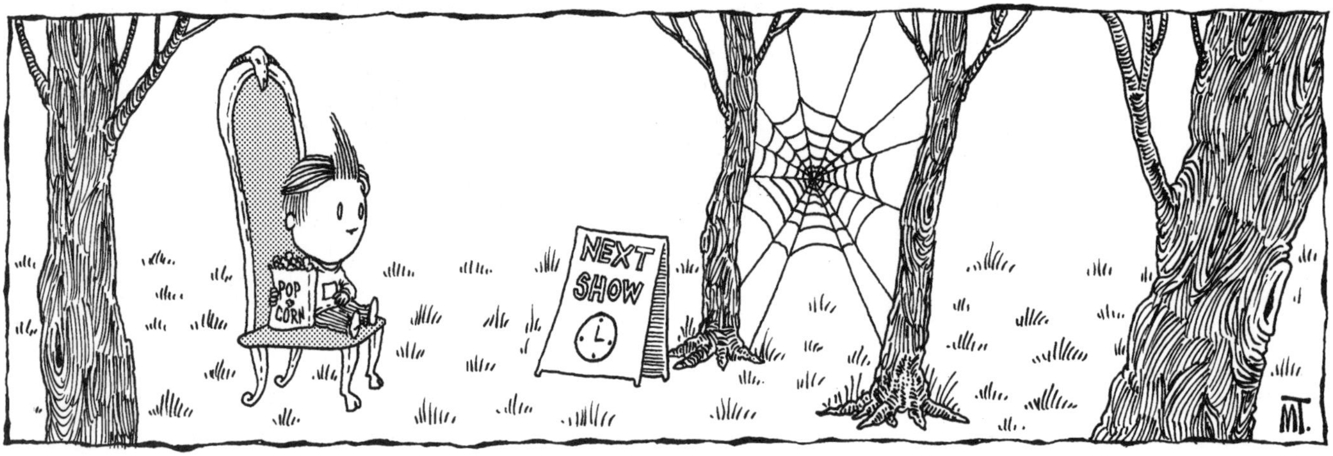
POP CORN
NEXT SHOW

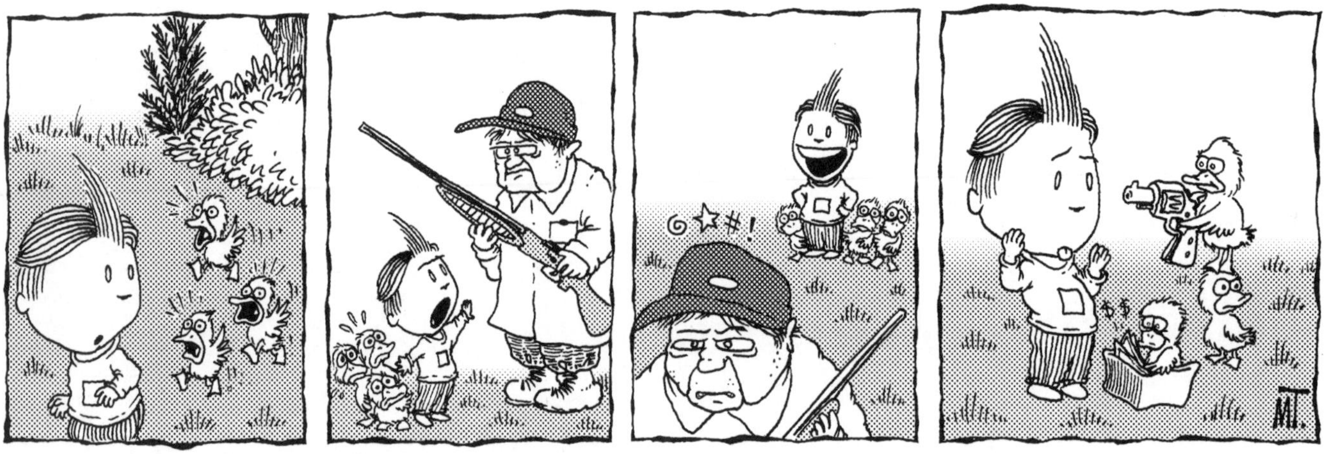

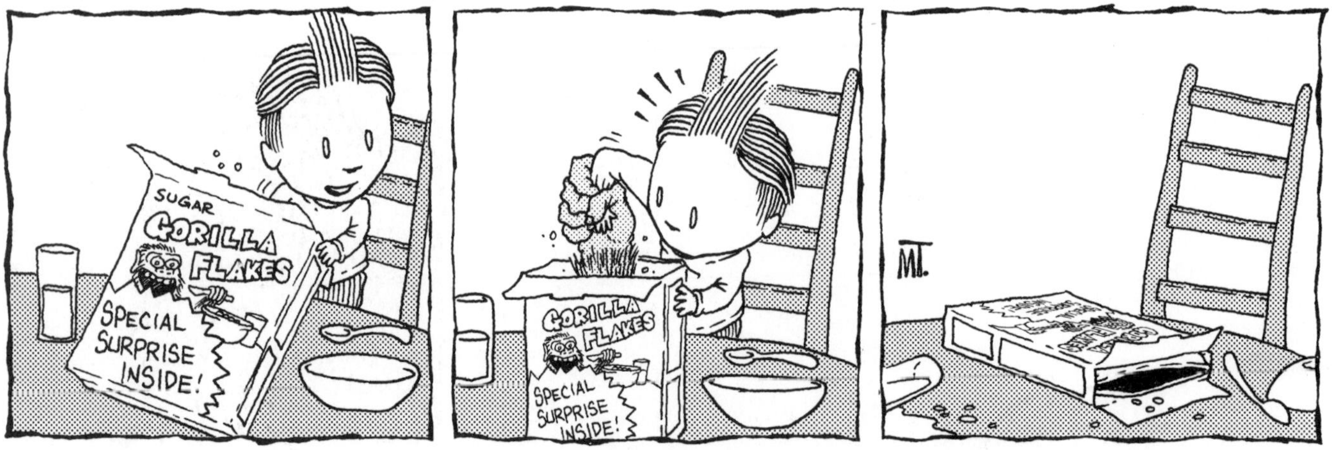
SUGAR GORILLA FLAKES
SPECIAL SURPRISE INSIDE!
GORILLA FLAKES
SPECIAL SURPRISE INSIDE!

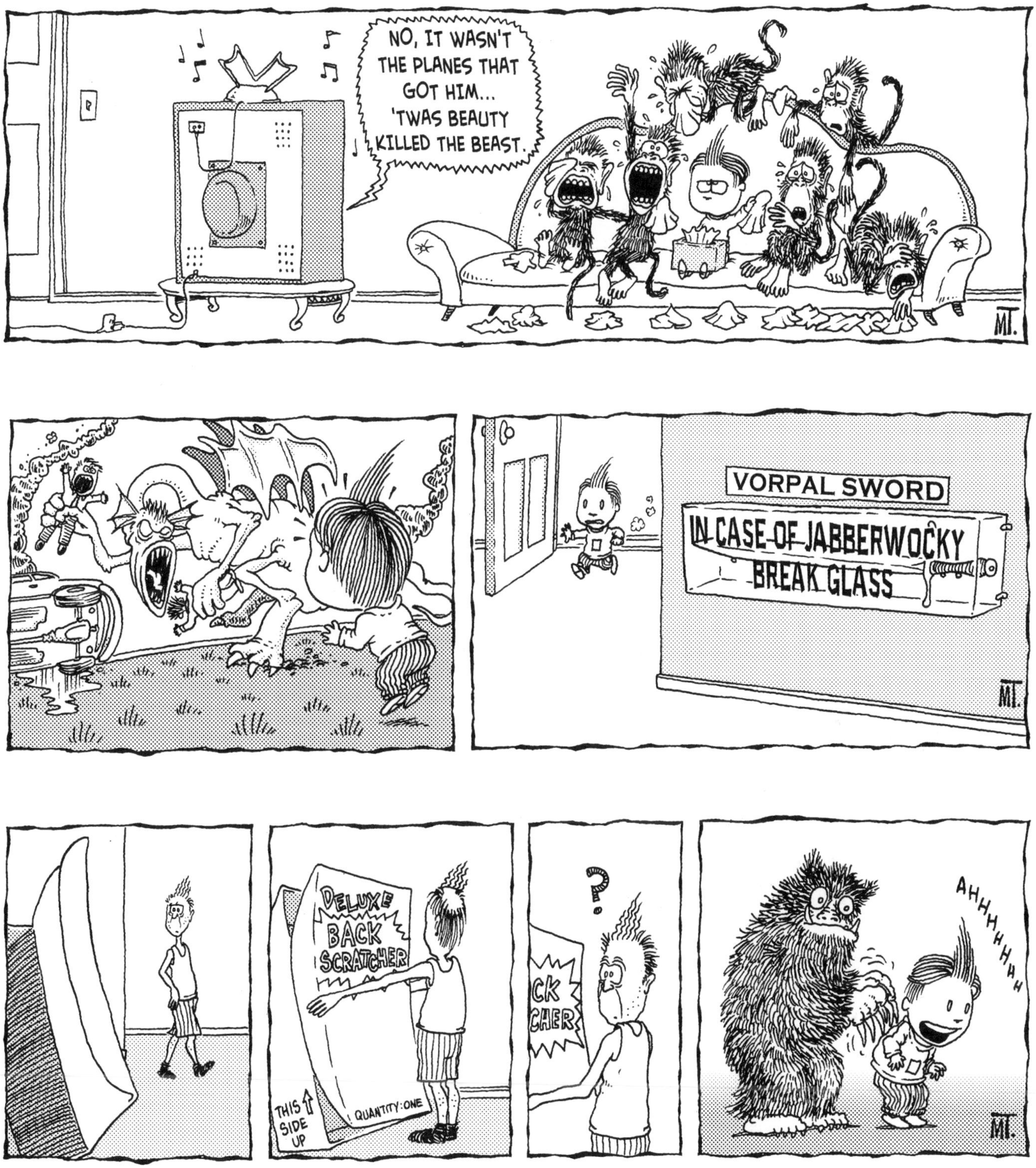
NO, IT WASN'T THE PLANES THAT GOT HIM... 'TWAS BEAUTY KILLED THE BEAST.
M.T.
VORPAL SWORD
IN CASE OF JABBERWOCKY BREAK GLASS
M.T.
DELUXE BACK SCRATCHER
THIS SIDE UP
QUANTITY: ONE
?
AHHHHHHHH
M.T.

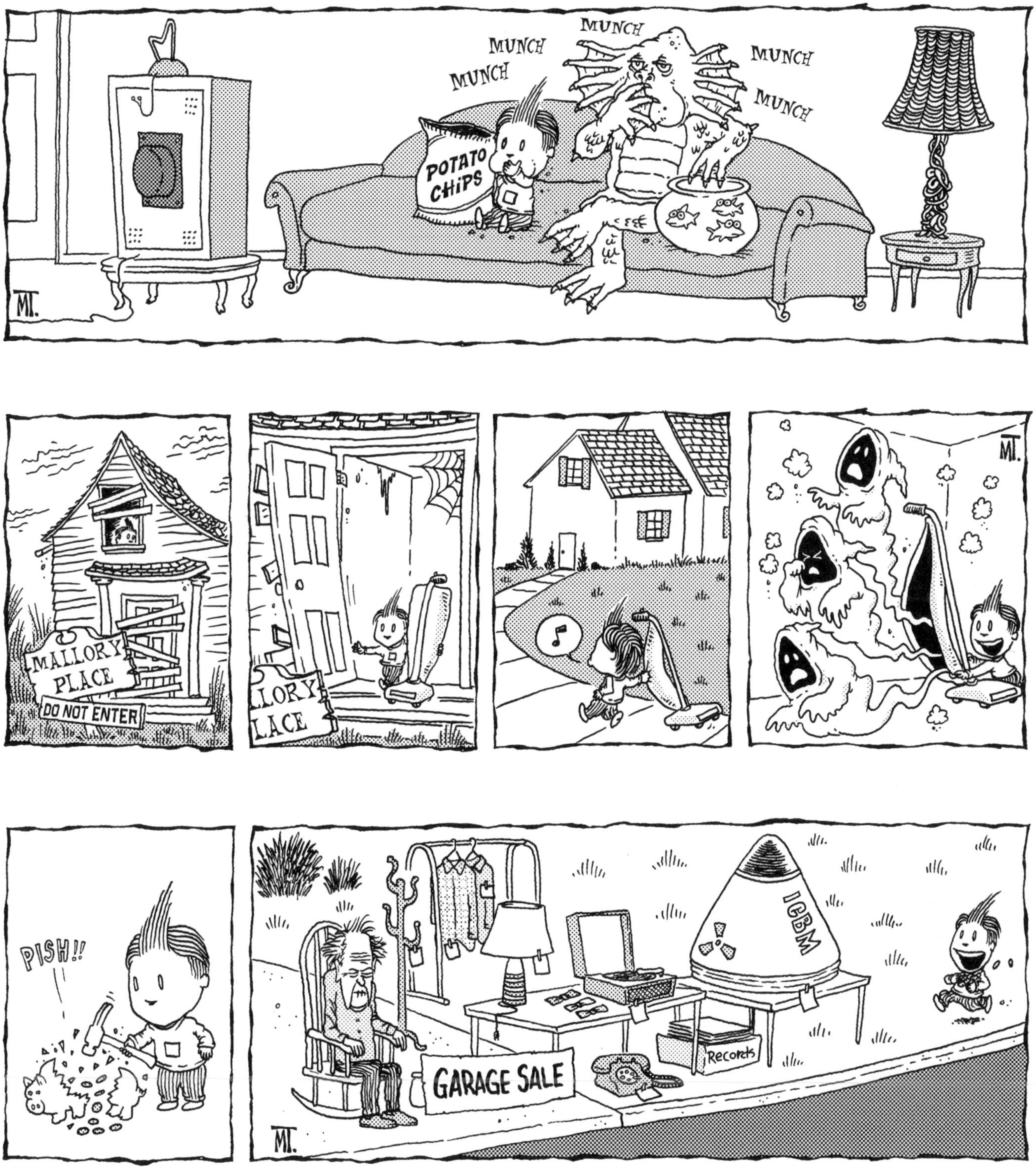
MUNCH
MUNCH
MUNCH
MUNCH
MUNCH
POTATO CHIPS
MT.
MALLORY PLACE
DO NOT ENTER
LLORY
LACE
MT.
PISH!!
IGBM
Records
GARAGE SALE
MT.

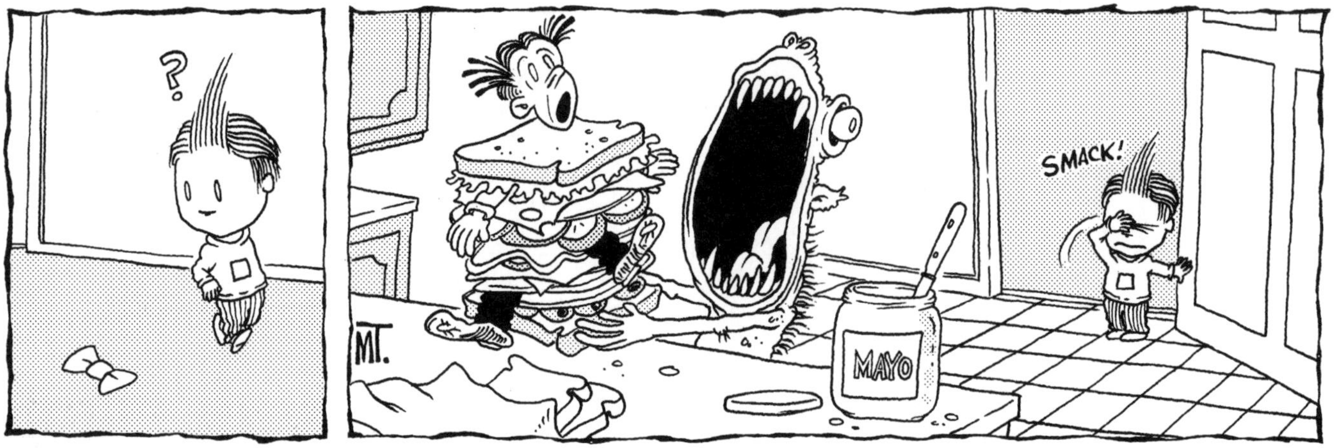
?
SMACK!
MT.
MAYO

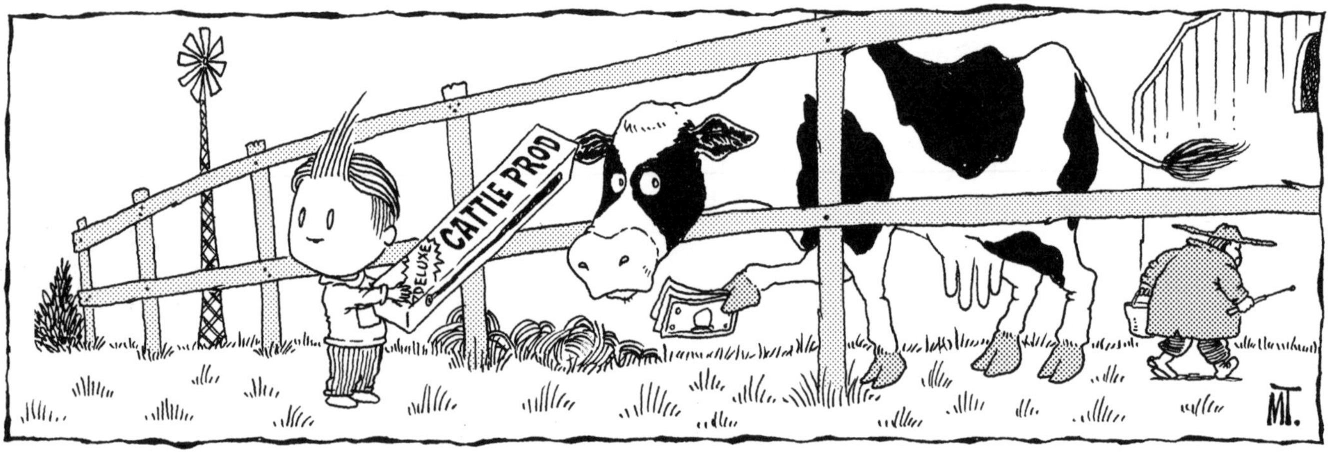
DELUXE
CATTLE PROD
MT.

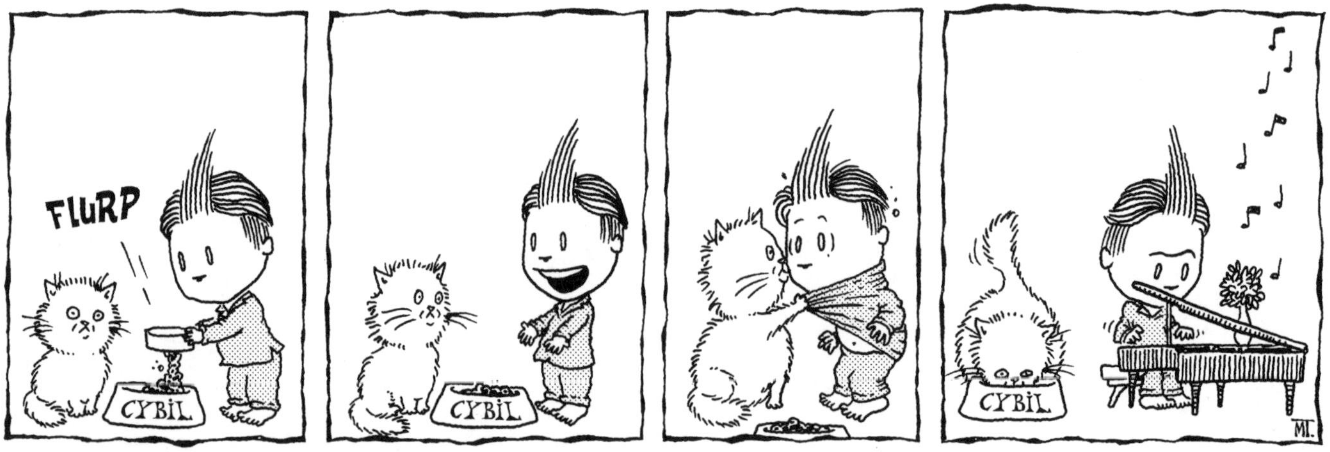
FLURP
CYBIL
CYBIL
CYBIL
MT.

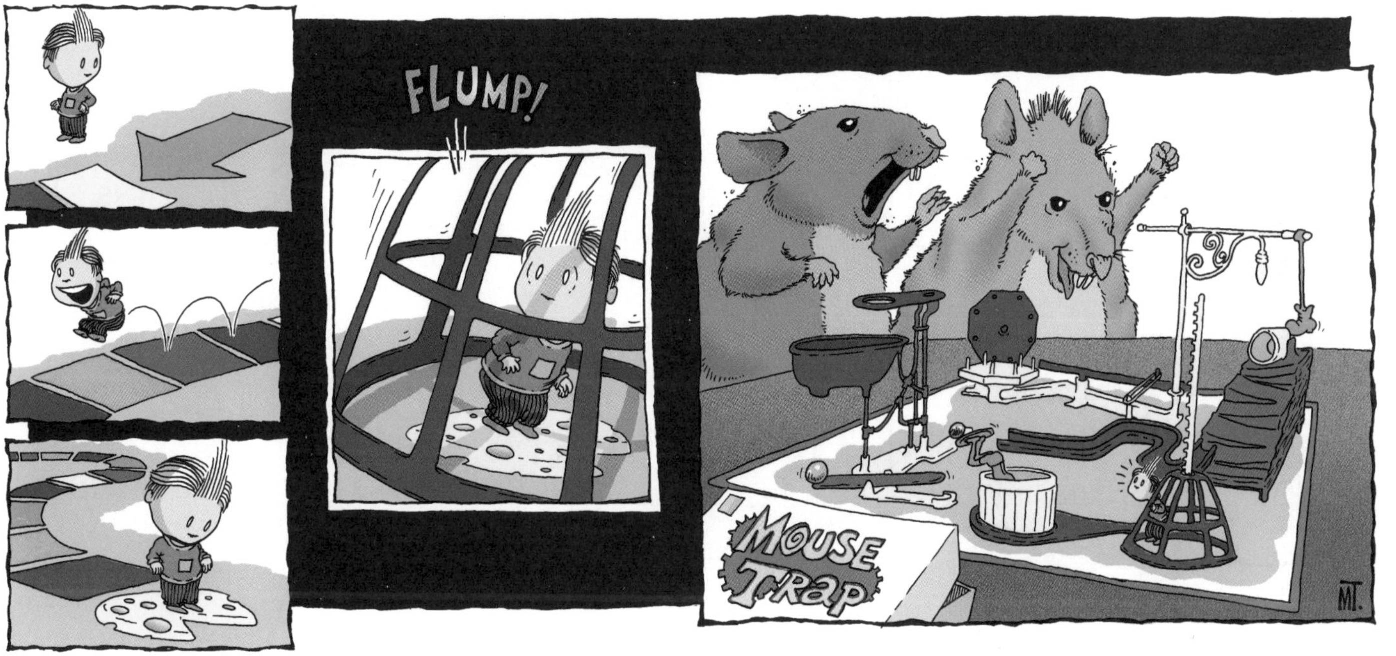
FLUMP!
MOUSE TRAP
MT.

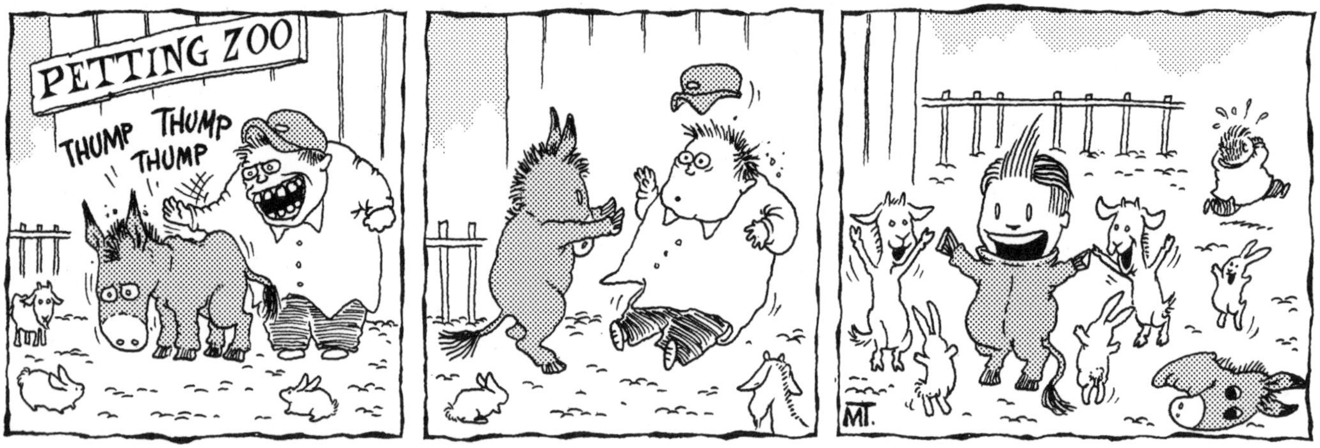
PETTING ZOO
THUMP THUMP
THUMP
MT.

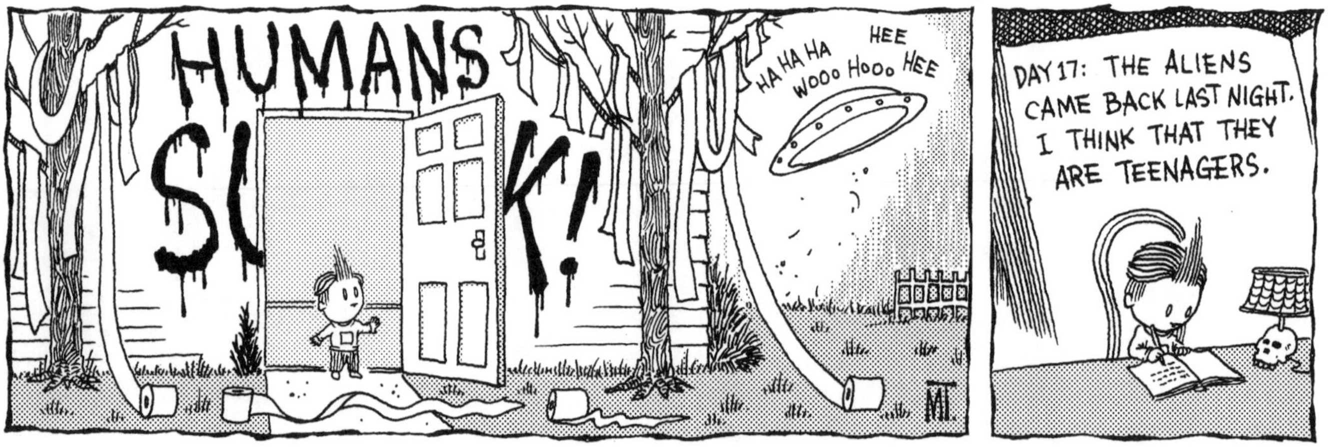
HUMANS
S K!
HA HA HA
WOOO HOOO
HEE
HEE
MT.
DAY 17: THE ALIENS CAME BACK LAST NIGHT. I THINK THAT THEY ARE TEENAGERS.

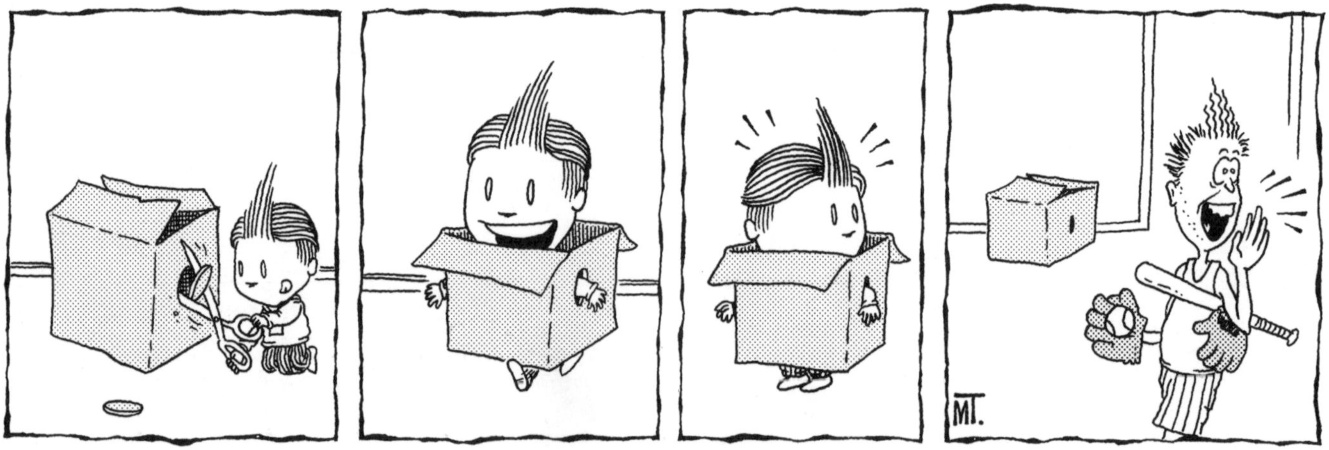
MT.

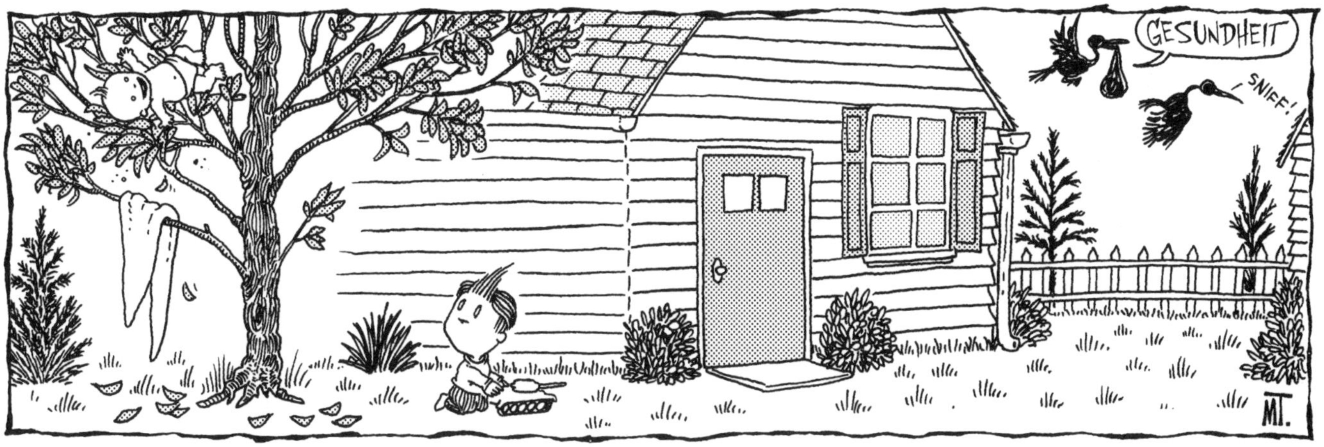
GESUNDHEIT
SNIFF!
MT.

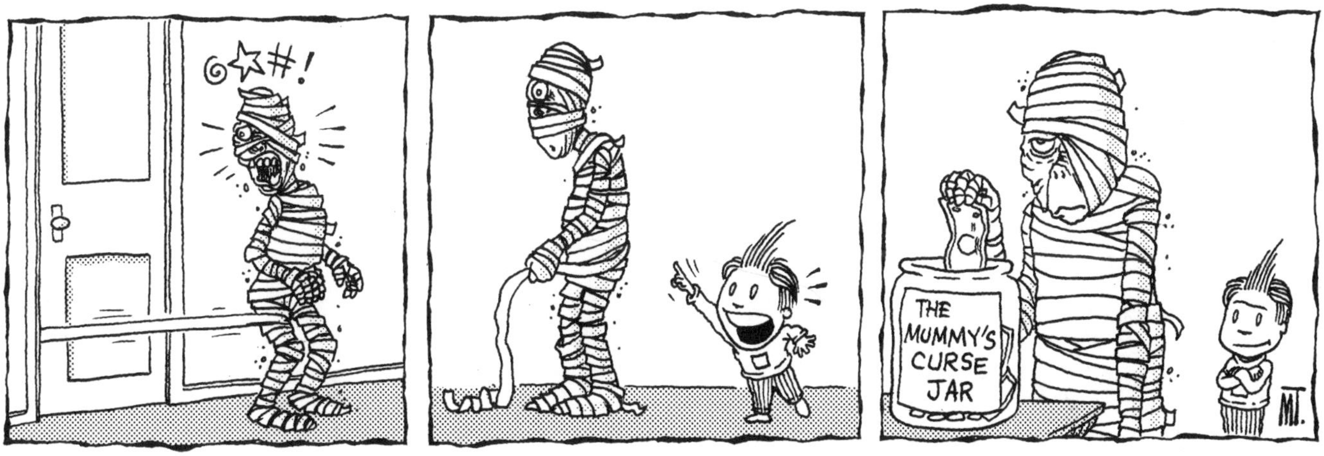
@☆#!
THE MUMMY'S CURSE JAR
MT.

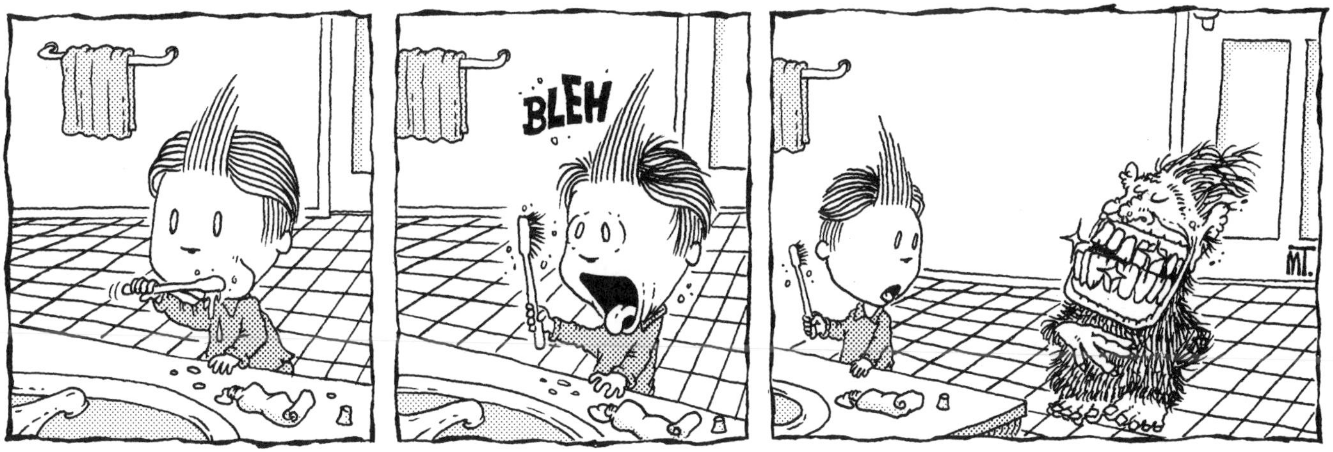
BLEH
MT.

THE BOO CKS
DROP QWIK
COMIC STRIP MOVING SERVICES
Lio
THERE GOES THE 'HOOD.
WORD.

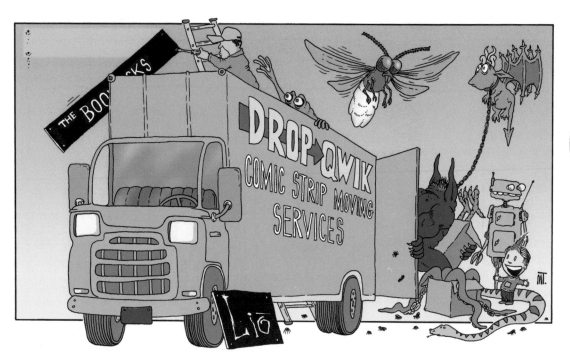

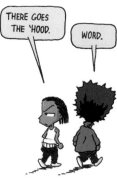

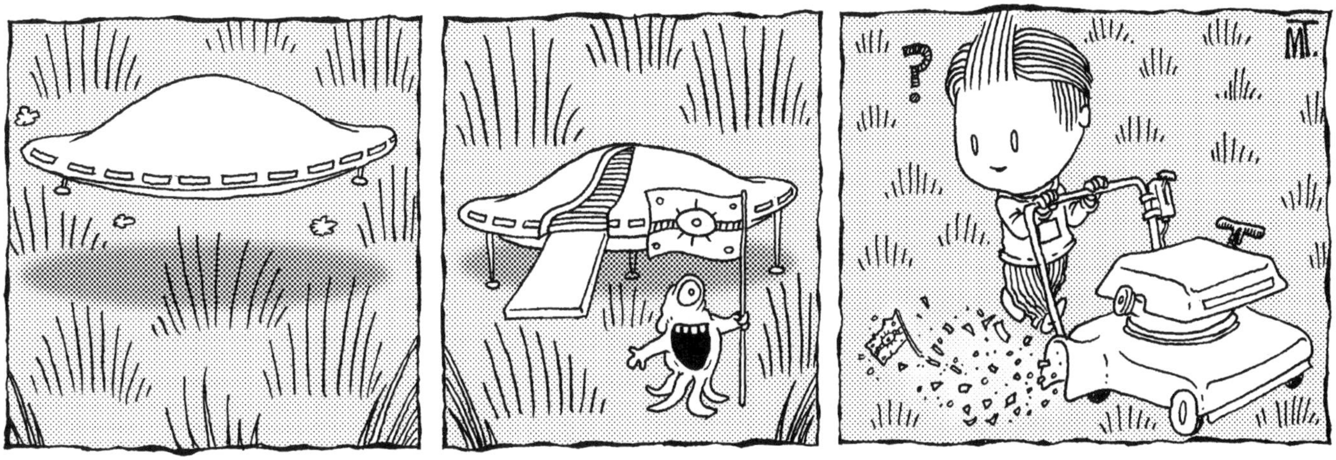
?
MT.

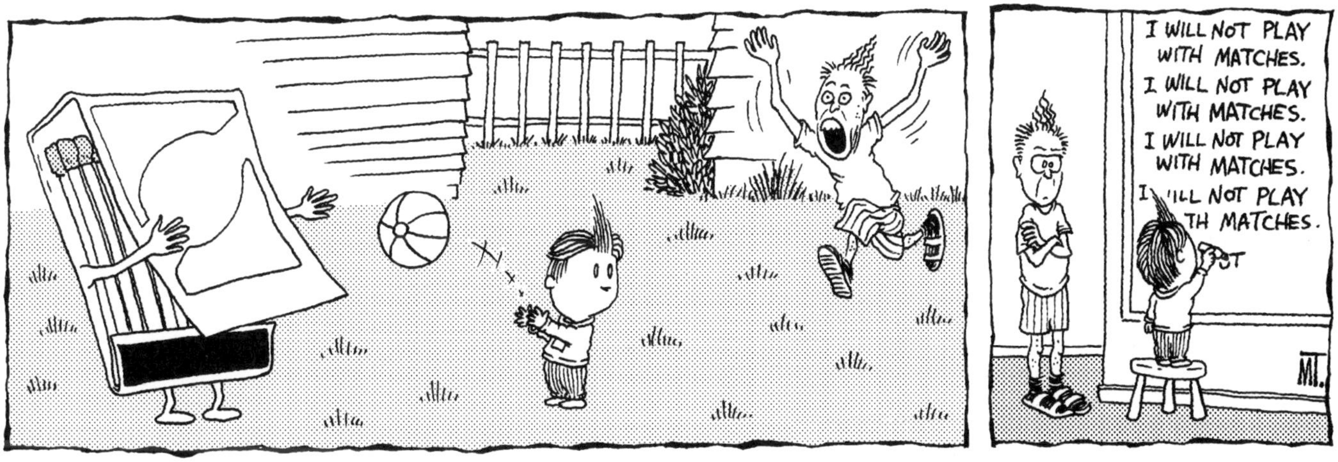
I WILL NOT PLAY WITH MATCHES.
I WILL NOT PLAY WITH MATCHES.
I WILL NOT PLAY WITH MATCHES.
MT.

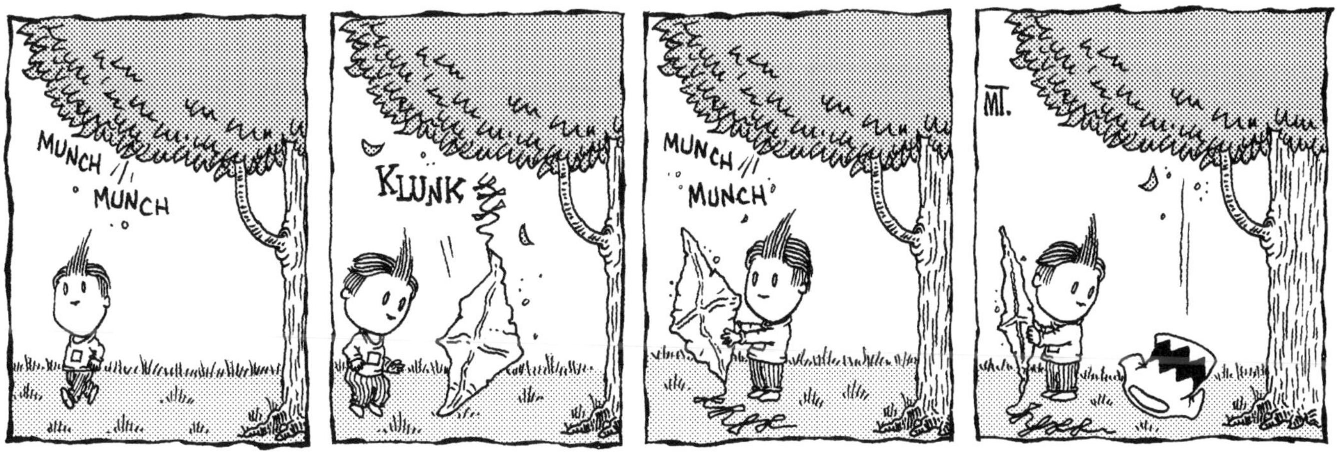
MUNCH
MUNCH
KLUNK
MUNCH
MUNCH
MT.

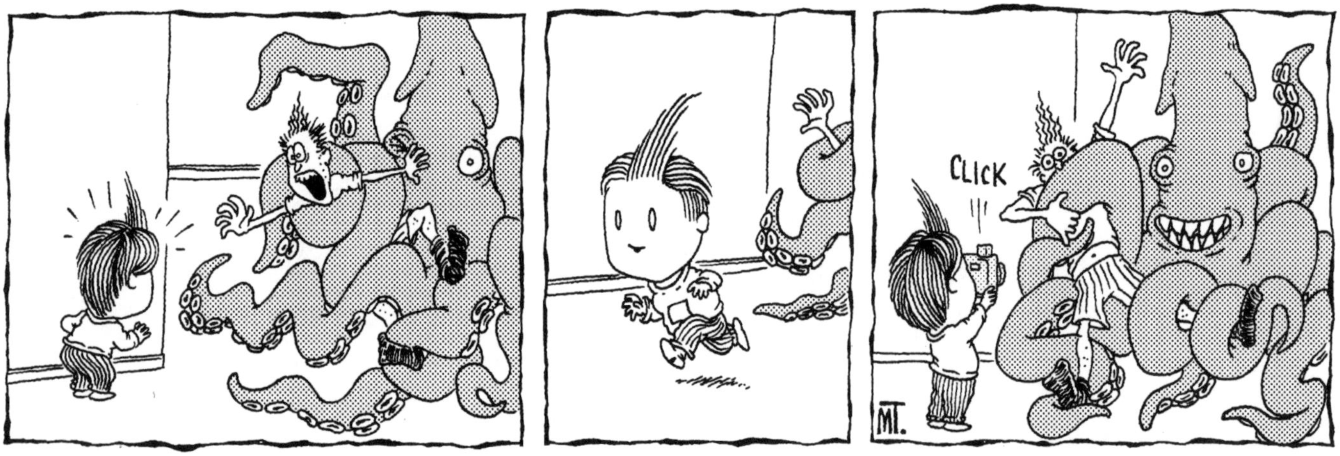
CLICK
MT.

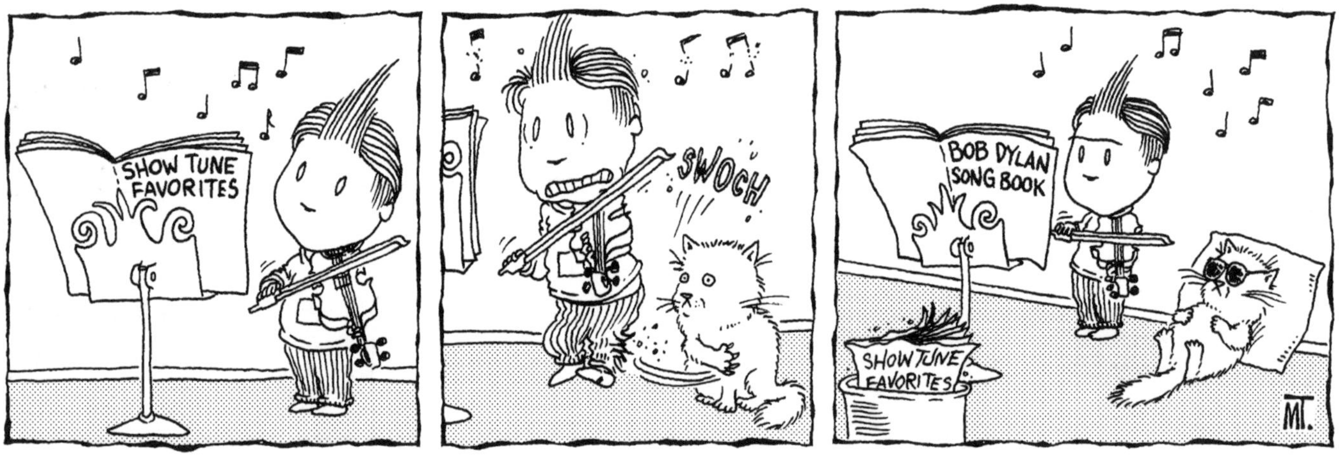
SHOW TUNE FAVORITES
SWOCH
BOB DYLAN SONG BOOK
SHOW TUNE FAVORITES
MT.

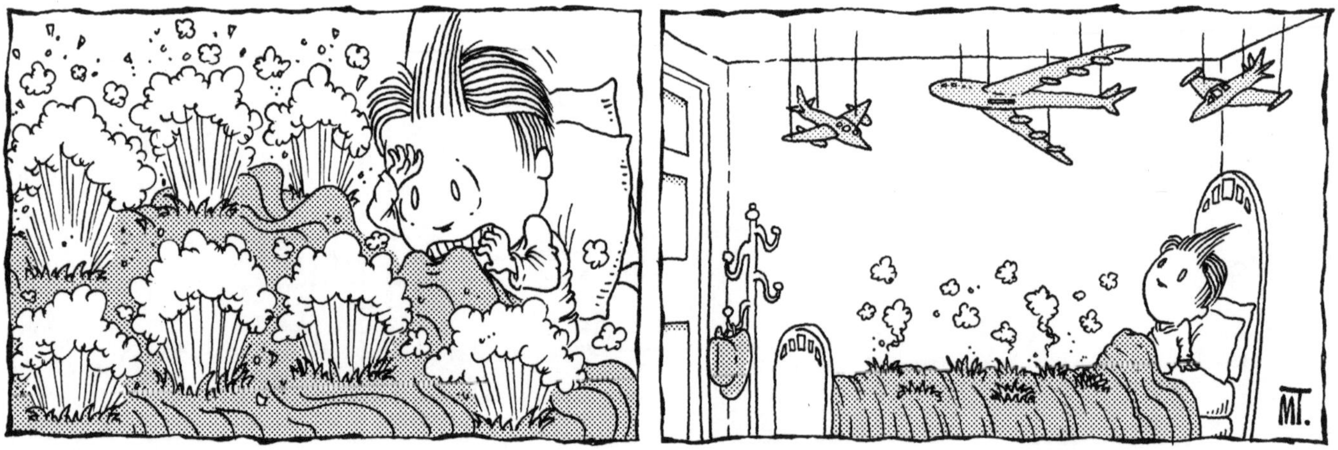
MT.

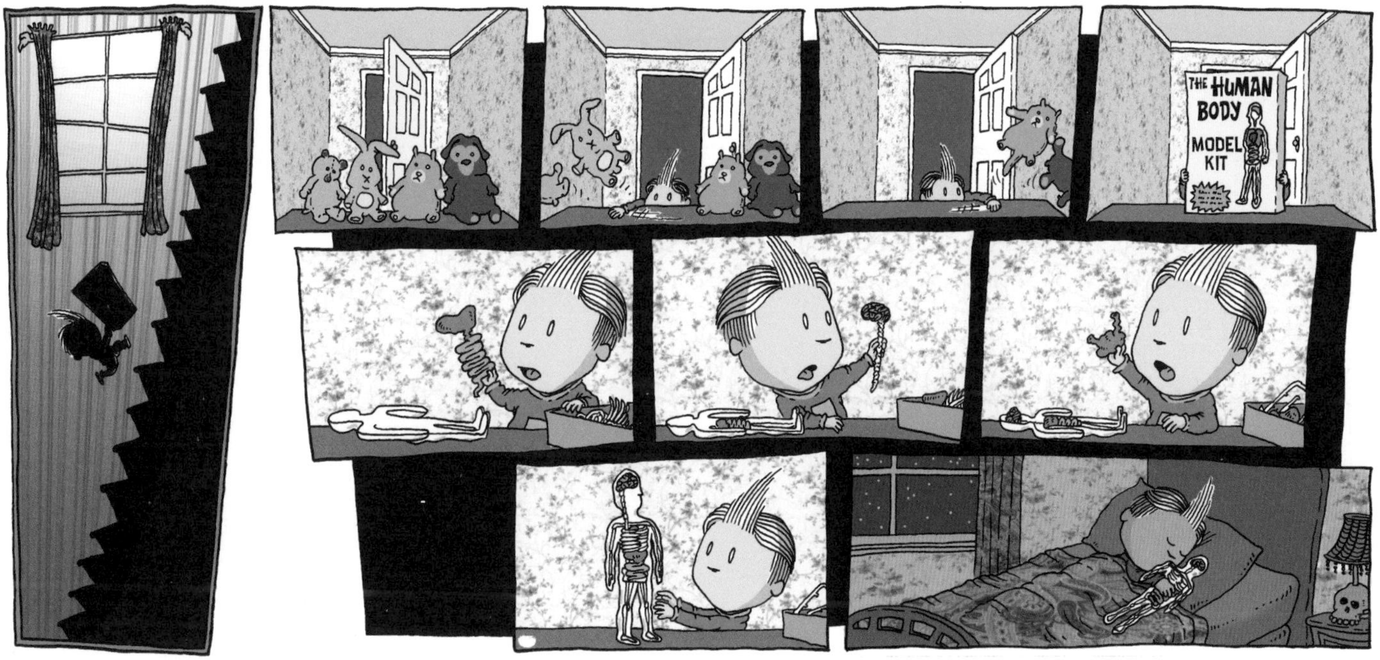
THE HUMAN BODY
MODEL KIT

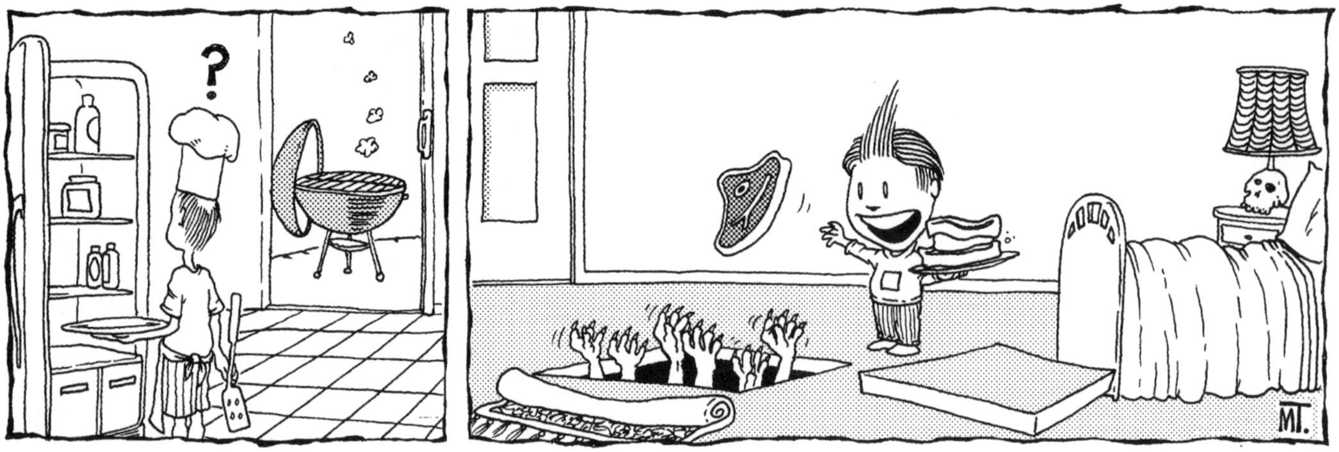

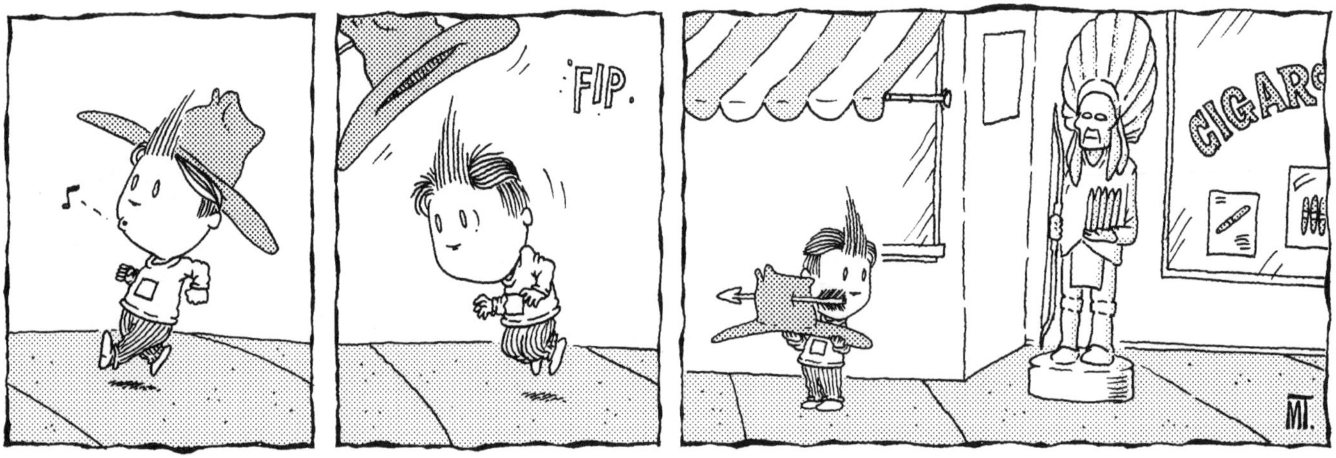
FIP.
CIGARS

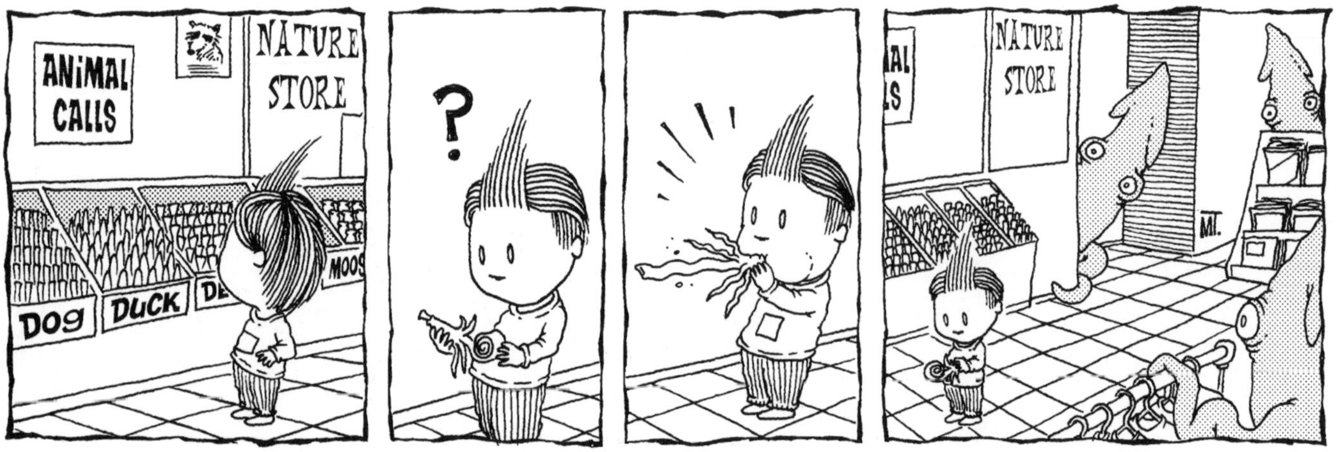
ANIMAL CALLS
NATURE STORE
DOG
DUCK
NATURE STORE

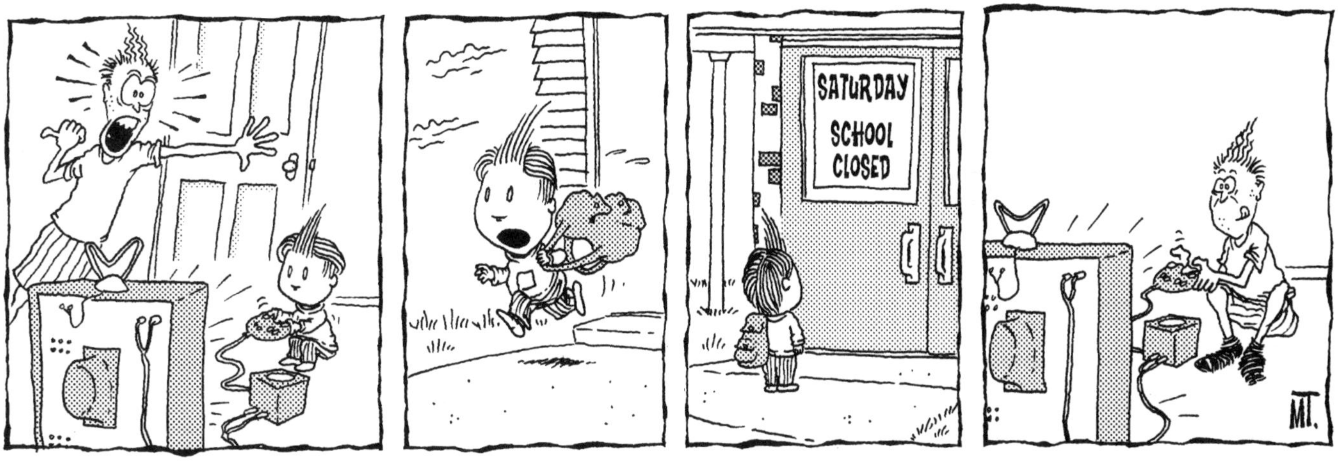
SATURDAY
SCHOOL
CLOSED
MT.

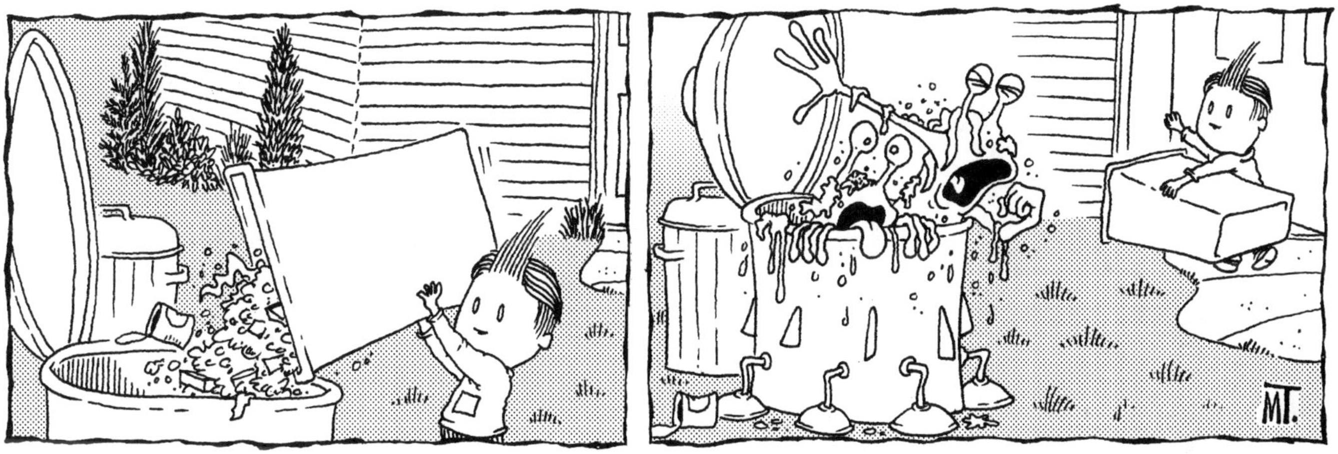
MT.

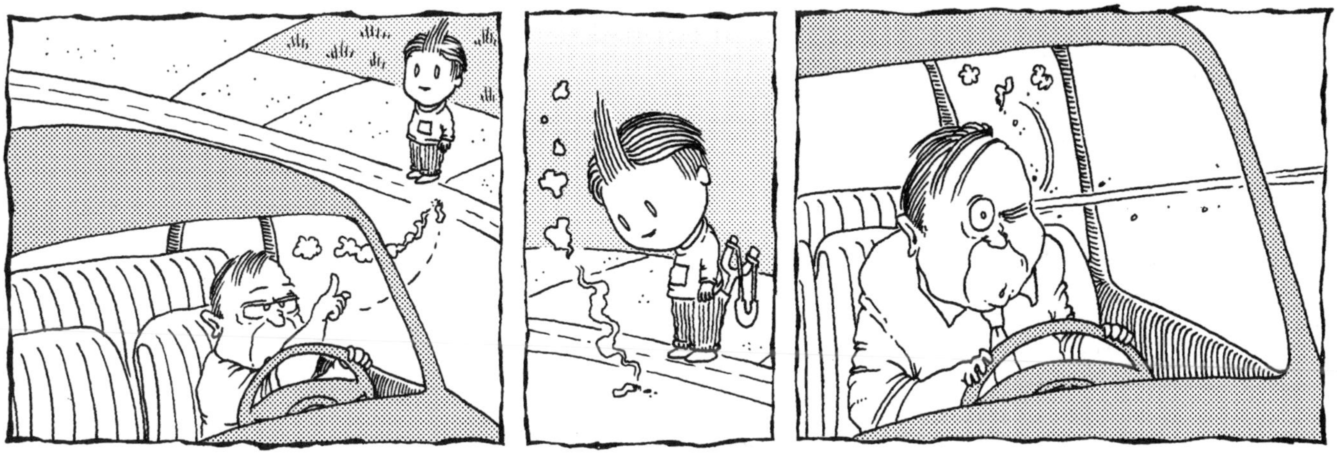

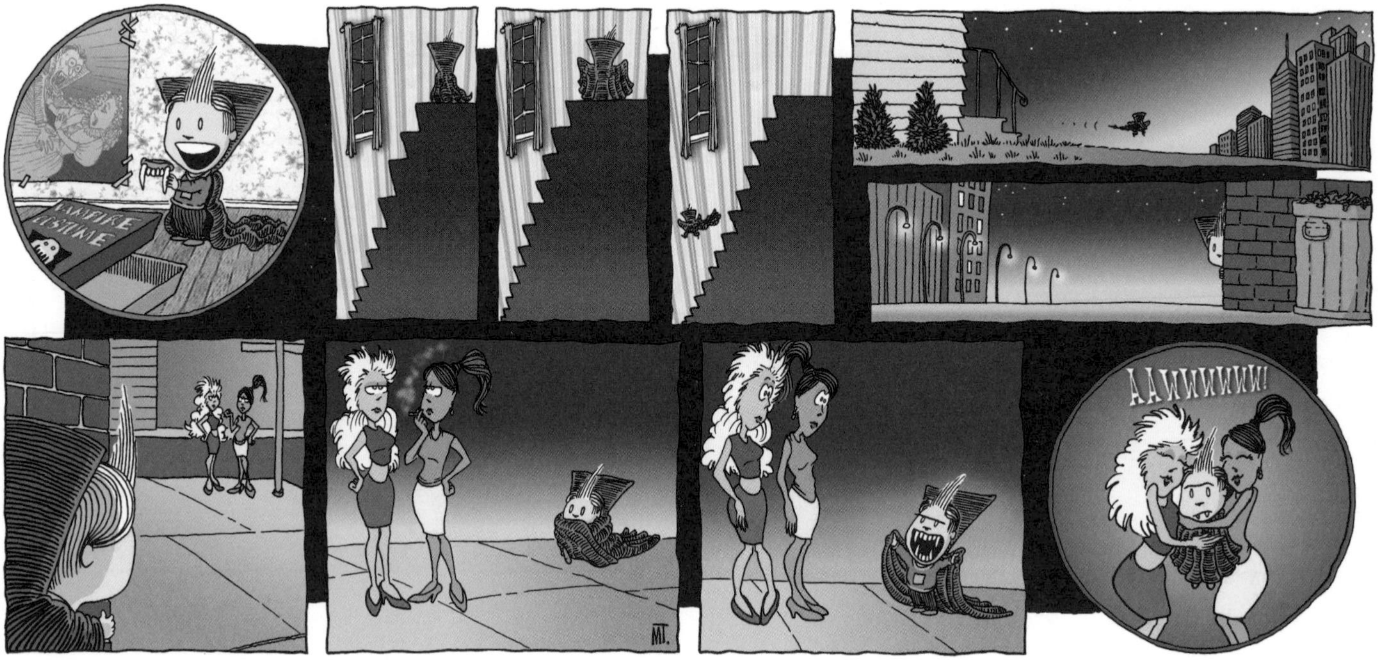
AAWWWWWWW!

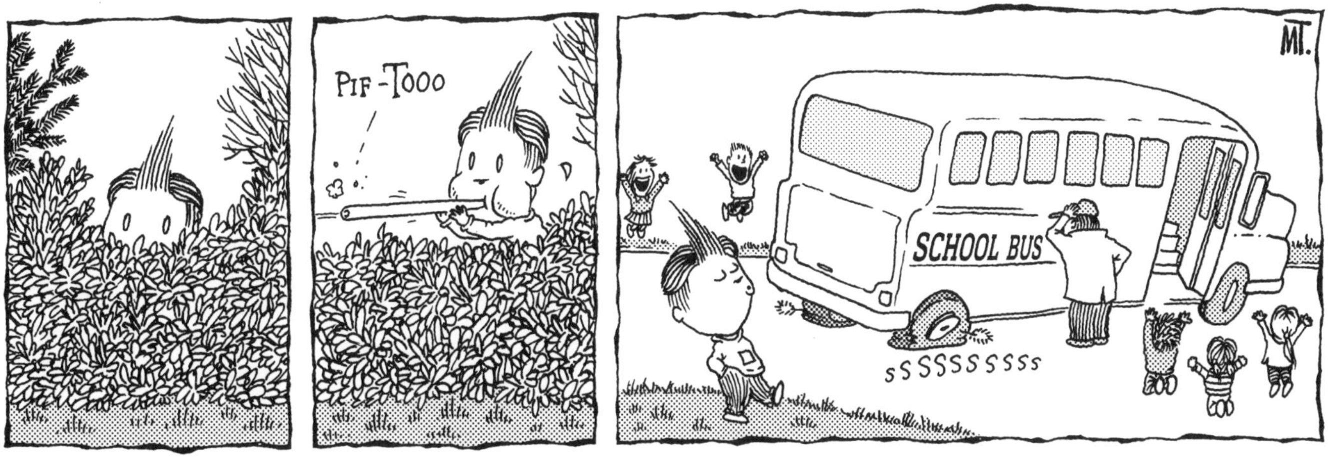
PIF-TOOO
MT.
SCHOOL BUS
sSSSSSSSSs

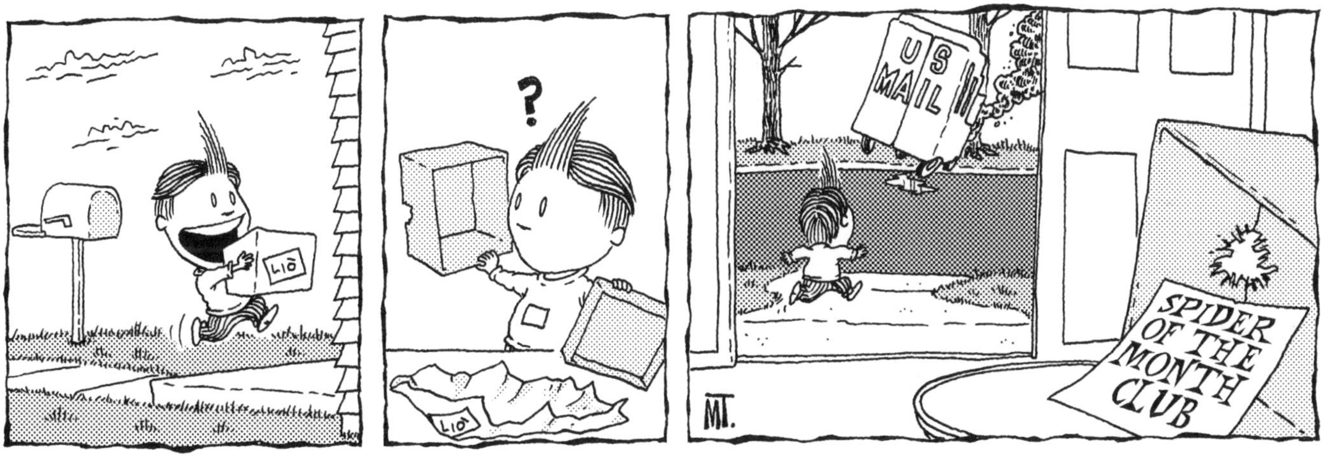
LIO
?
LIO
US MAIL
SPIDER OF THE MONTH CLUB
MT.

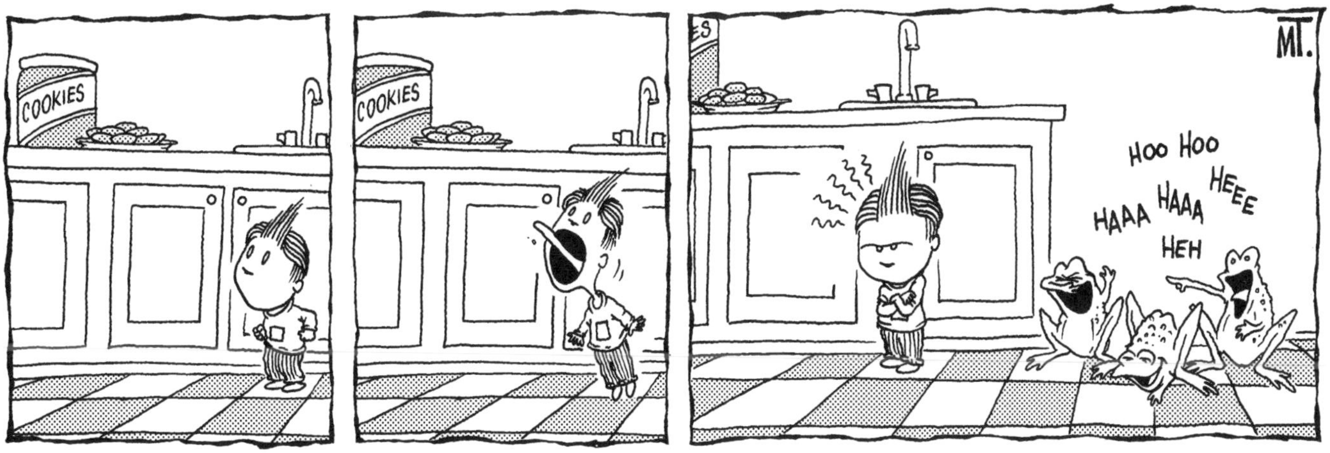
COOKIES
COOKIES
MT.
HOO HOO
HEEE
HAAA
HAAA
HEH

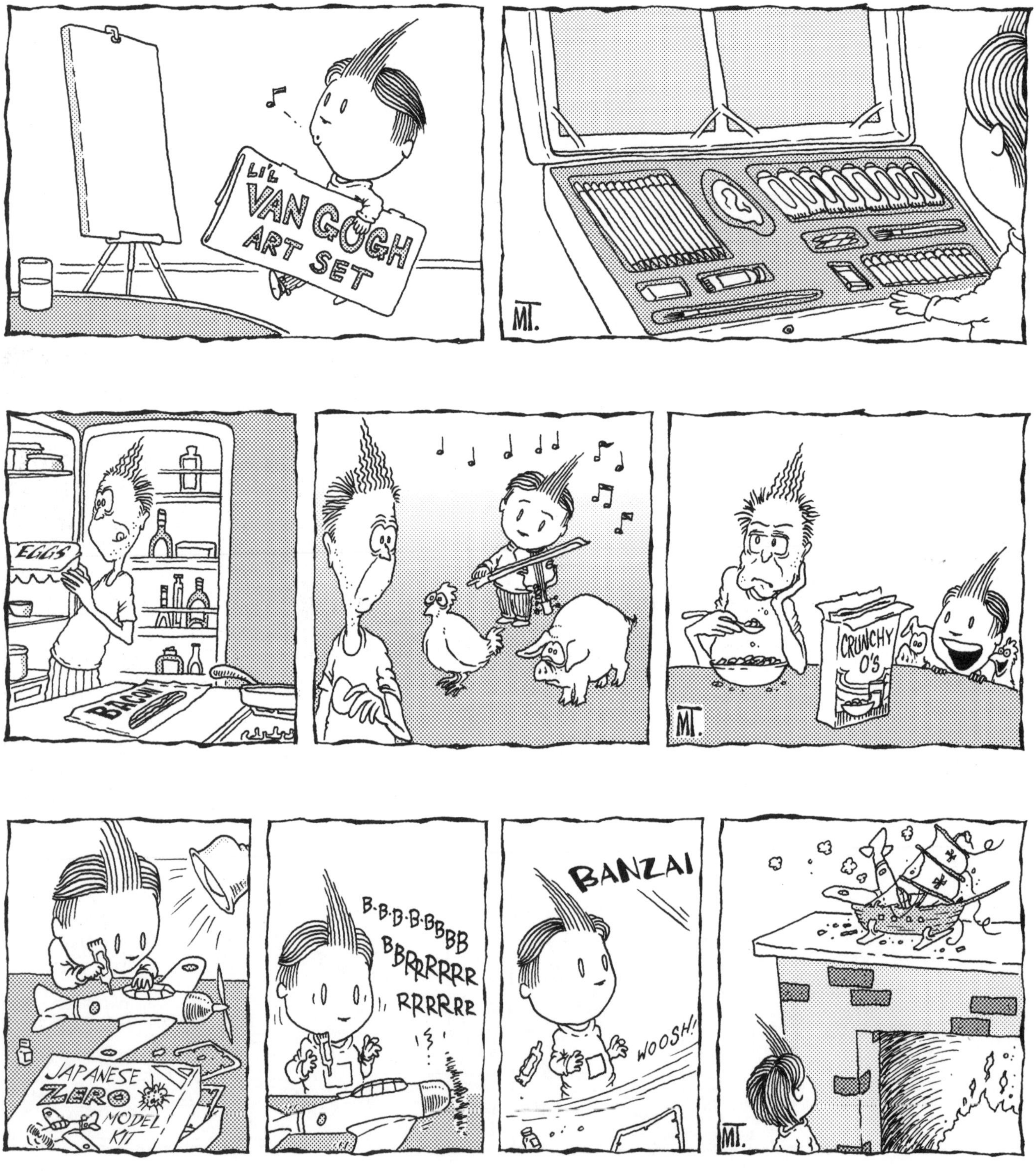
LI'L VAN GOGH ART SET
MT.
EGGS
BACON
CRUNCHY O'S
MT.
JAPANESE ZERO MODEL KIT
B-B-B-B-BBBB
BBRRRRRRR
RRRRRRR
BANZAI
WOOSH!
MT.

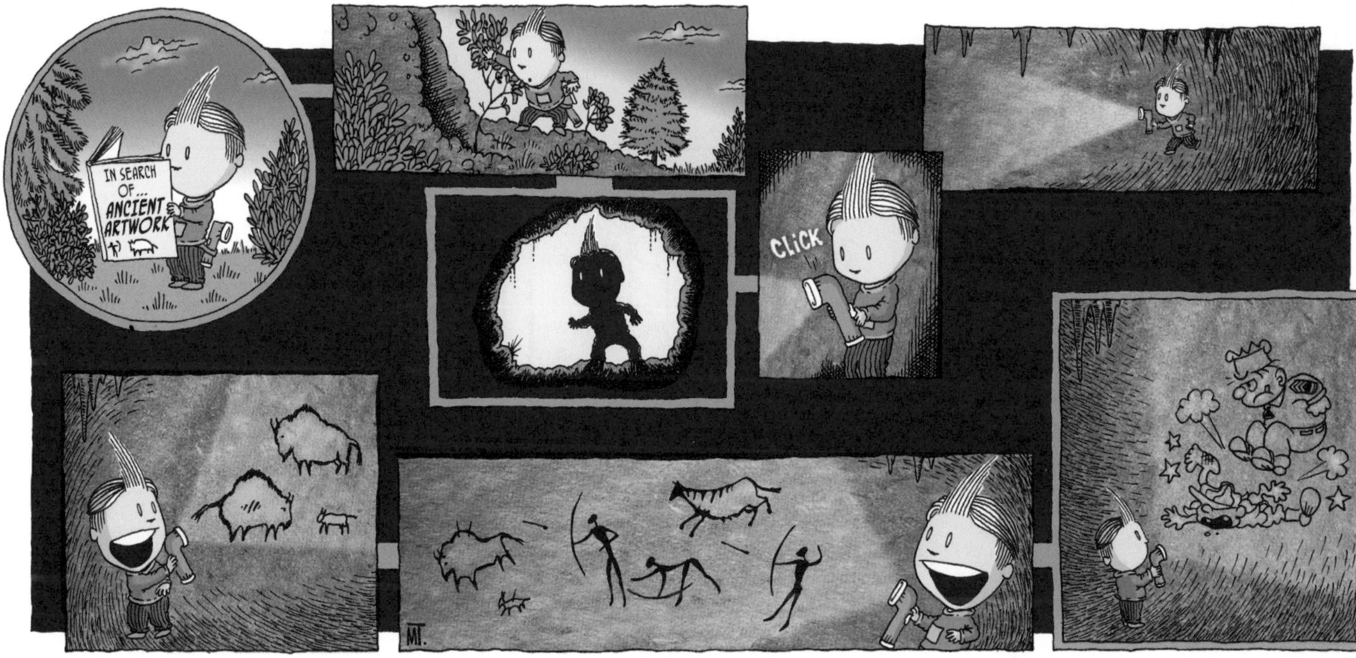
IN SEARCH OF... ANCIENT ARTWORK
CLICK
MT.

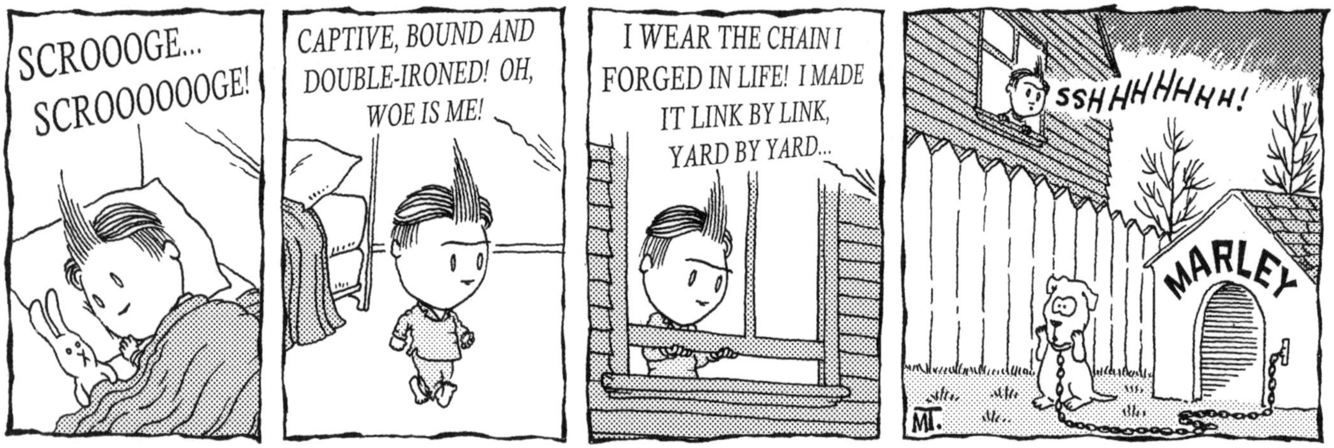
SCROOOGE...
SCROOOOOOGE!
CAPTIVE, BOUND AND DOUBLE-IRONED! OH, WOE IS ME!
I WEAR THE CHAIN I FORGED IN LIFE! I MADE IT LINK BY LINK, YARD BY YARD...
SSHHHHHHH!
MARLEY
MT.

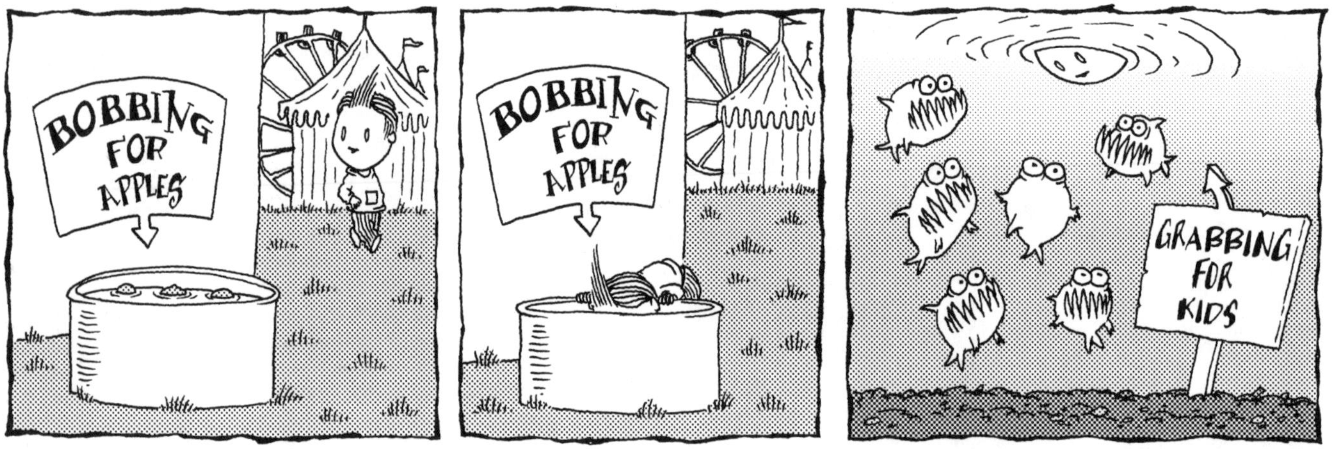
BOBBING FOR APPLES
BOBBING FOR APPLES
GRABBING FOR KIDS

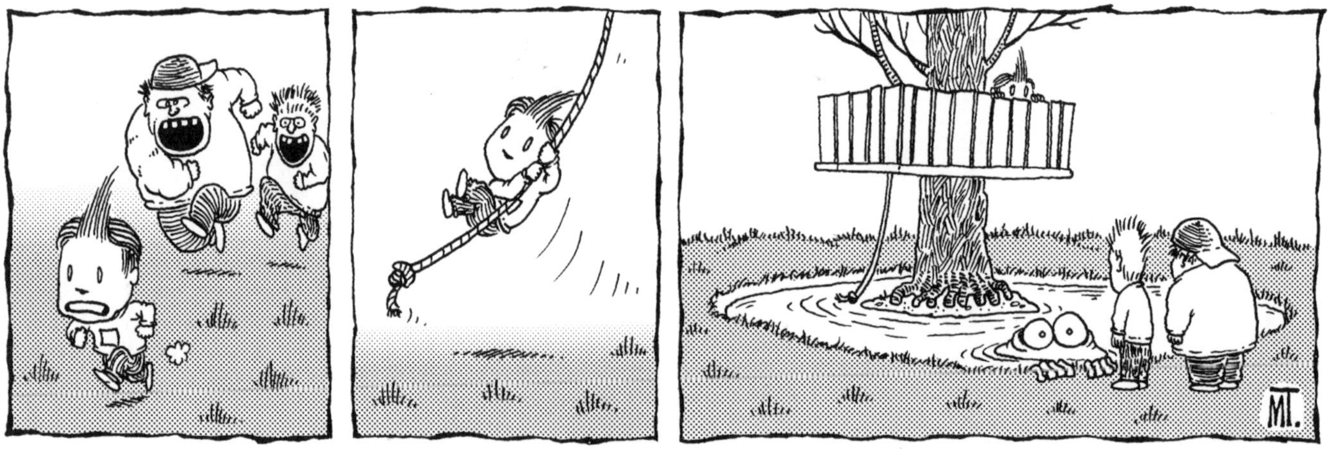
MT.

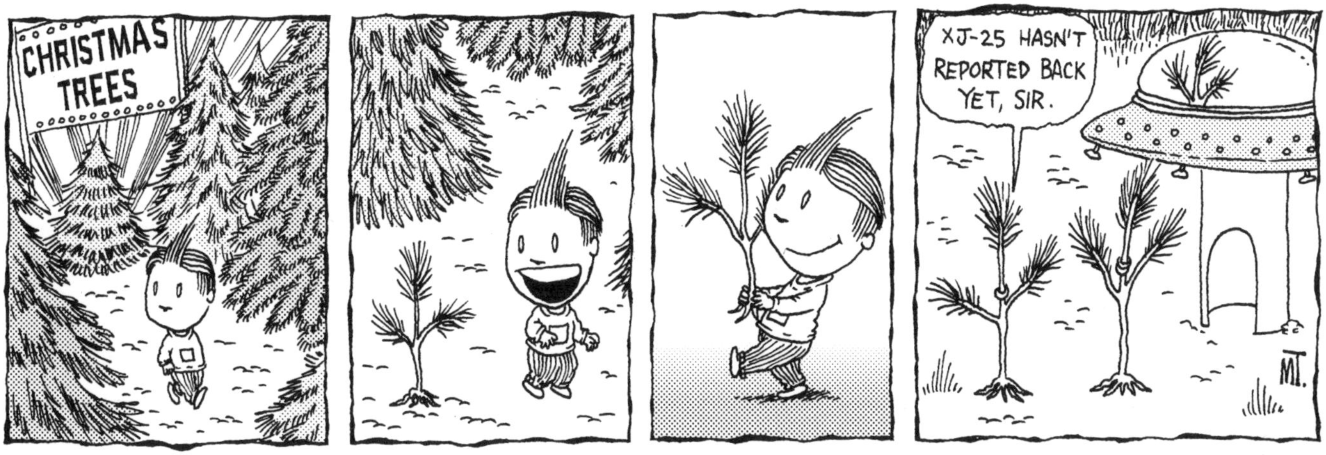
CHRISTMAS TREES
XJ-25 HASN'T REPORTED BACK YET, SIR.
MT.

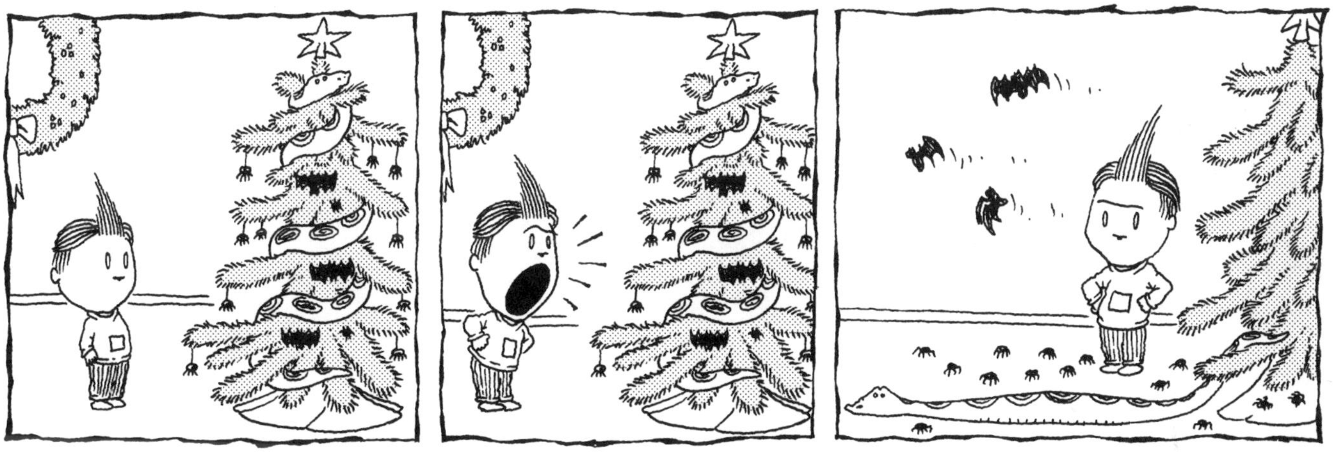

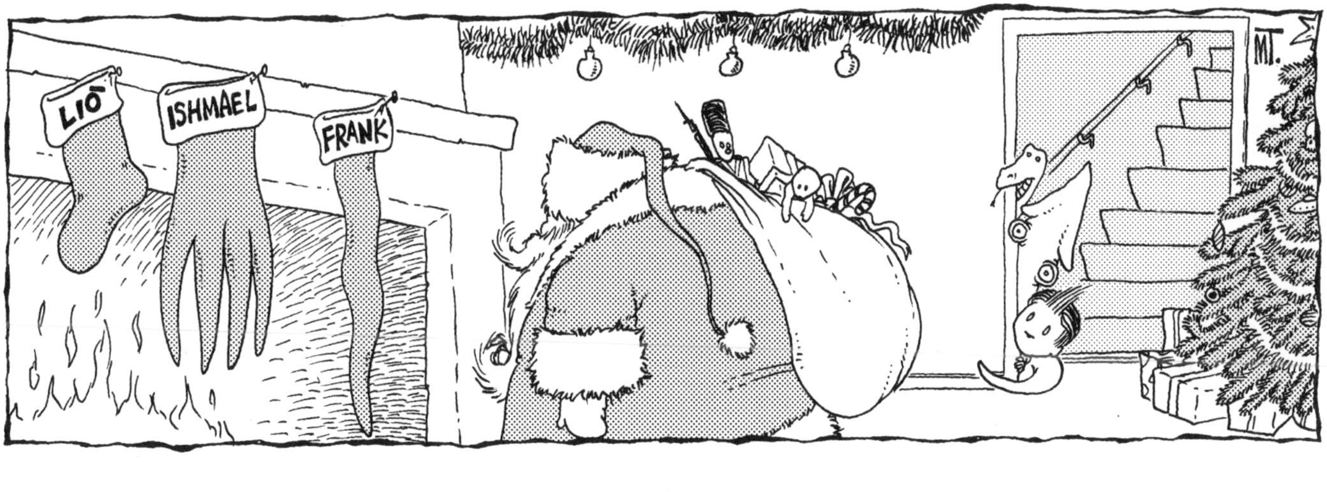
LIO
ISHMAEL
FRANK
MT.

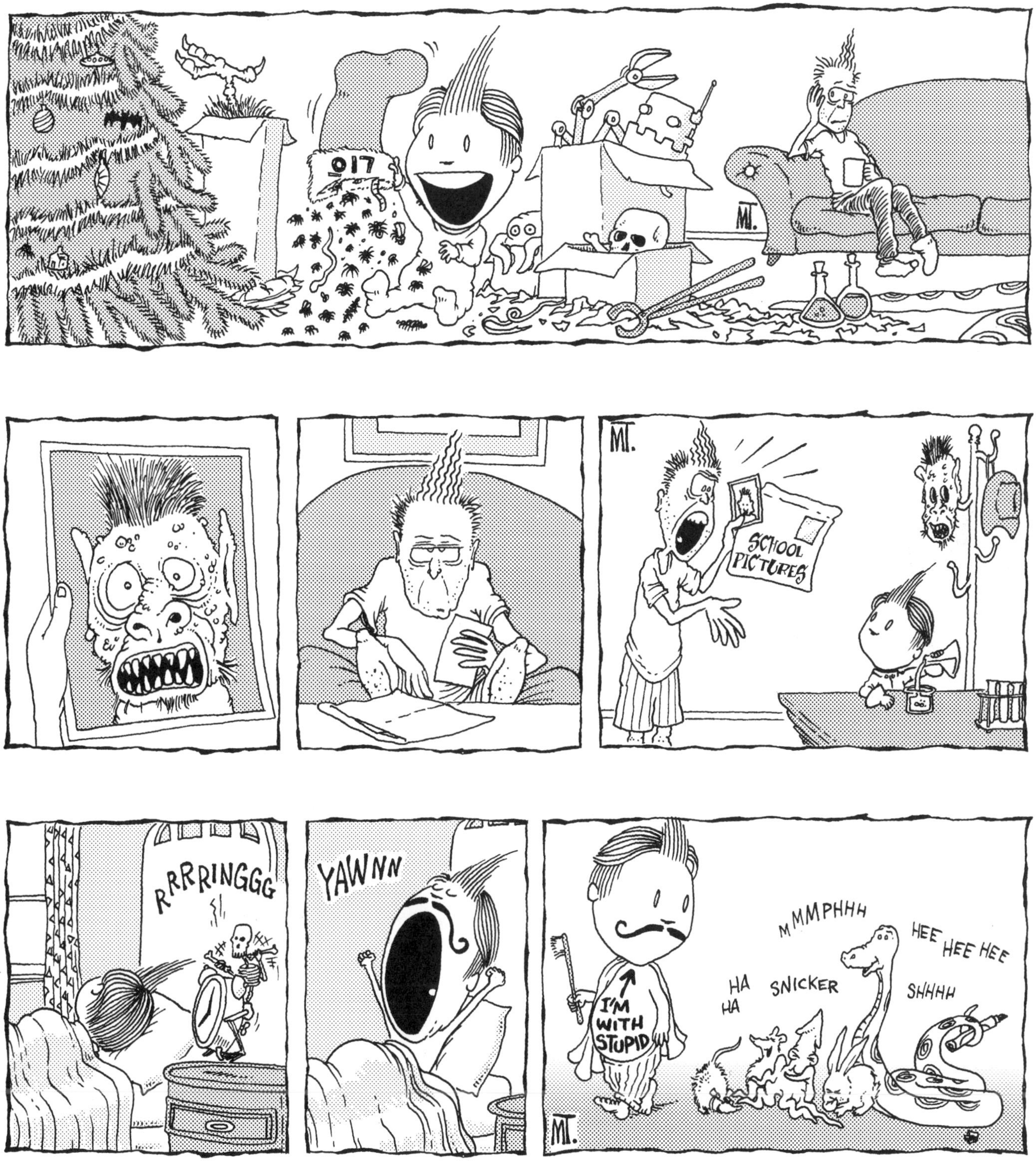
SCHOOL PICTURES
RRRRINGGG
YAWNN
I'M WITH STUPID
MMMPHHH
HEE HEE HEE
HA HA
SNICKER
SHHHH

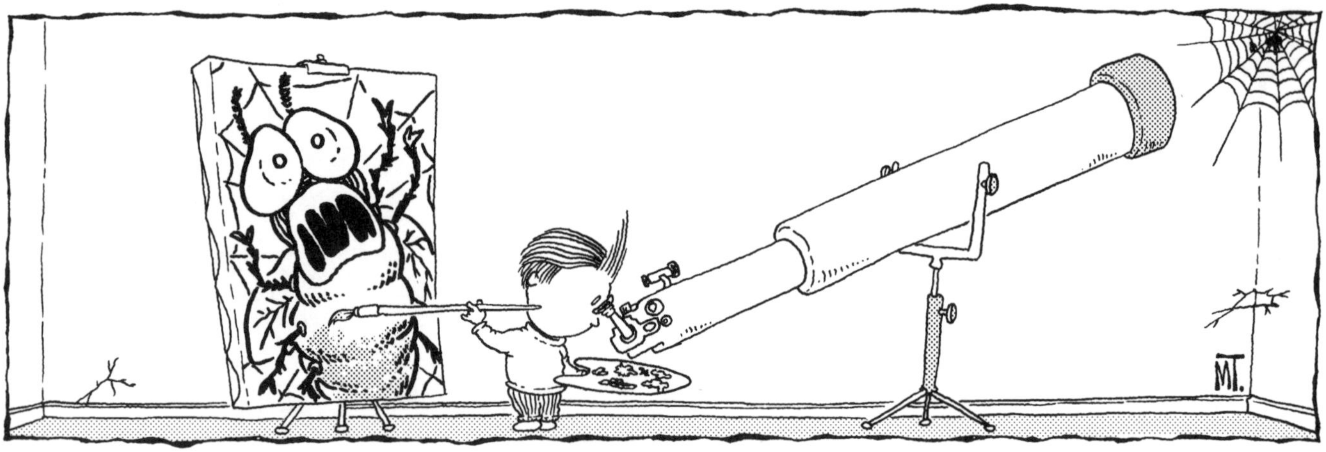
MT.

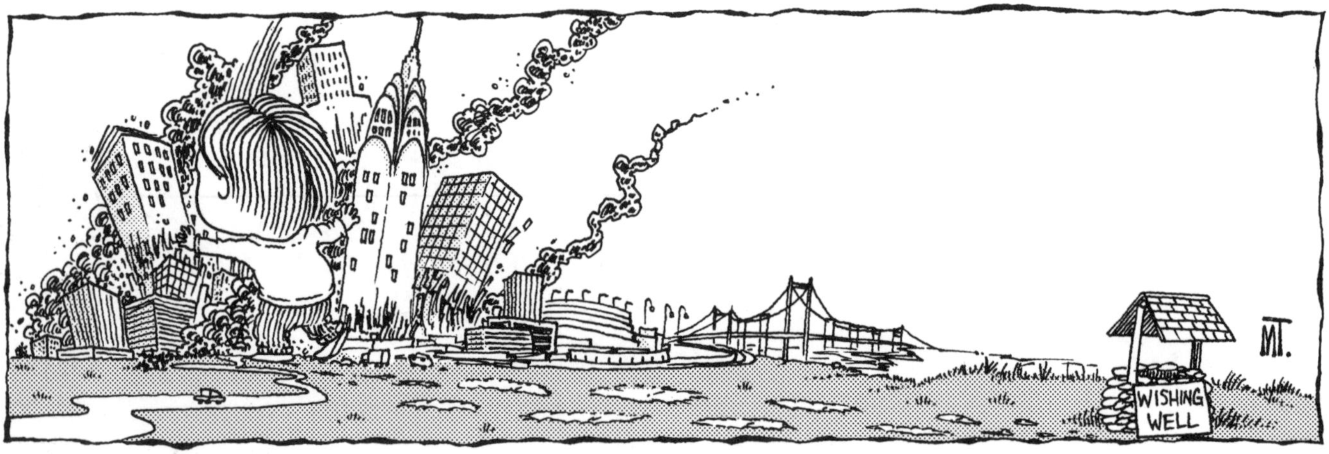
WISHING WELL
MT.

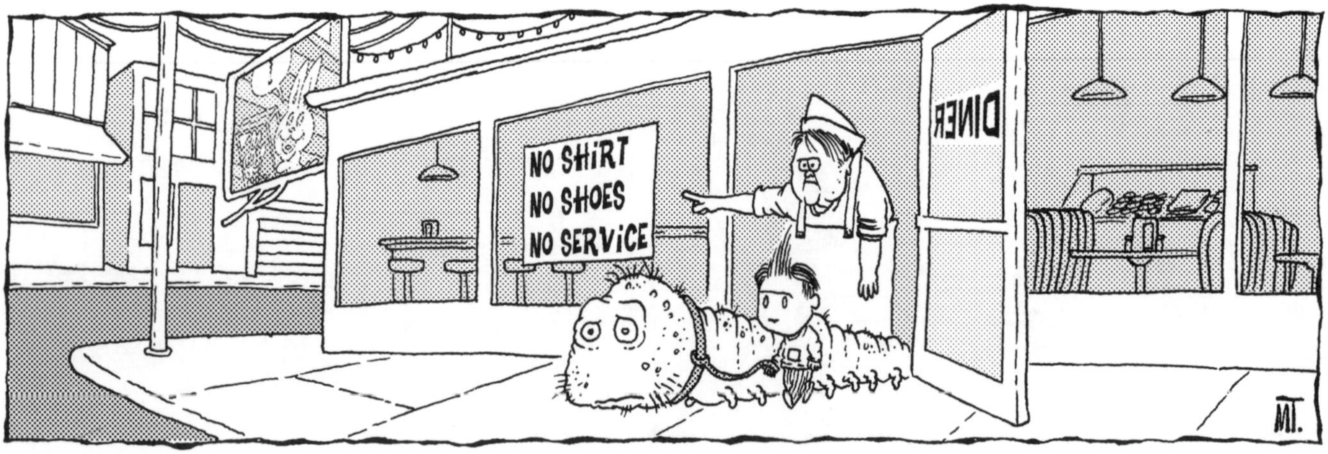
NO SHIRT
NO SHOES
NO SERVICE
DINER
MT.

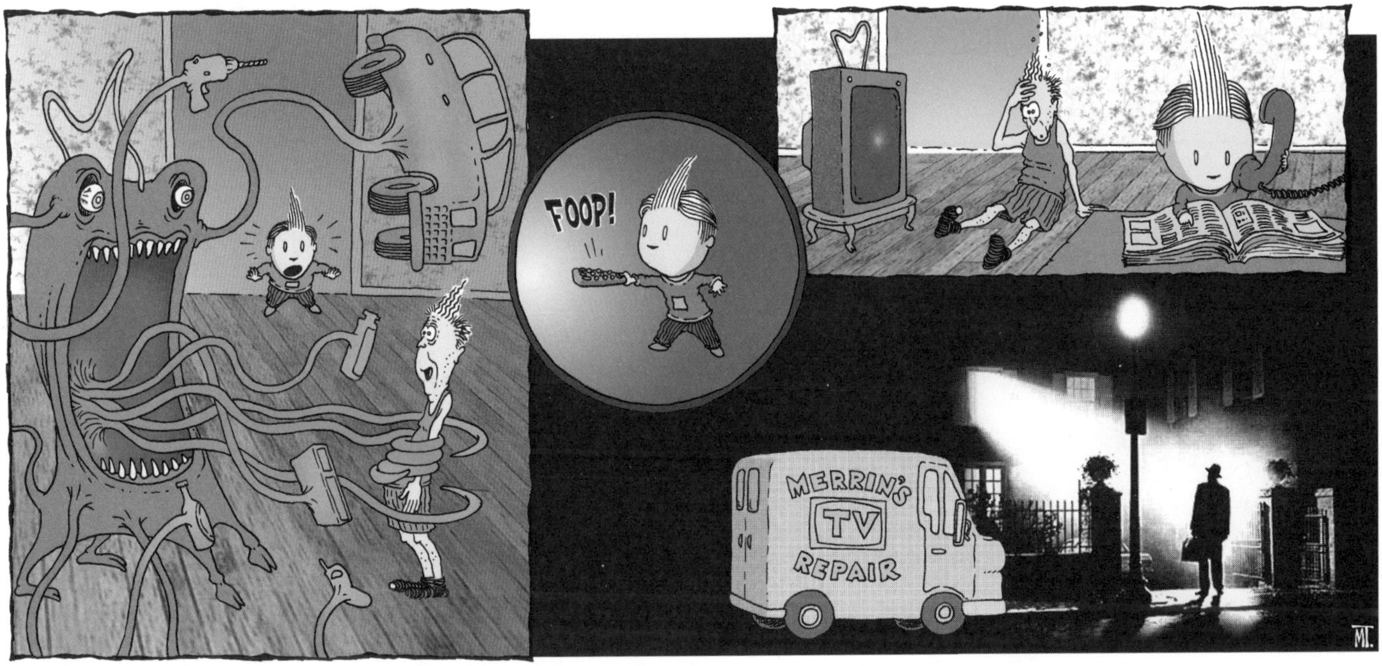
FOOP!
MERRIN'S
TV
REPAIR
MT.

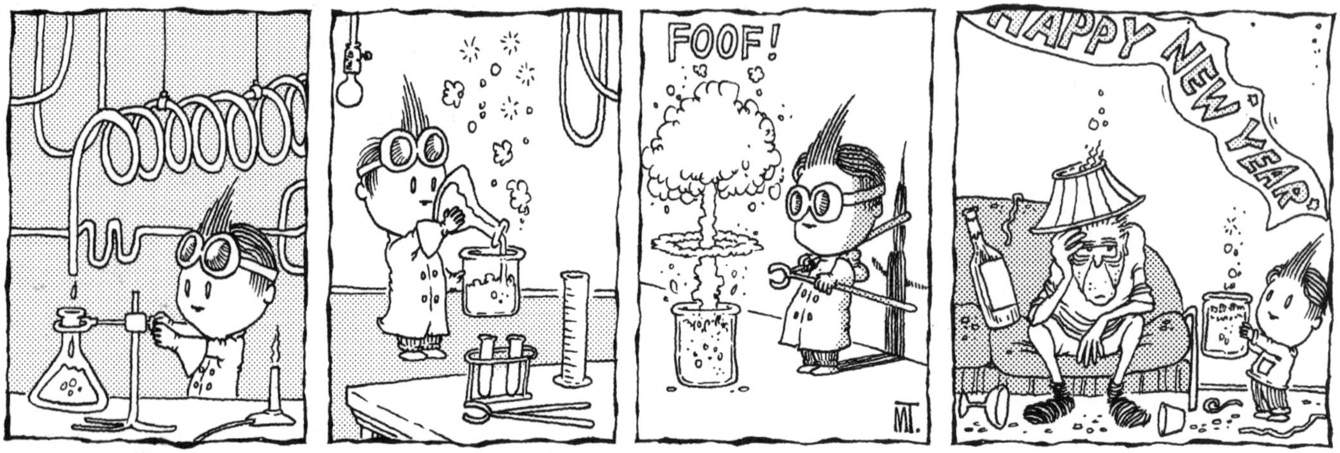
FOOF!
HAPPY NEW YEAR
MT.

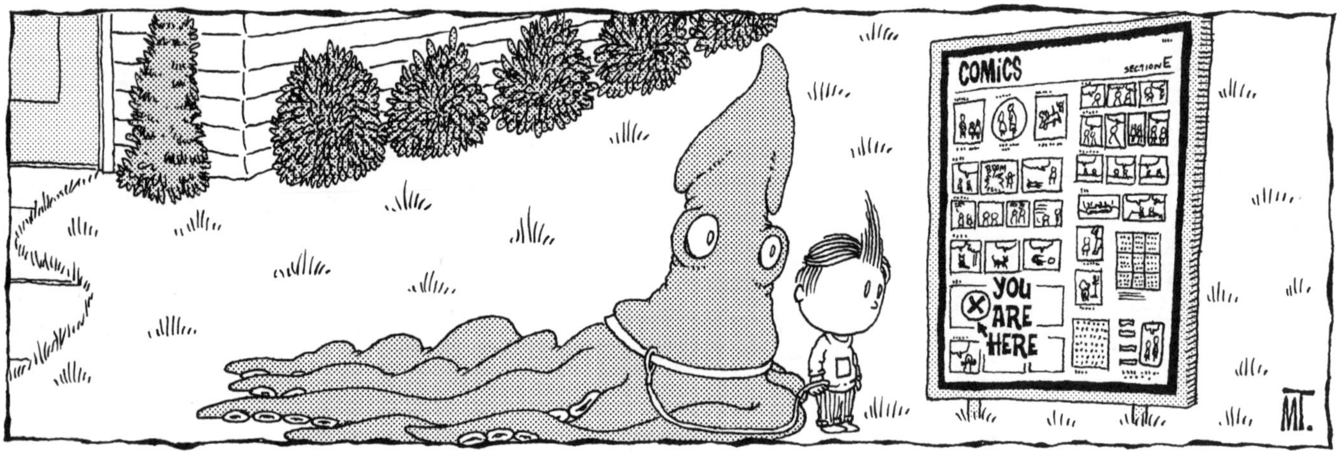
COMICS
SECTION E
YOU ARE HERE
MT.

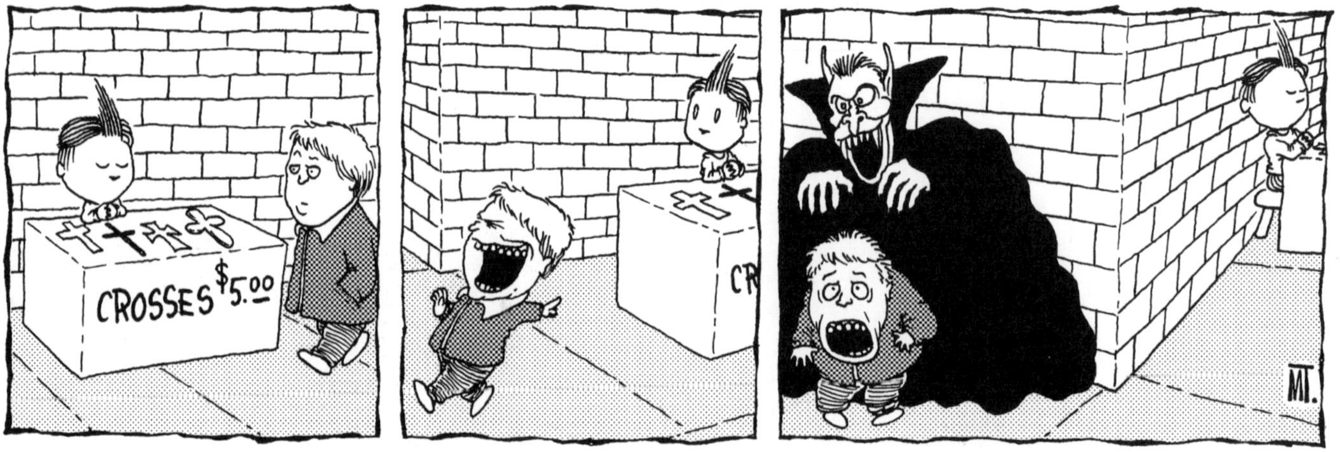
CROSSES $5.00
CR
MT.

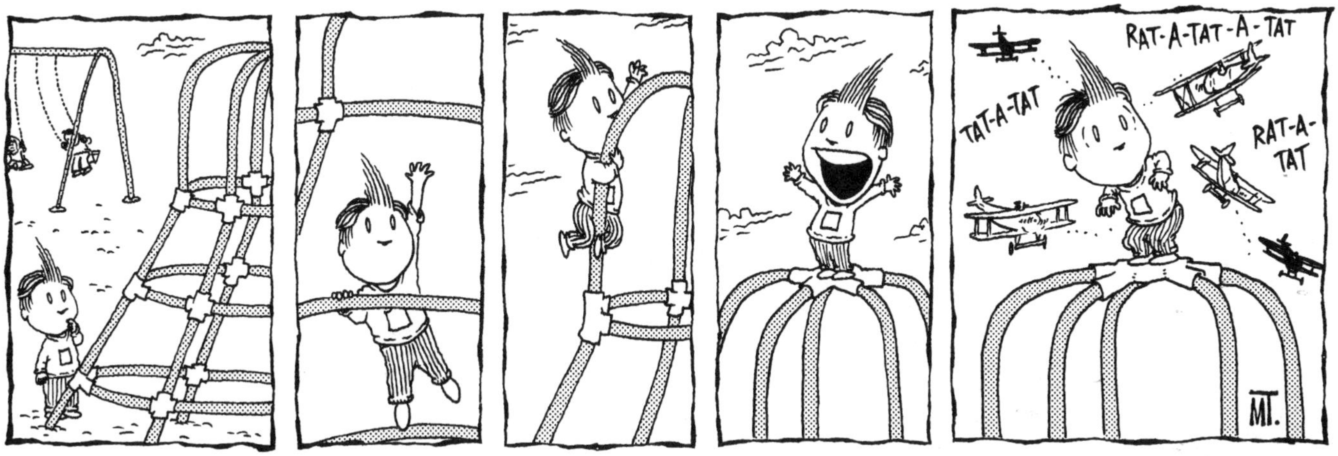
TAT-A-TAT
RAT-A-TAT-A-TAT
RAT-A-TAT

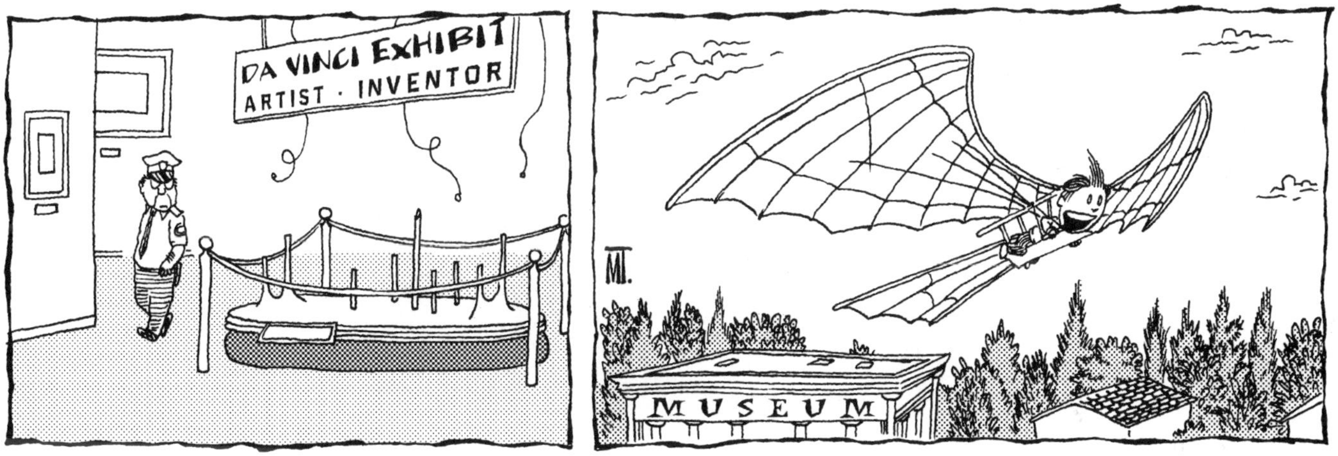
DA VINCI EXHIBIT
ARTIST · INVENTOR
MUSEUM

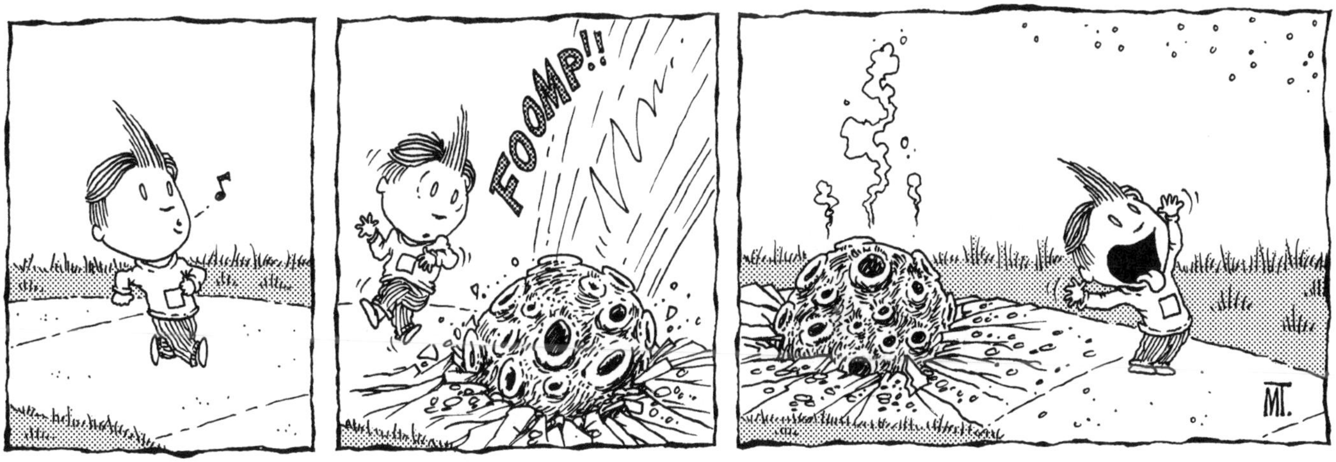
FOOMP!!

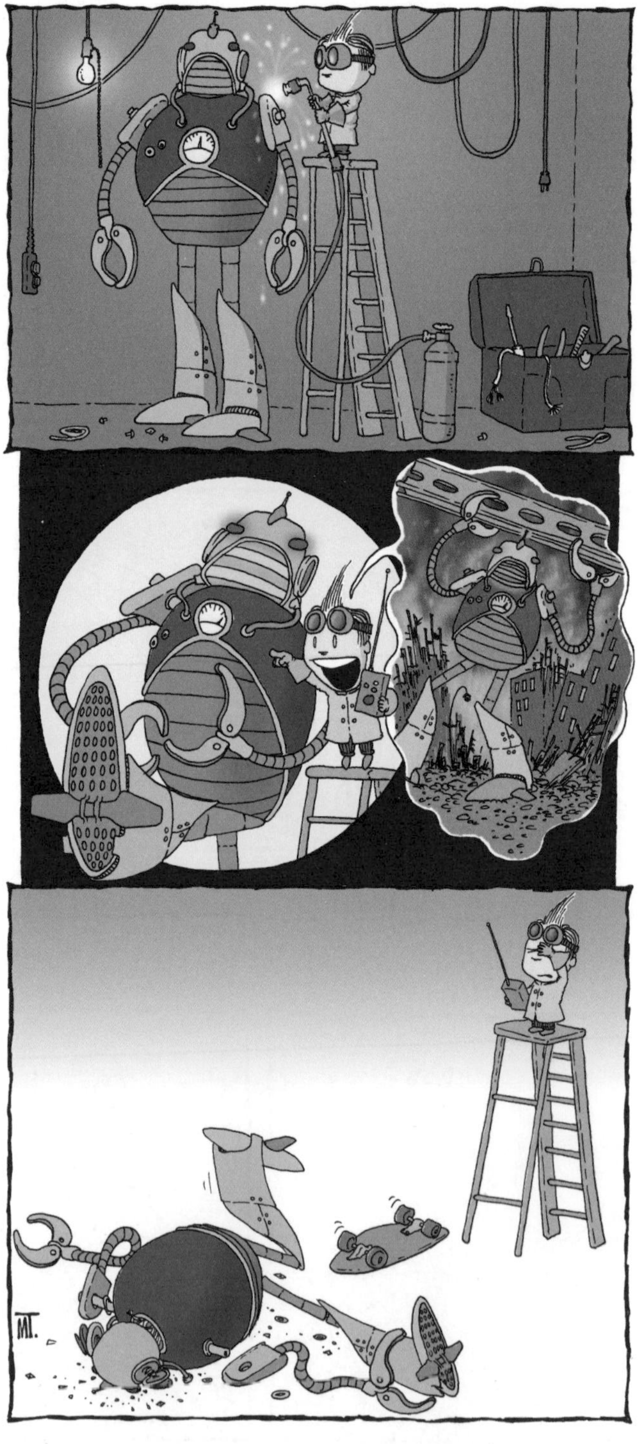
MT.

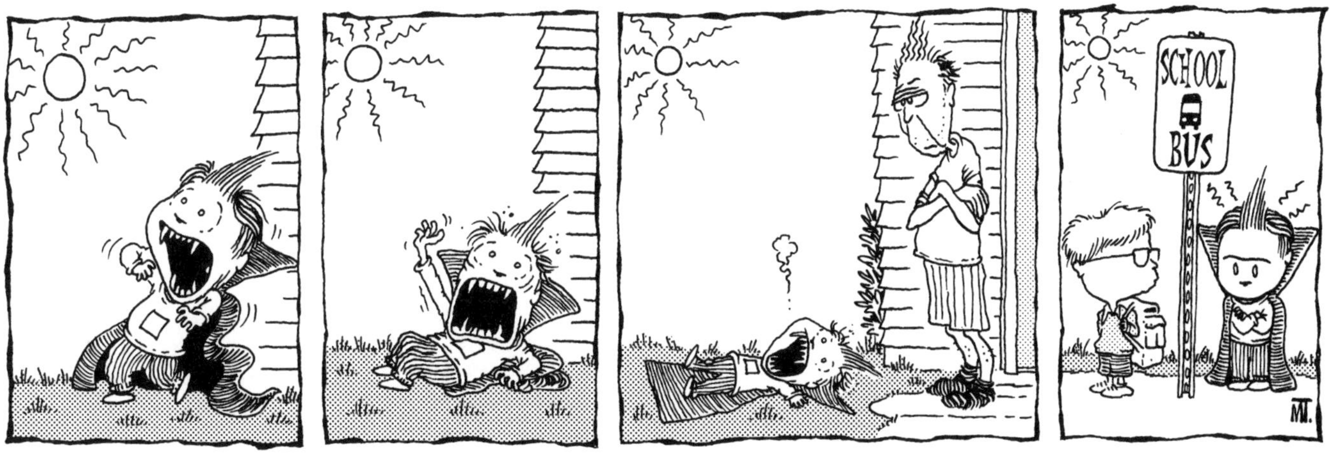
SCHOOL
BUS
MT.

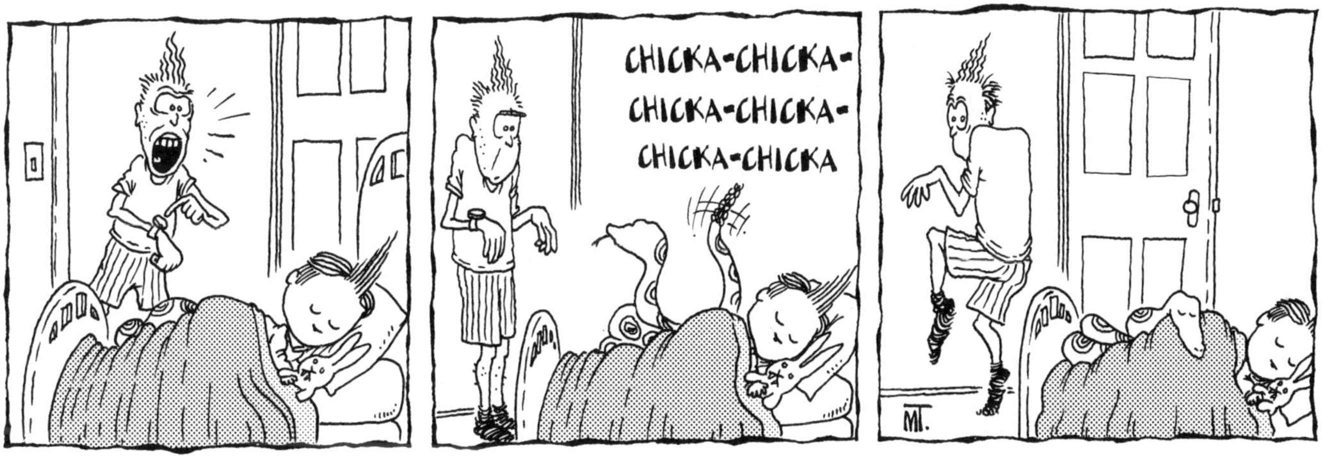
CHICKA-CHICKA-
CHICKA-CHICKA-
CHICKA-CHICKA
MT.

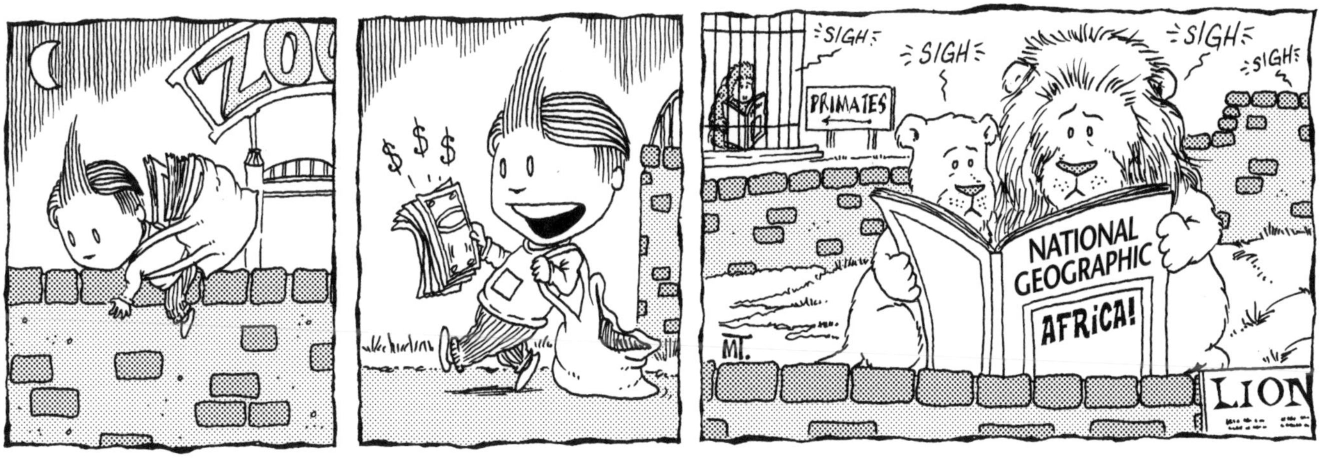
ZOO
PRIMATES
SIGH
SIGH
SIGH
SIGH
NATIONAL GEOGRAPHIC
AFRICA!
LION
MT.

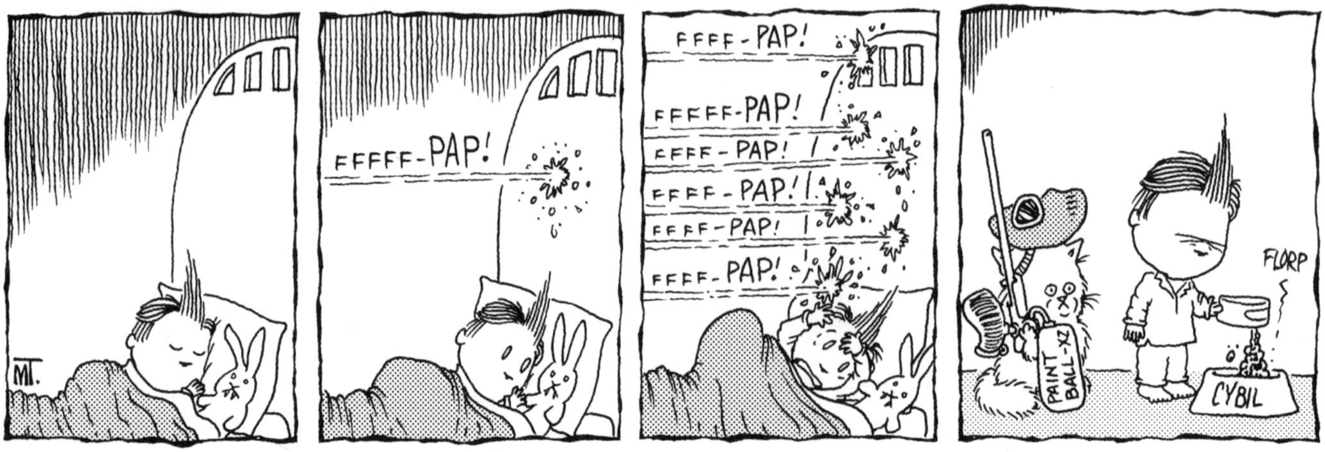
MT.
FFFFF-PAP!
FFFF-PAP!
FFFFF-PAP!
FFFF-PAP!
FFFF-PAP!
FFFF-PAP!
FFFF-PAP!
PAINT BALL-X2
FLORP
CYBIL

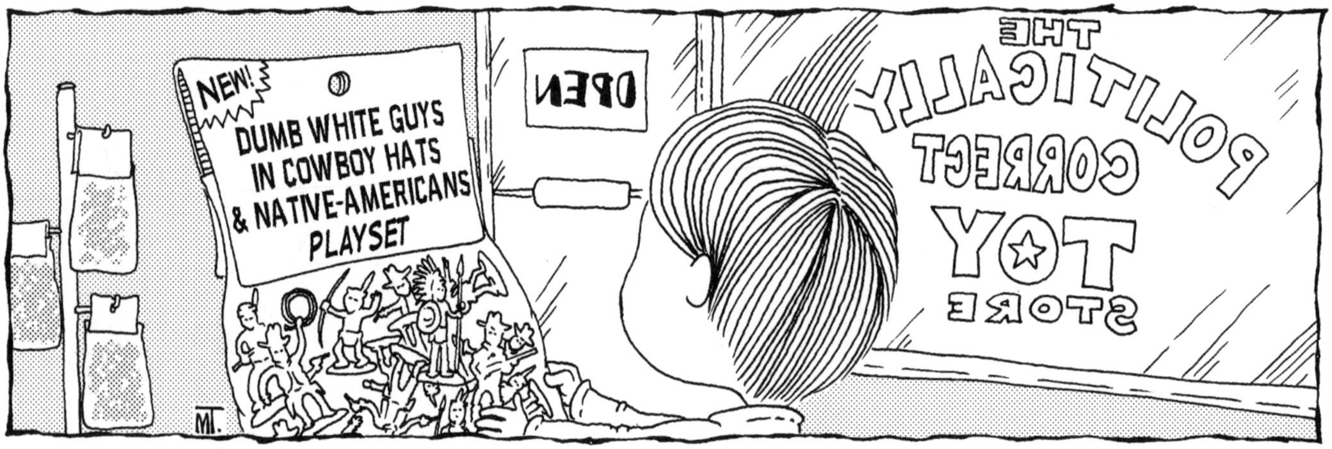
NEW!
DUMB WHITE GUYS
IN COWBOY HATS
& NATIVE-AMERICANS
PLAYSET
OPEN
THE POLITICALLY CORRECT TOY STORE
MT.

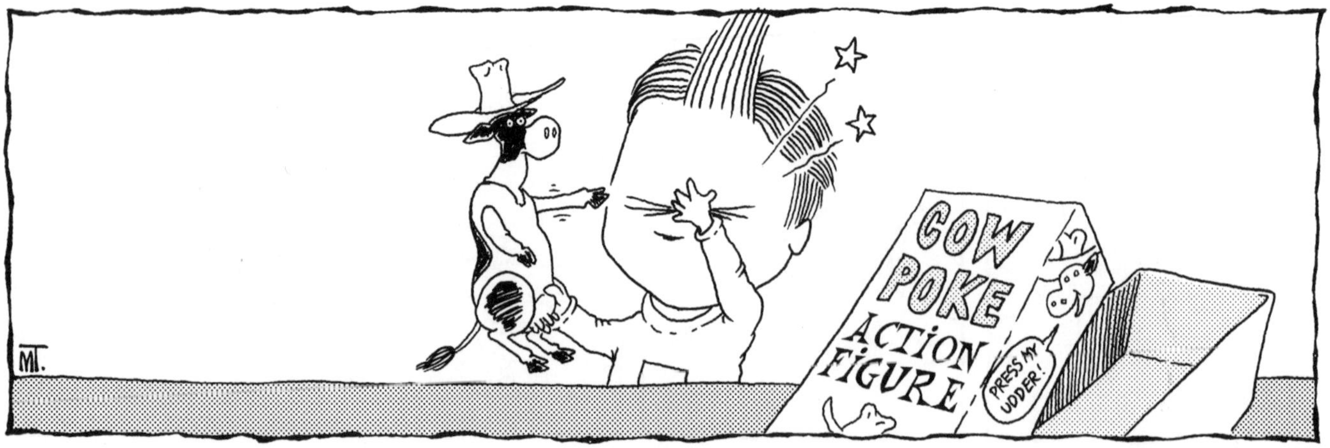
MT.
COW POKE ACTION FIGURE
PRESS MY UDDER!

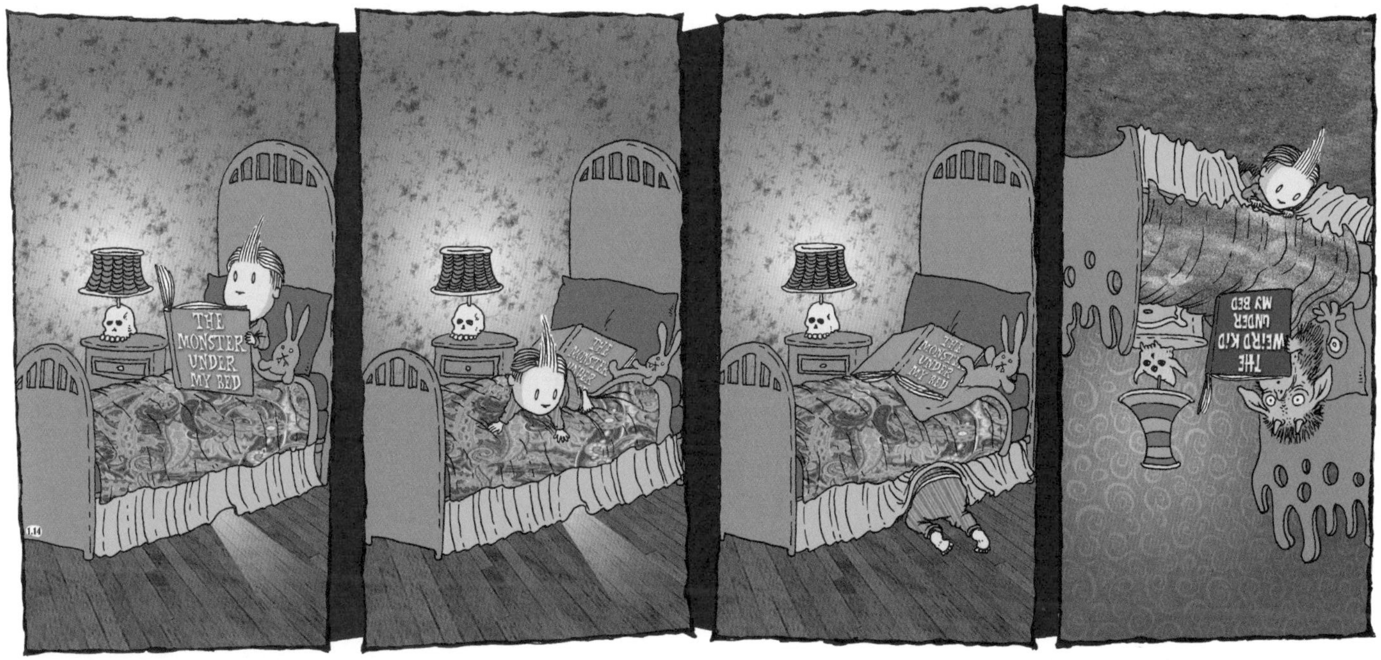
THE MONSTER UNDER MY BED
THE MONSTER UNDER MY BED
THE WEIRD KID UNDER MY BED

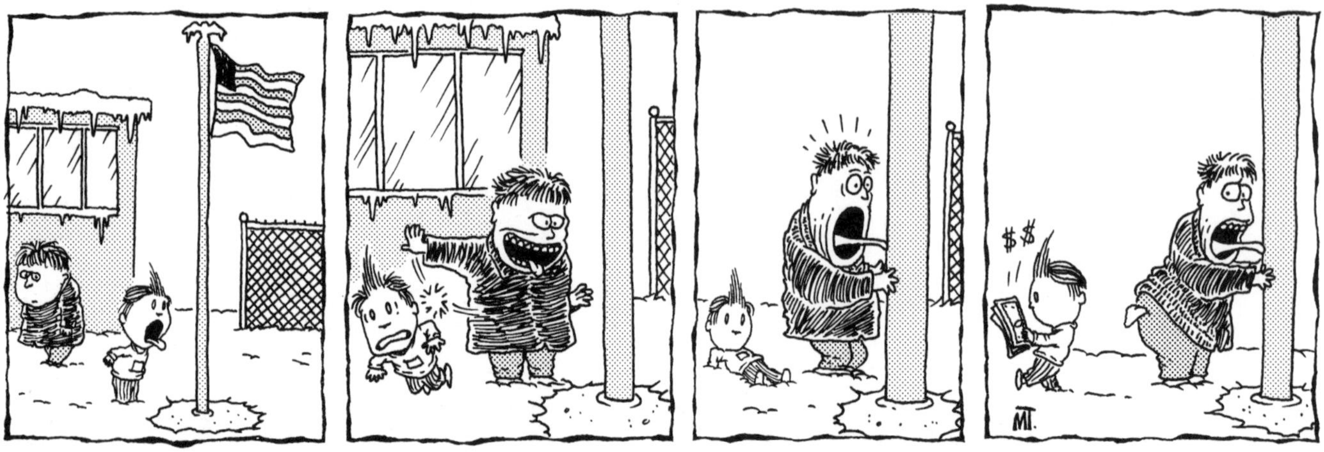

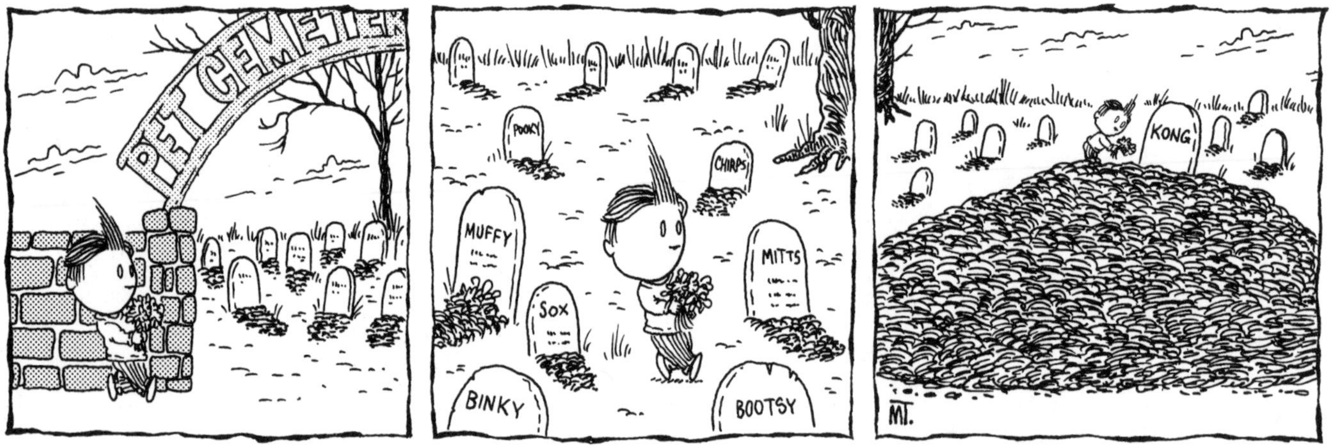
PET CEMETER
POOKY
CHIRPS
MUFFY
MITTS
SOX
BINKY
BOOTSY
KONG

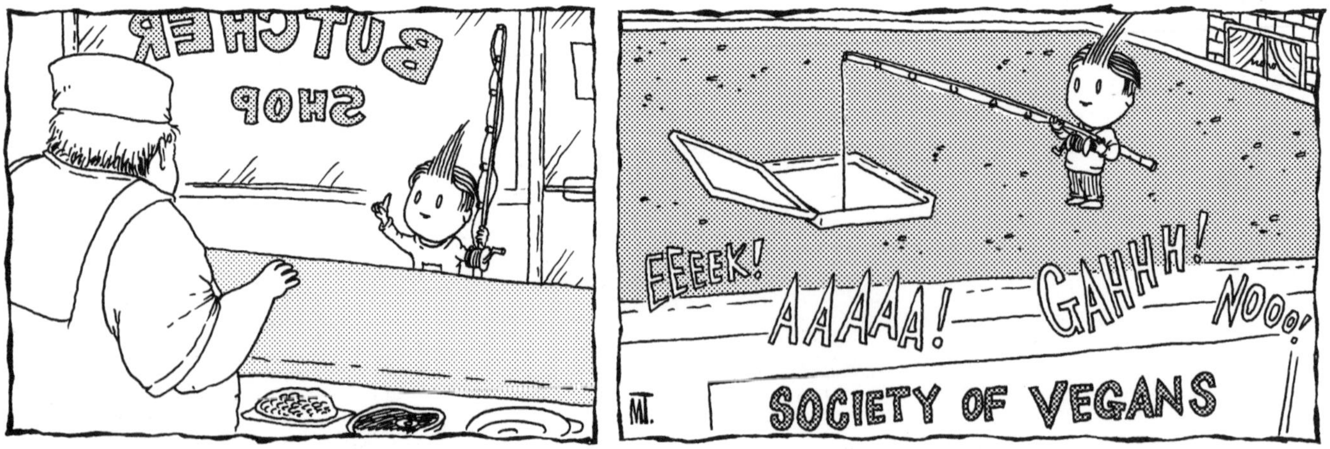
BUTCHER
SHOP
EEEEK!
AAAAA!
GAHHH!
NOoo!
SOCIETY OF VEGANS

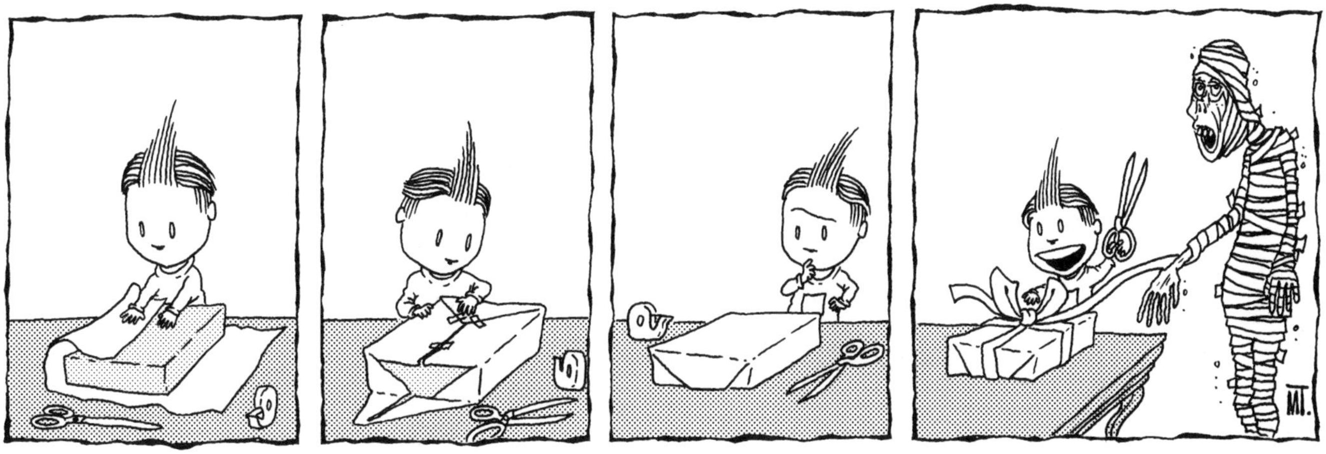
MT.

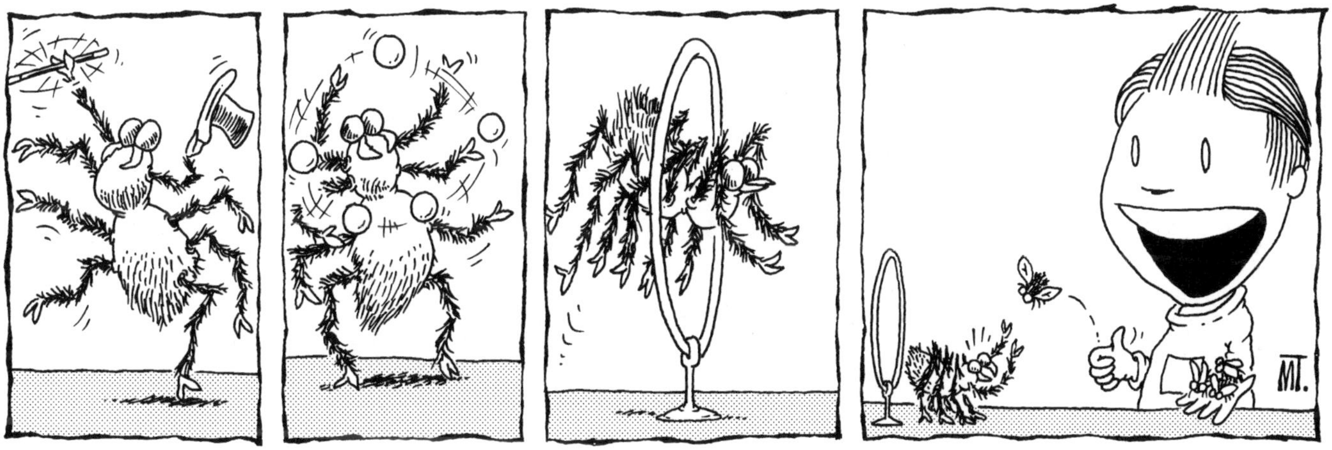
MT.

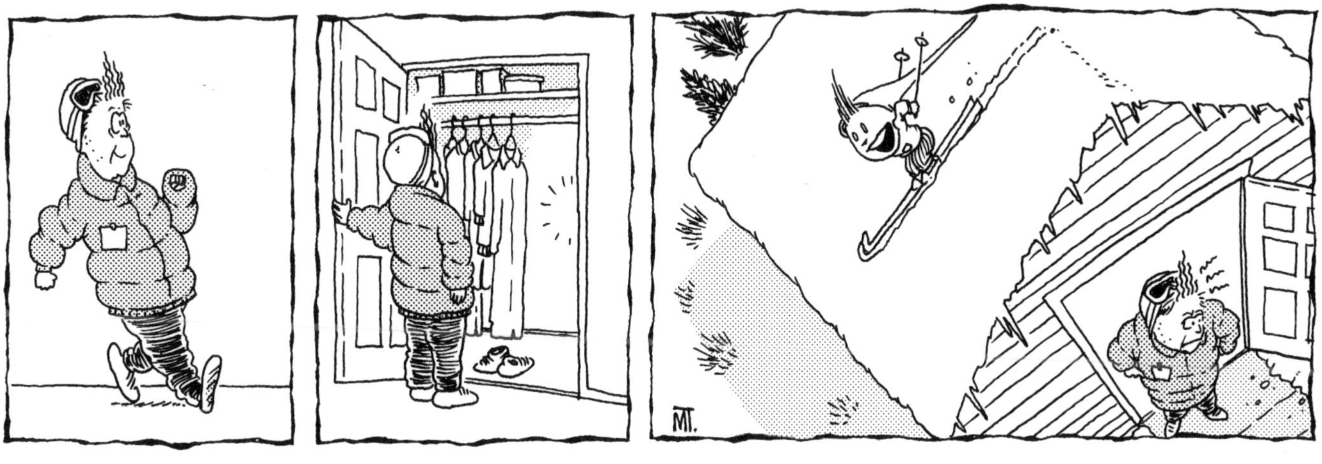
MT.

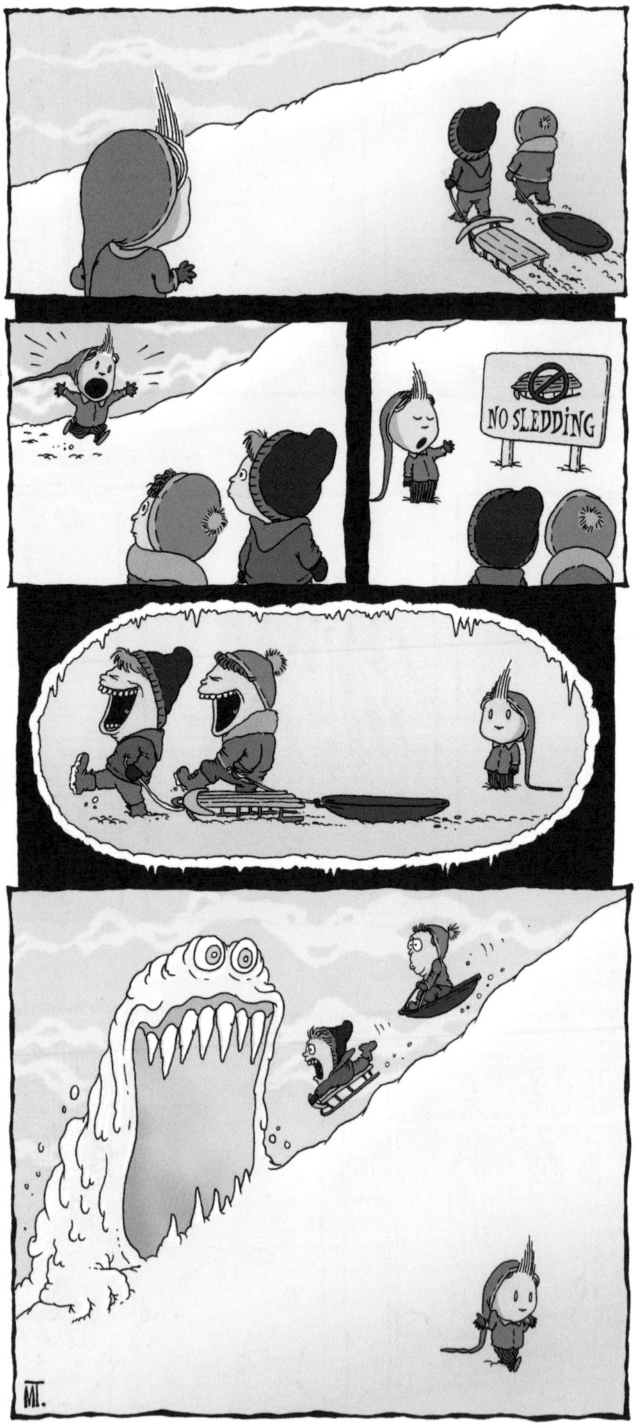
NO SLEDDING
MT.

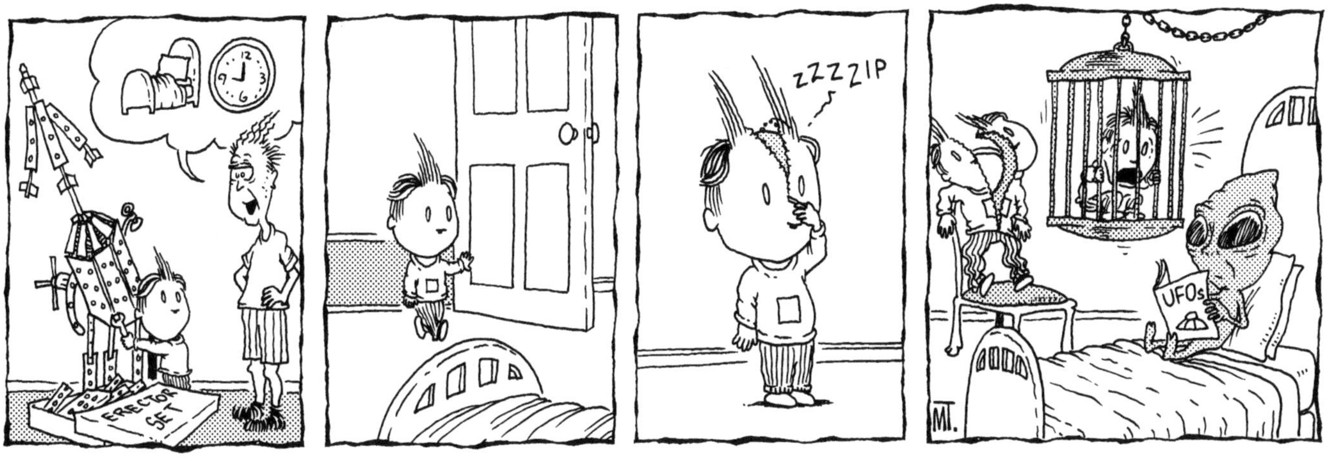
ERECTOR SET
ZZZZIP
UFOs
MT.

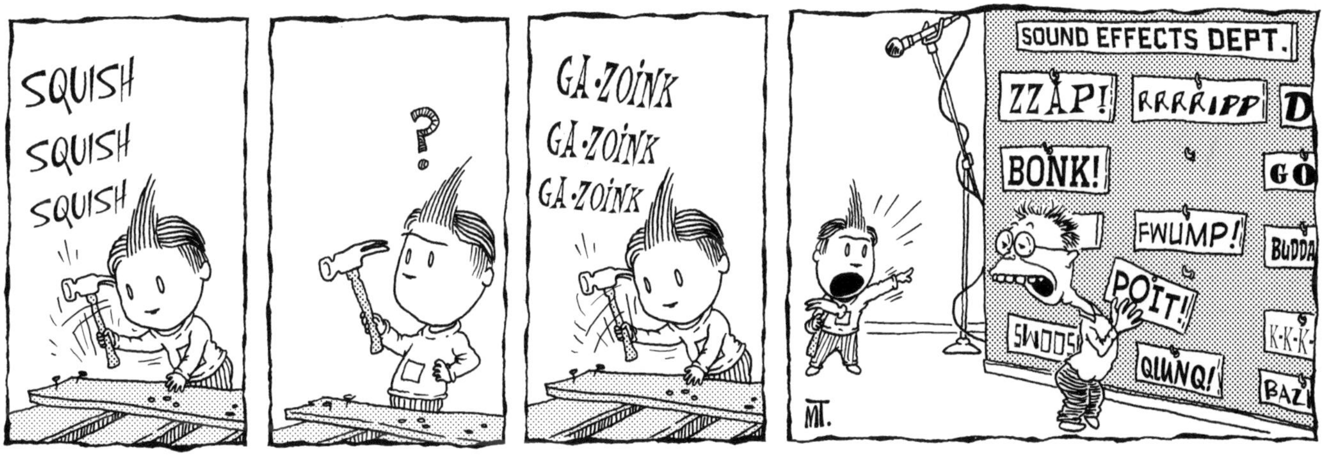
SQUISH
SQUISH
SQUISH
?
GA·ZOINK
GA·ZOINK
GA·ZOINK
SOUND EFFECTS DEPT.
ZZAP!
RRRRIPP
BONK!
FWUMP!
POIT!
MT.

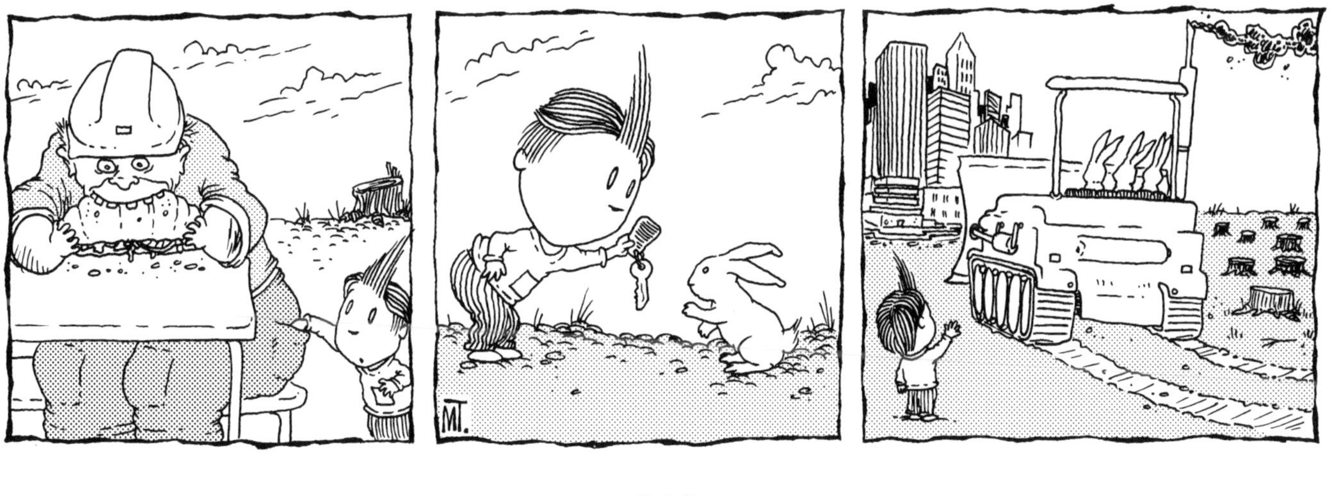
MT.

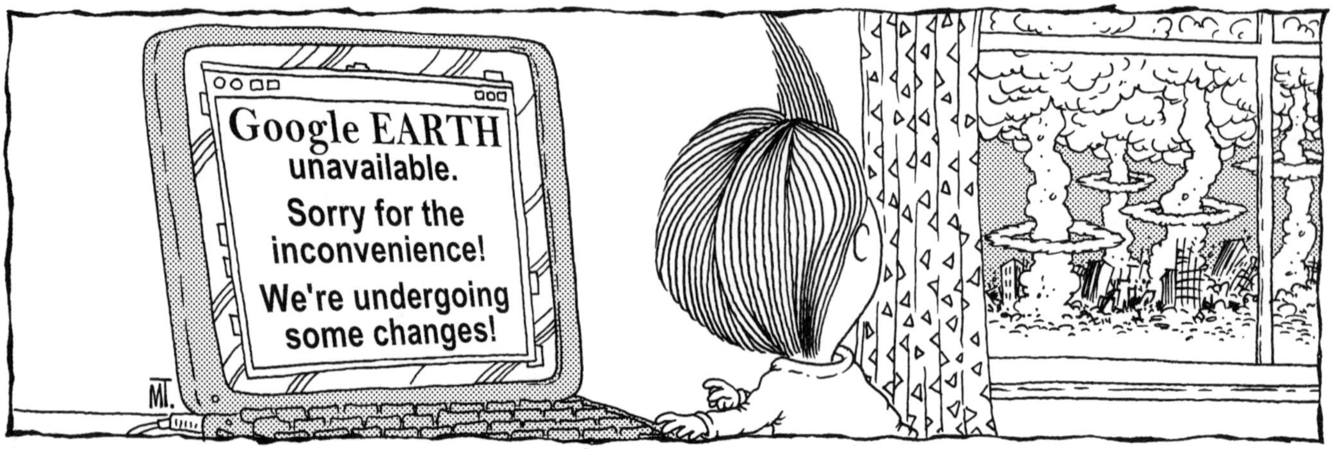
Google EARTH
unavailable.
Sorry for the inconvenience!
We're undergoing some changes!
MT.

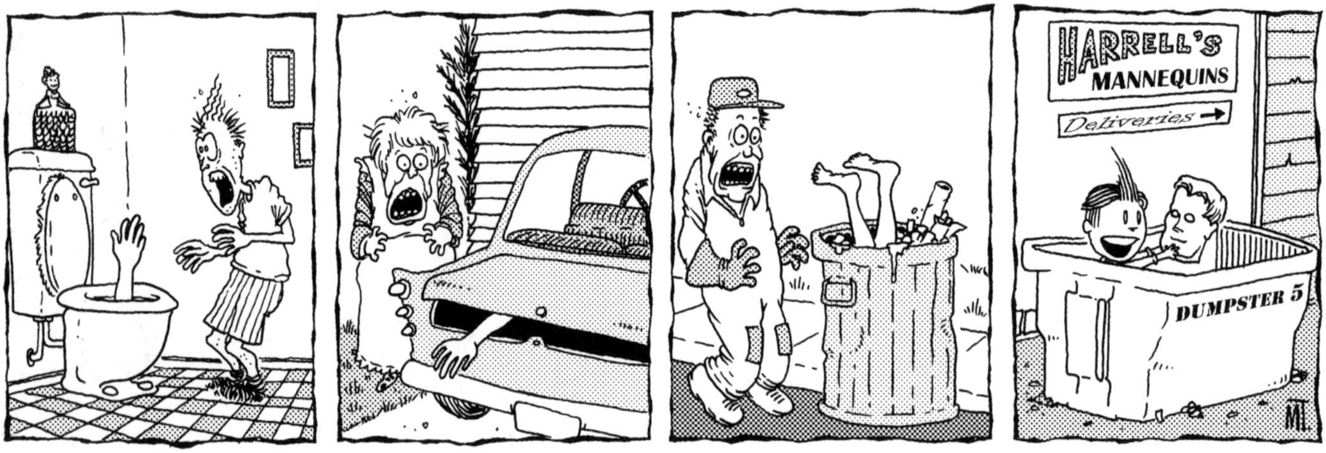
HARRELL'S
MANNEQUINS
Deliveries
DUMPSTER 5
MT.

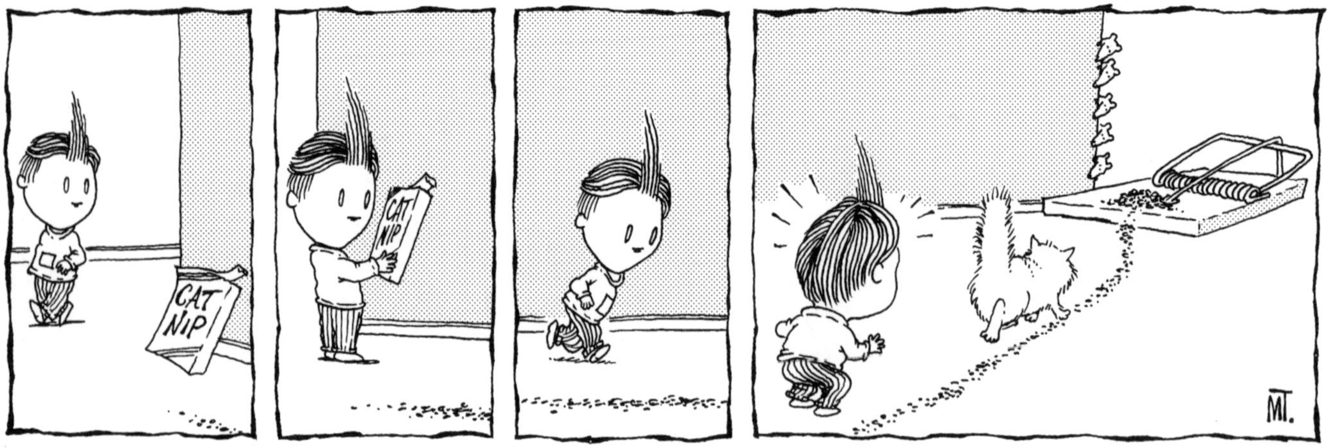
CAT NIP
CAT NIP
MT.

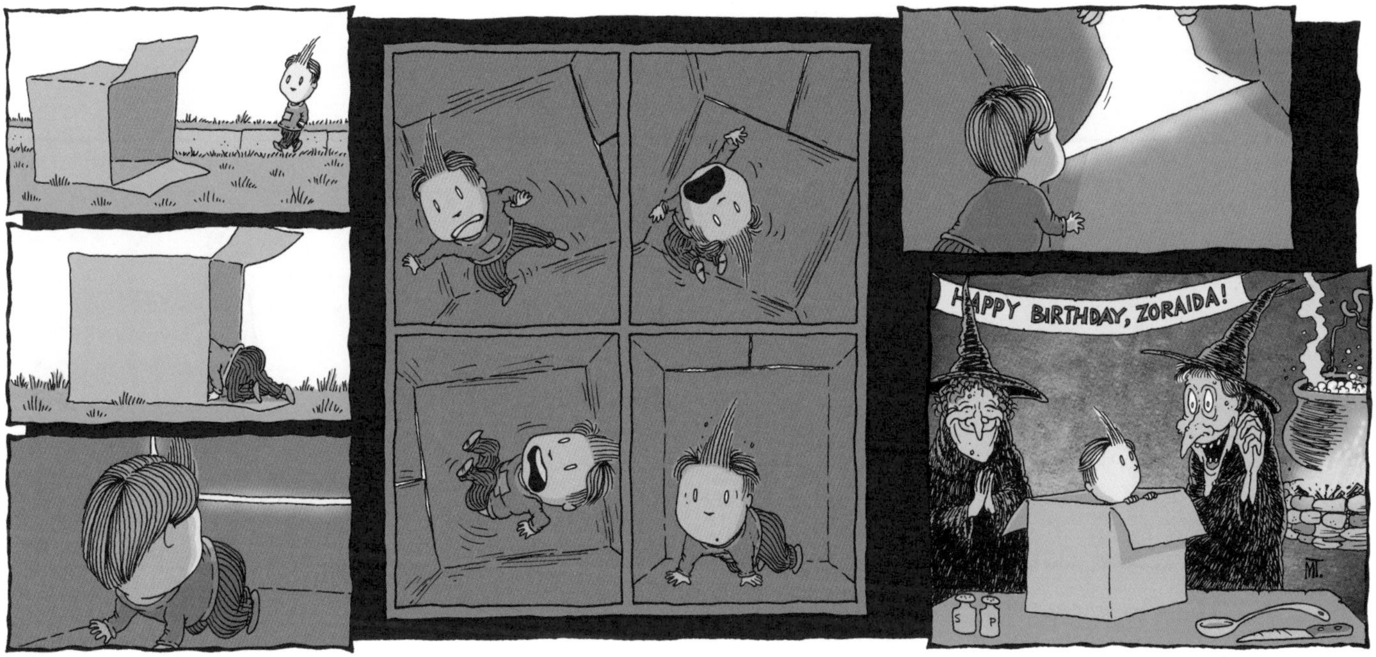
HAPPY BIRTHDAY, ZORAIDA!
S
P

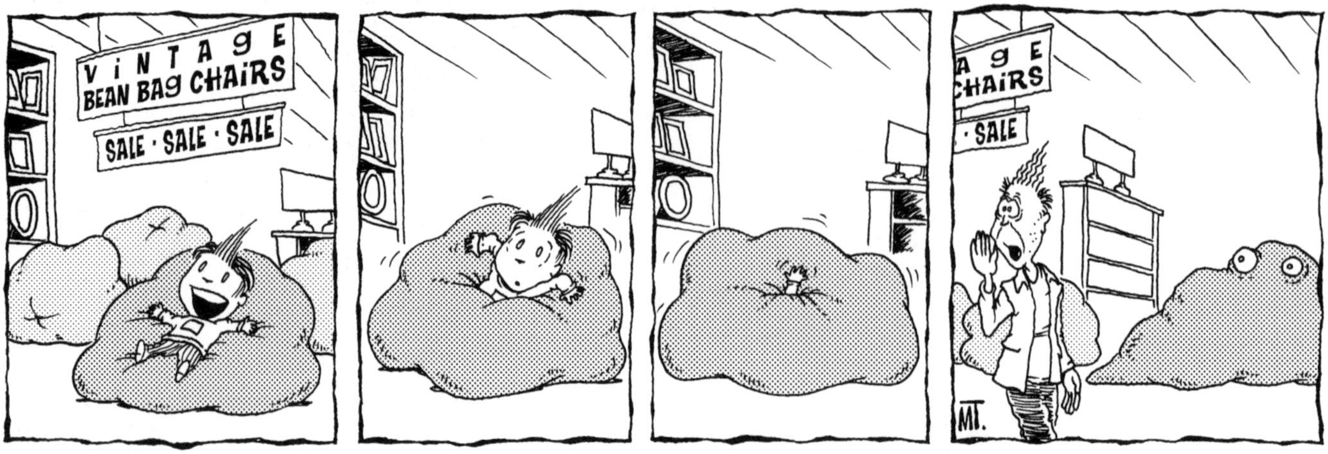
ViNTAGE
BEAN BAG CHAiRS
SALE · SALE · SALE
MT.

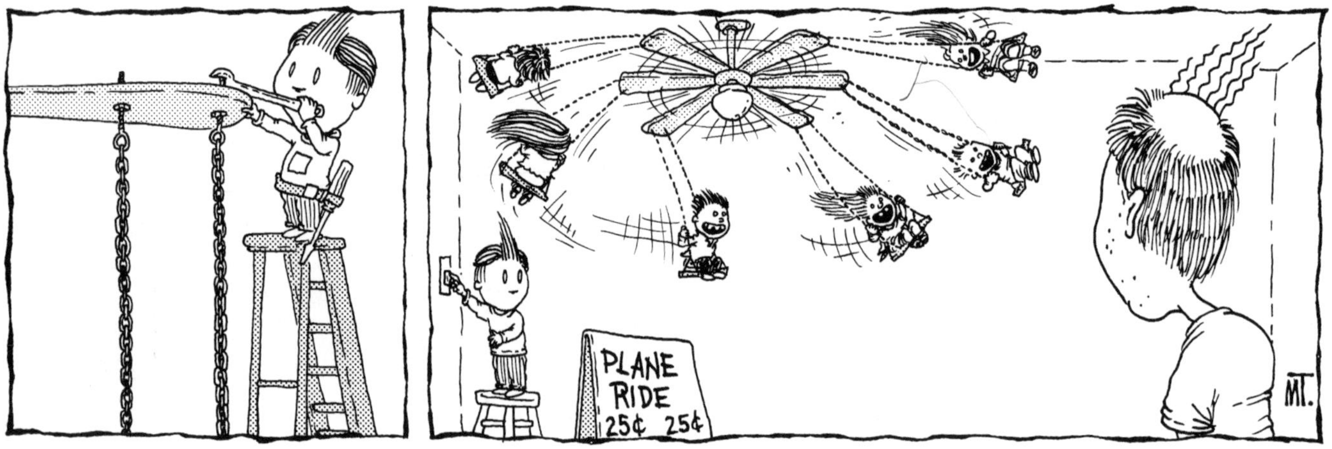
PLANE
RIDE
25¢ 25¢
MT.

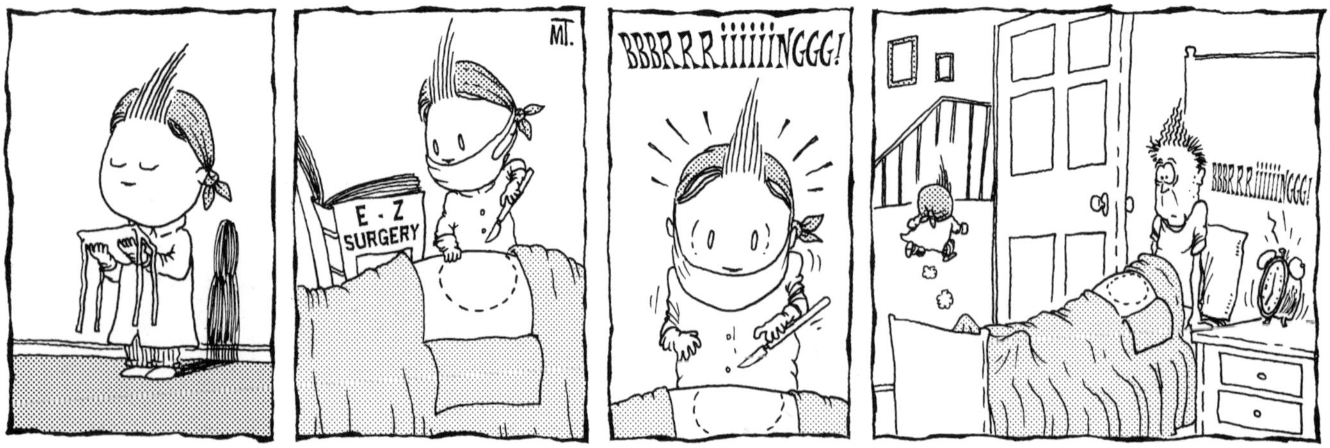
MT.
E-Z
SURGERY
BBBRRRiiiiiiNGGG!
BBBRRRiiiiiiNGGG!

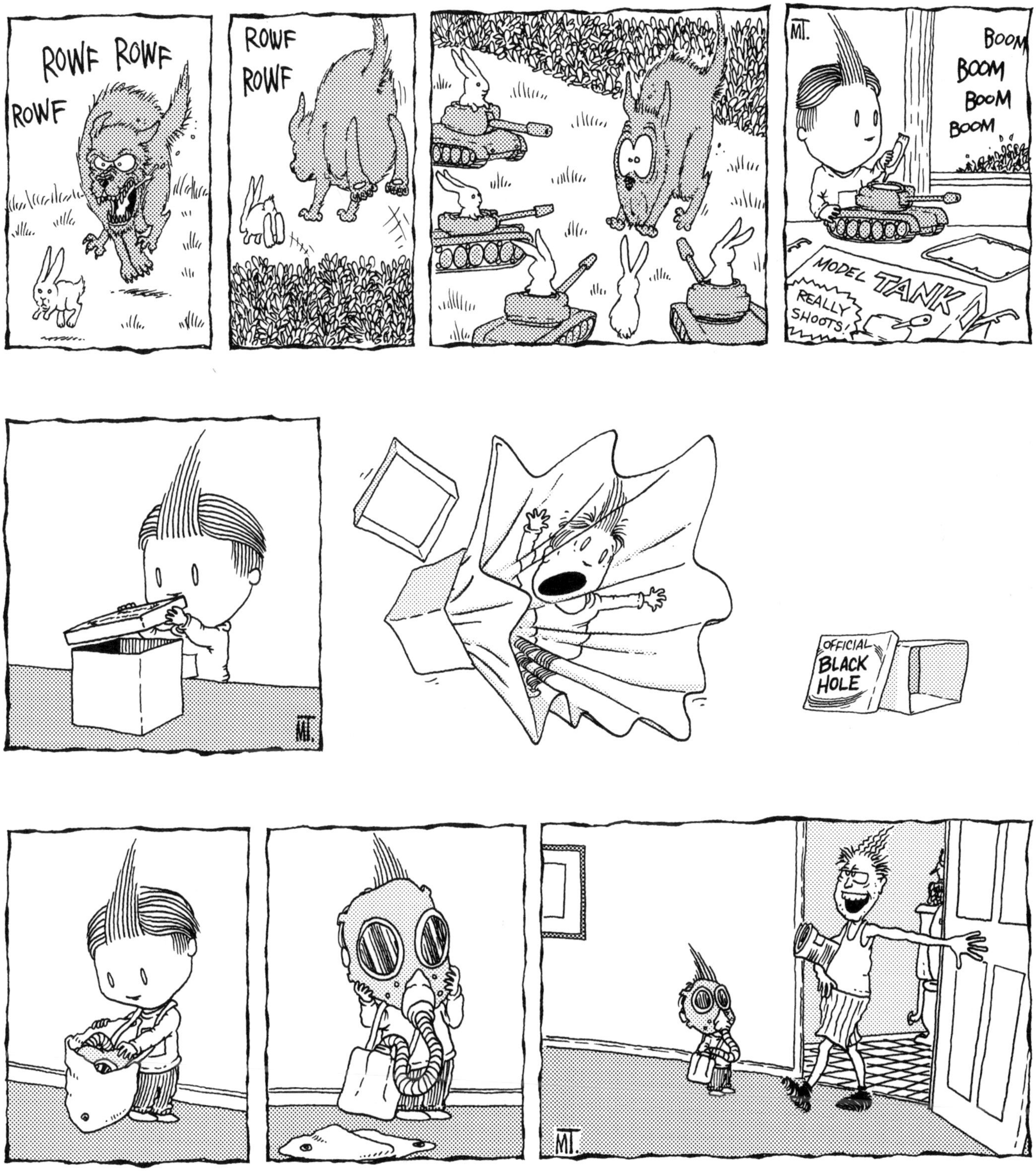
ROWF ROWF
ROWF
ROWF
ROWF
MT.
BOOM
BOOM
BOOM
BOOM
MODEL TANK
REALLY SHOOTS!
MT.
OFFICIAL BLACK HOLE
MT.

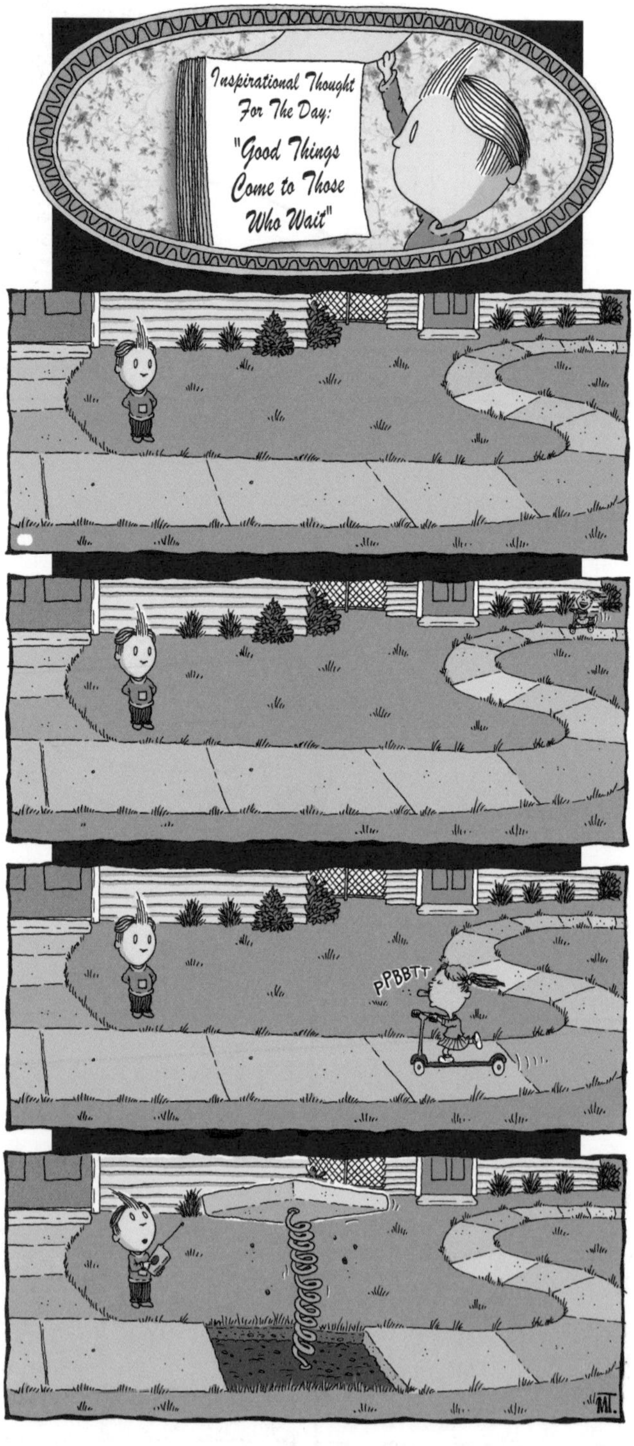
Inspirational Thought For The Day:
"Good Things Come to Those Who Wait"
PPBBTT

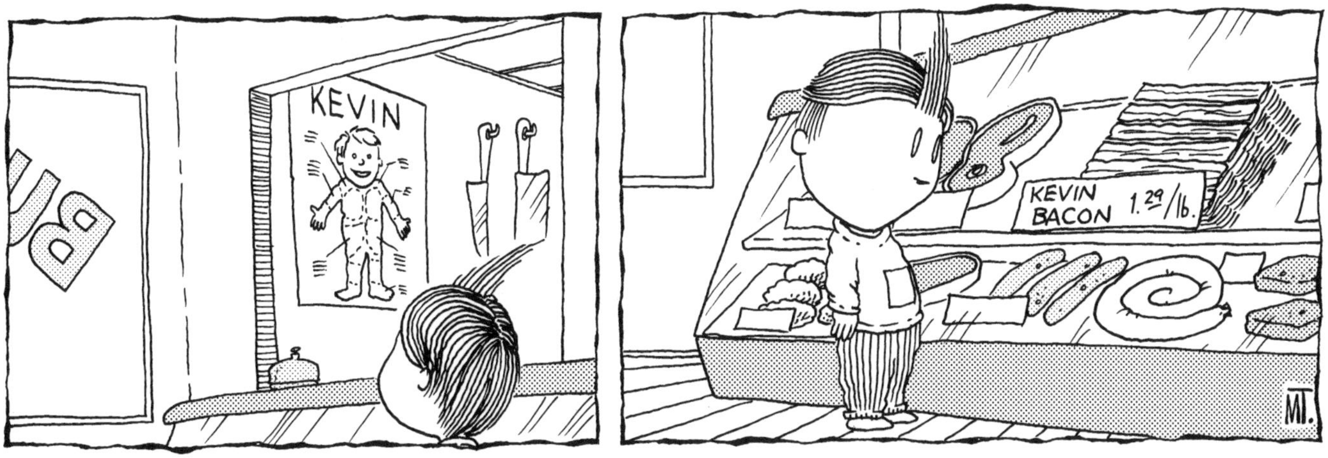
KEVIN
KEVIN BACON 1.29/lb.
MT.

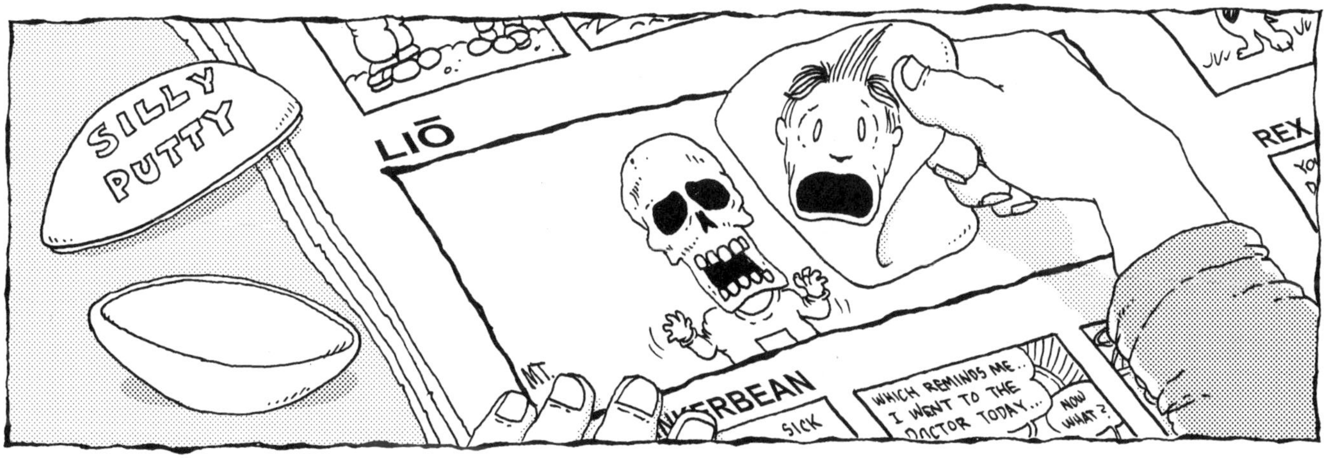
SILLY PUTTY
LIŌ
REX
MT.
WHICH REMINDS ME... I WENT TO THE DOCTOR TODAY...
NOW WHAT?
SICK

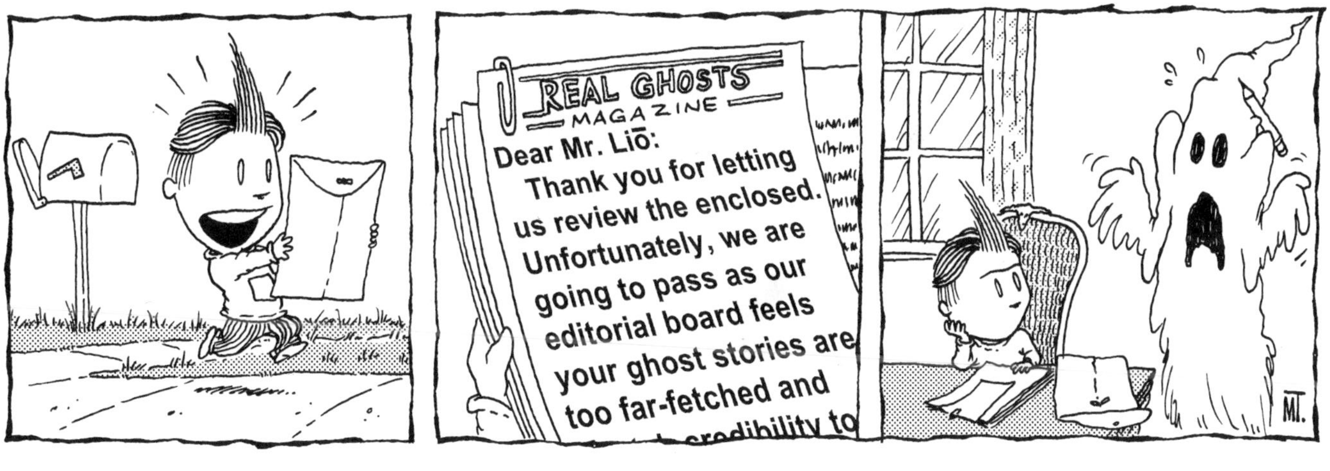
REAL GHOSTS MAGAZINE
Dear Mr. Liō:
Thank you for letting us review the enclosed. Unfortunately, we are going to pass as our editorial board feels your ghost stories are too far-fetched and
MT.

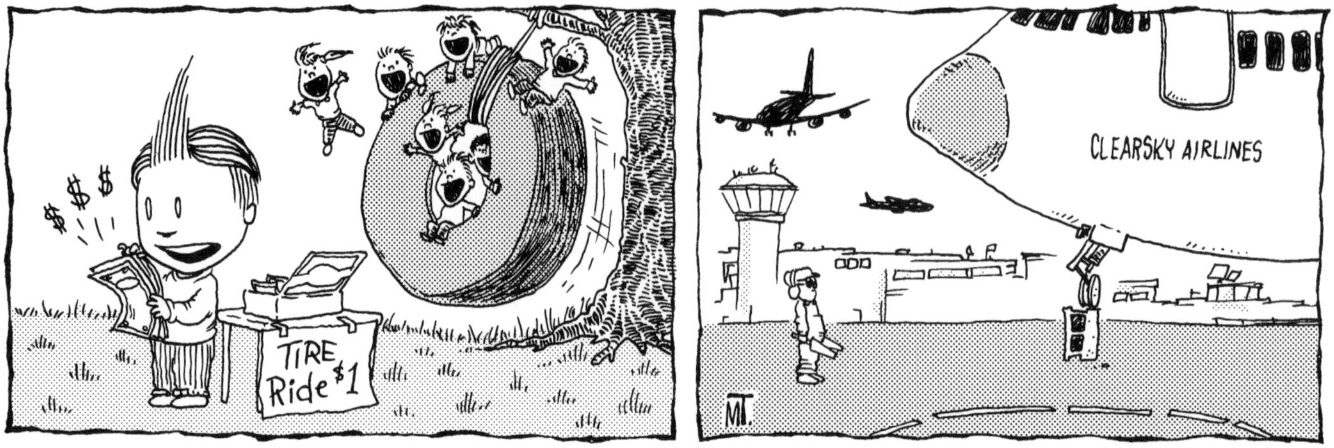
$ $ $
TIRE
Ride $1
CLEARSKY AIRLINES
MT.

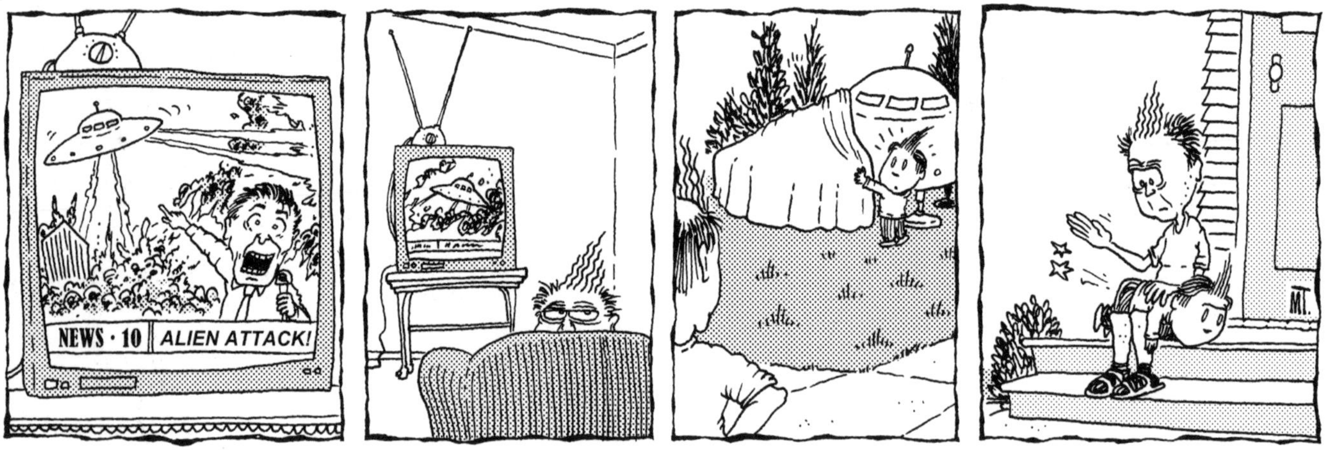
NEWS · 10
ALIEN ATTACK!
MT.

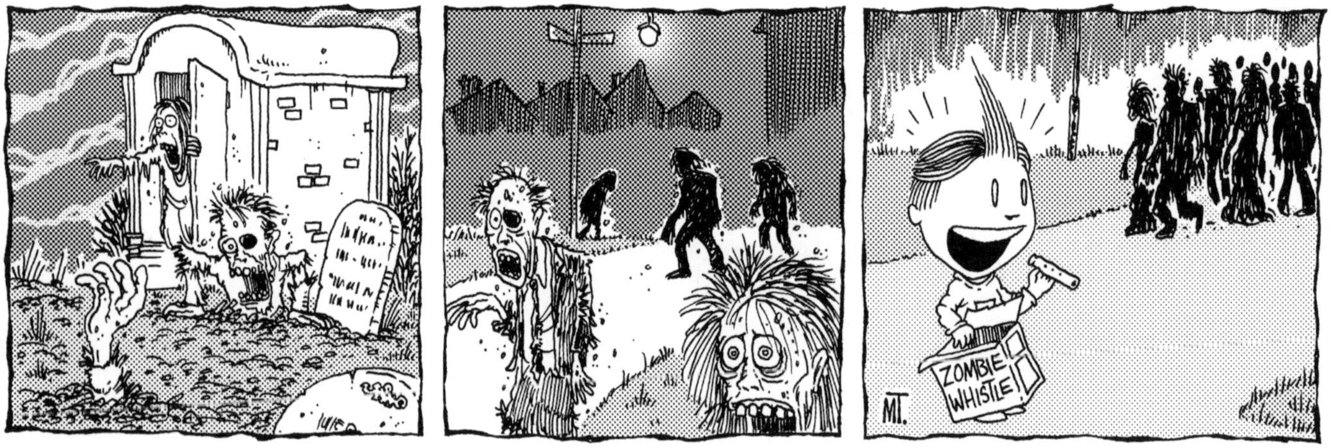
ZOMBIE
WHISTLE
MT.

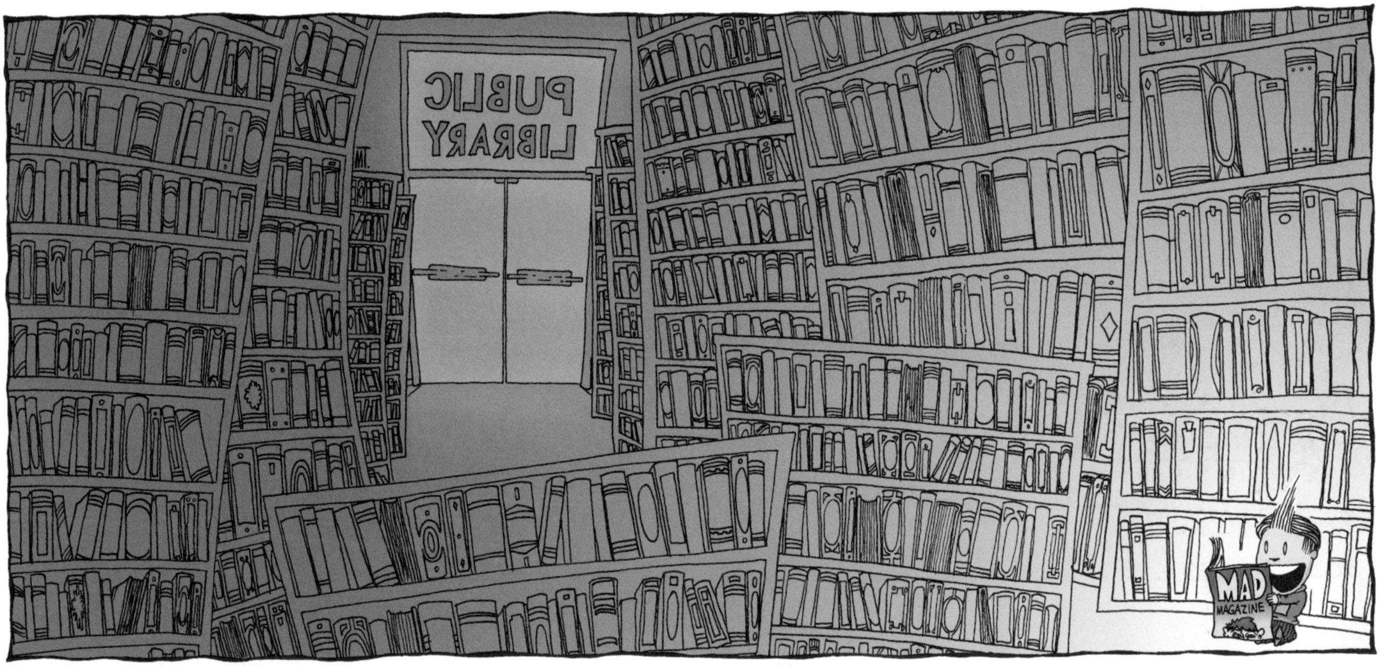
PUBLIC
LIBRARY
MAD
MAGAZINE

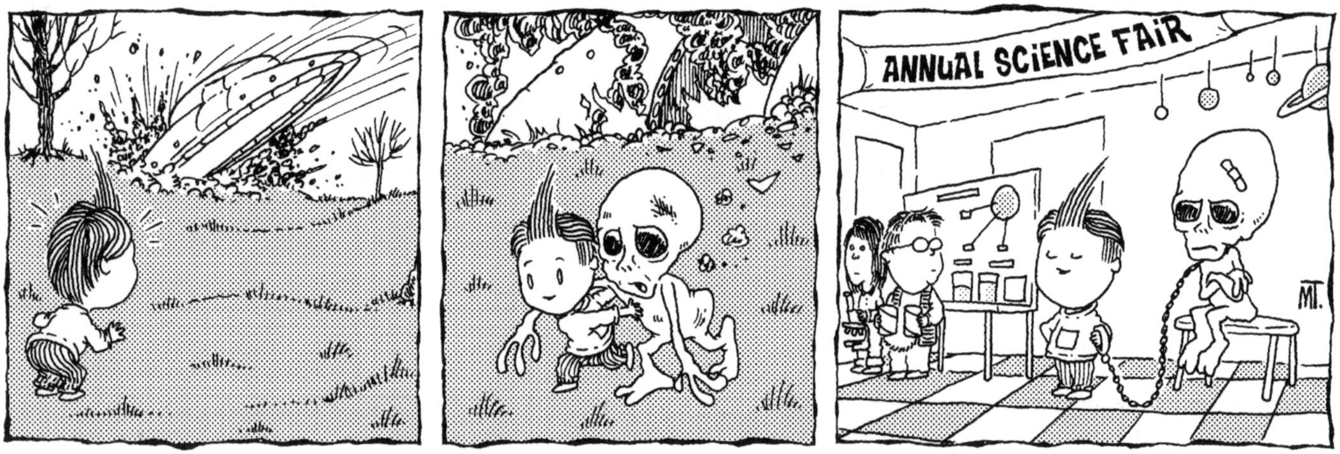
ANNUAL SCIENCE FAIR

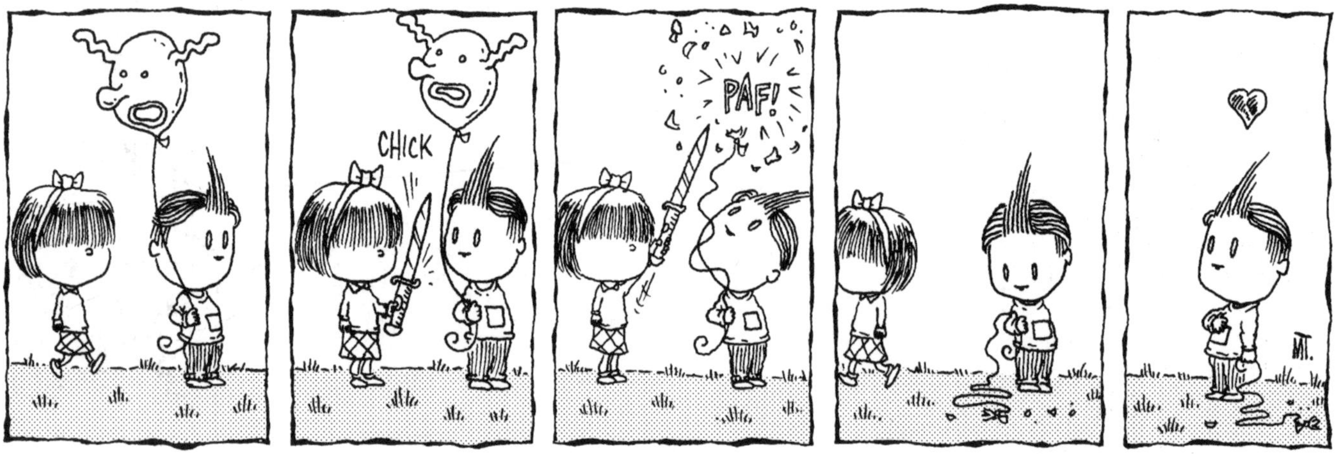
CHICK
PAF!

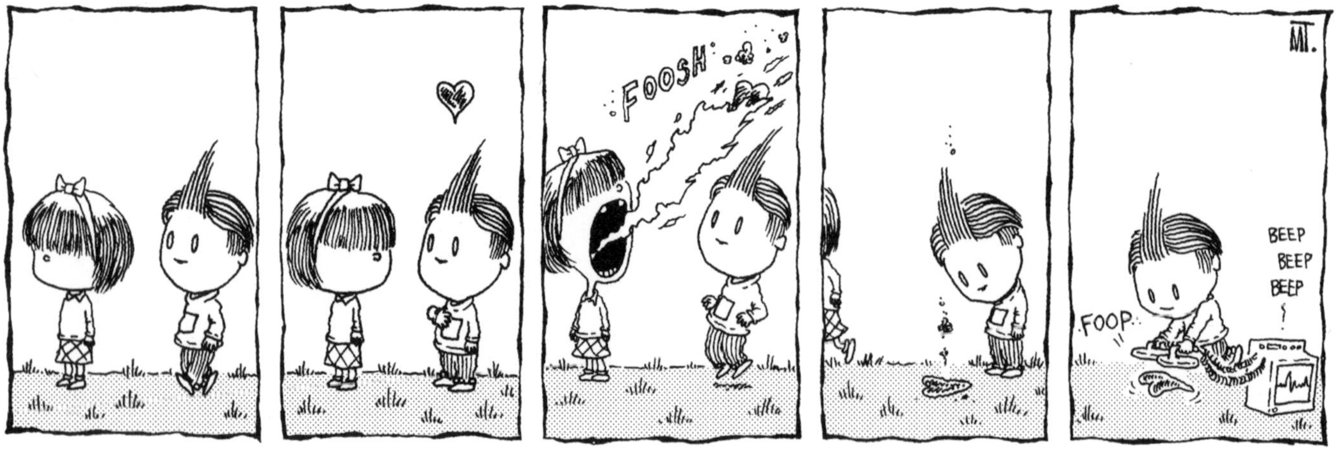
FOOSH
FOOP
BEEP
BEEP
BEEP

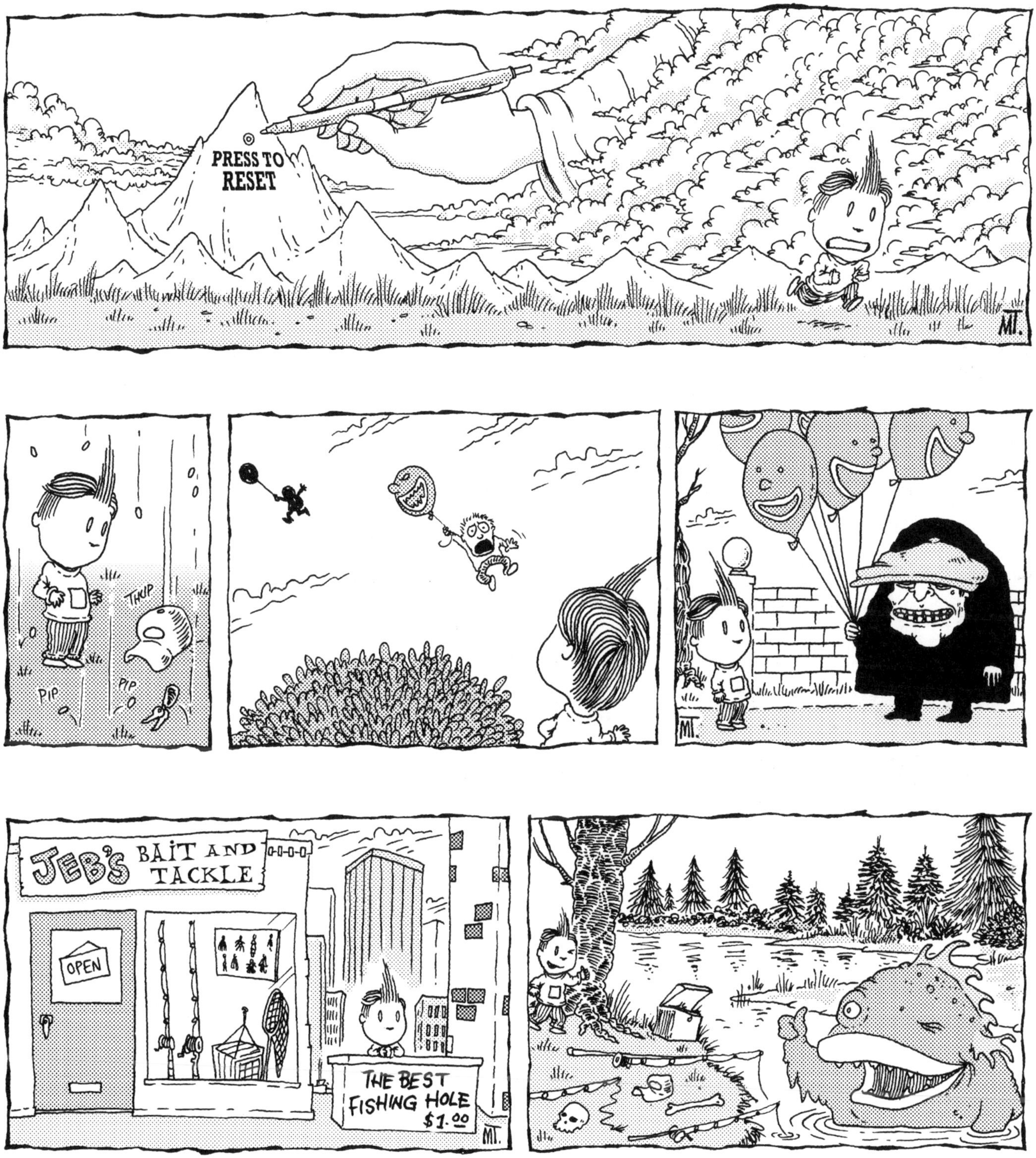
PRESS TO RESET
THUP
PIP
PIP
JEB'S BAIT AND TACKLE
OPEN
THE BEST FISHING HOLE $1.00

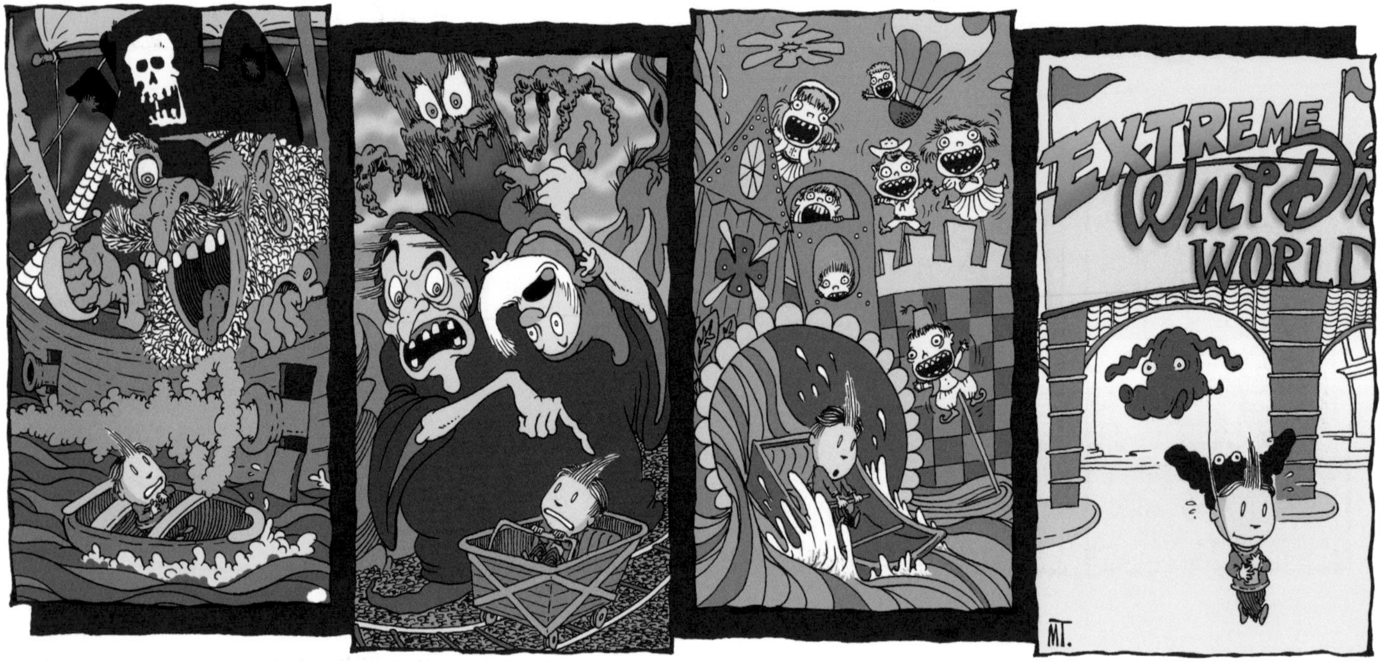
EXTREME
WALT DIS
WORLD
MT.

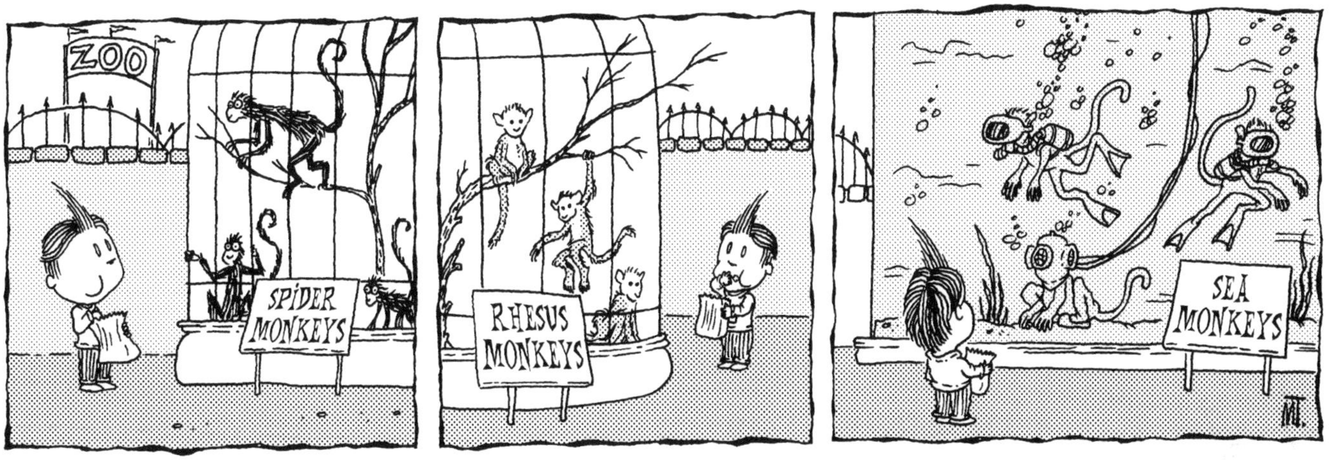
ZOO
SPIDER MONKEYS
RHESUS MONKEYS
SEA MONKEYS
MT.

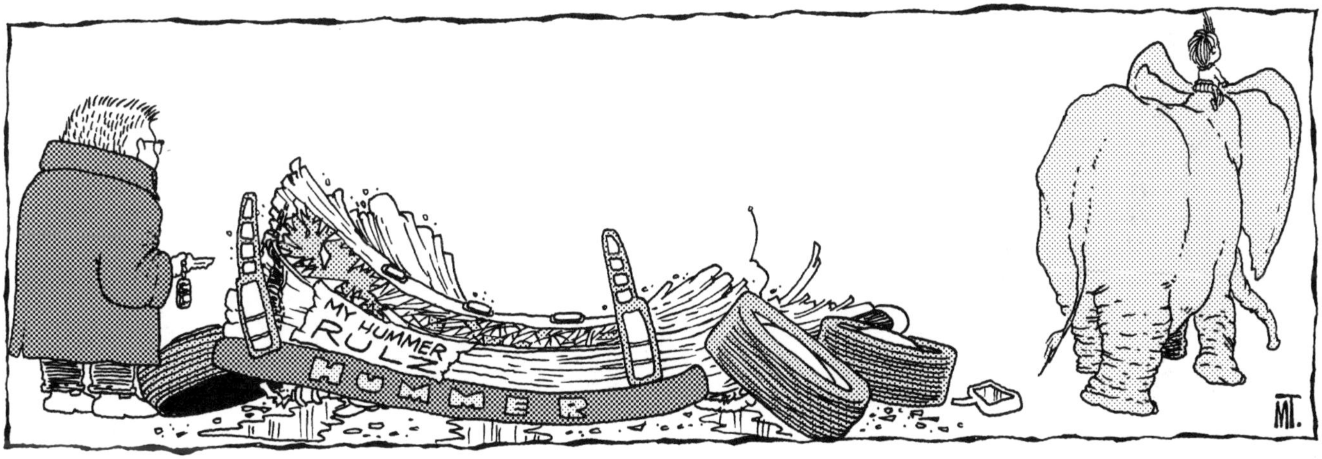
MY HUMMER RULZ
HUMMER
MT.

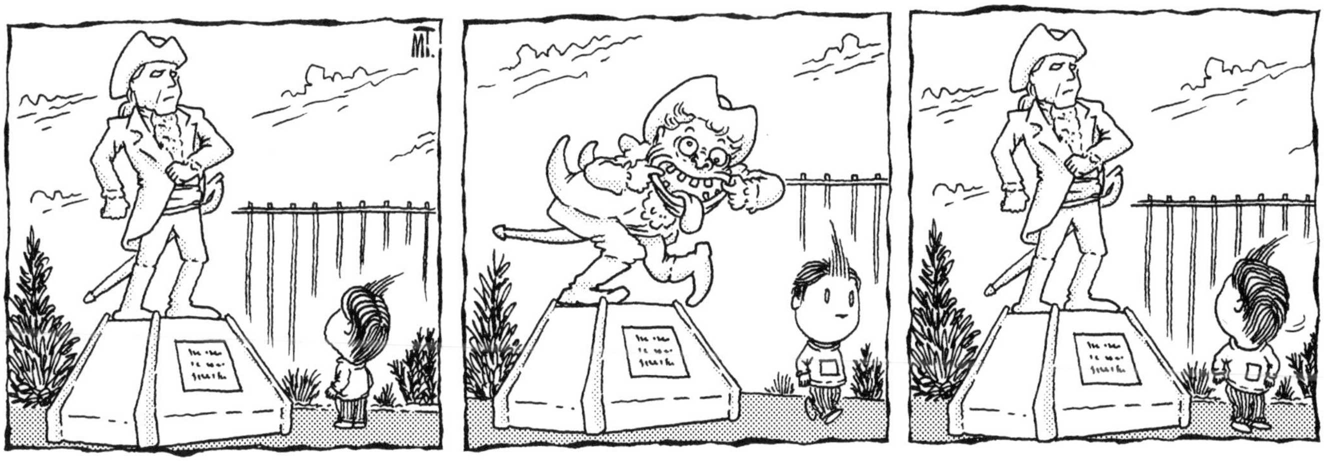
MT.

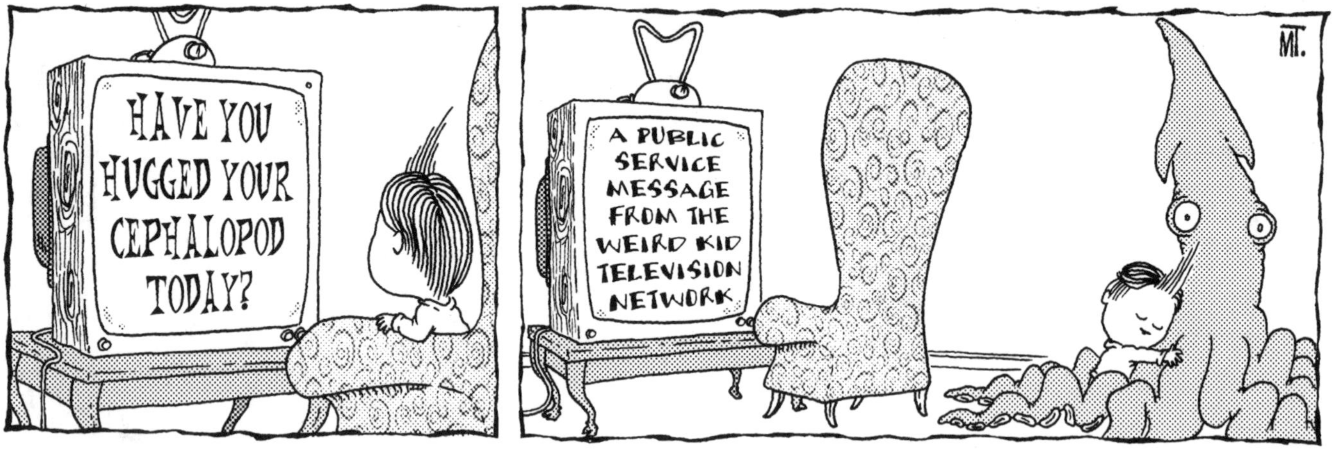
HAVE YOU HUGGED YOUR CEPHALOPOD TODAY?
A PUBLIC SERVICE MESSAGE FROM THE WEIRD KID TELEVISION NETWORK
MT.

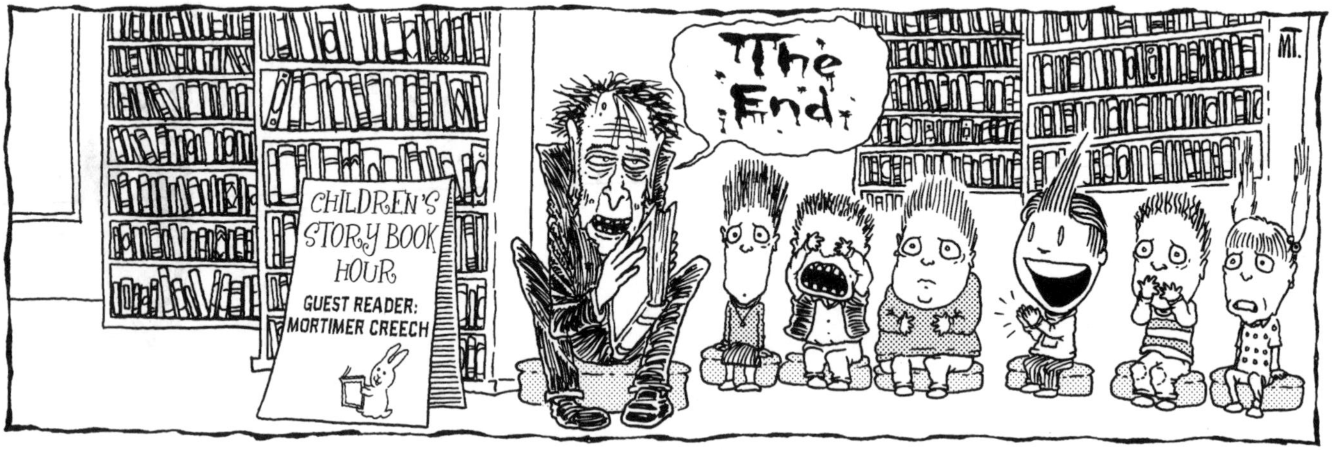
CHILDREN'S STORY BOOK HOUR
GUEST READER: MORTIMER CREECH
The End
MT.

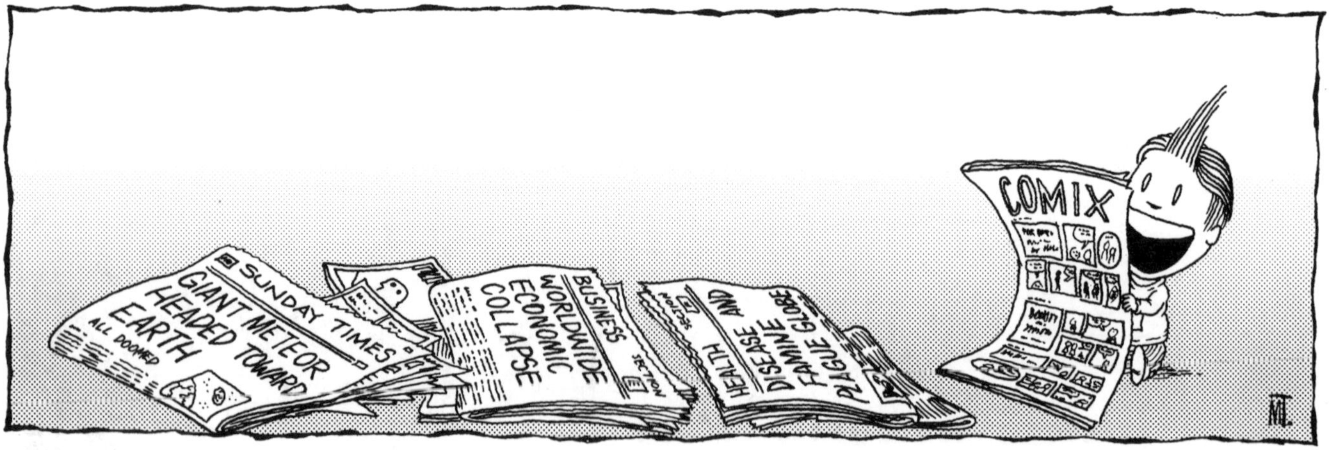
SUNDAY TIMES
GIANT METEOR HEADED TOWARD EARTH
ALL DOOMED
BUSINESS
WORLDWIDE ECONOMIC COLLAPSE
SECTION
HEALTH AND
DISEASE
FAMINE
PLAGUE
COMIX
MT.